SYMPATHY IN PERCEPTION

The philosophy of perception has been an important topic through-out history, appealing to thinkers in antiquity and the Middle Ages as well as to figures such as Kant, Bergson, and others. In this wide-ranging study, Mark Eli Kalderon presents multiple perspectives on the general nature of perception, discussing touch and hearing, as well as vision. He draws on the rich history of the subject and shows how analytic and continental approaches to it are connected, provid-ing readers with insights from both traditions and arguing for new orientations when thinking about the presentation of perception. His discussion addresses issues including tactile metaphors, sympathy in relation to the concept of fellow-feeling, and the Wave Theory of sound. His comprehensive and thoughtful study presents bold and systematic investigations into current theory, informed by centuries of philosophical inquiry, and will be important for those working on ontological and metaphysical aspects of perception and feeling.

MARK ELI KALDERON is Professor of Philosophy at University College London. His publications include *Moral Fictionalism* (2005) and *Form without Matter: Empedocles and Aristotle on Colour Perceptions* (2015).

T0371051

SYMPATHY IN PERCEPTION

MARK ELI KALDERON

University College London

CAMBRIDGE
UNIVERSITY PRESS

CAMBRIDGE
UNIVERSITY PRESS

University Printing House, Cambridge CB2 8BS, United Kingdom

One Liberty Plaza, 20th Floor, New York, NY 10006, USA

477 Williamstown Road, Port Melbourne, VIC 3207, Australia

314-321, 3rd Floor, Plot 3, Splendor Forum, Jasola District Centre, New Delhi - 110025, India

79 Anson Road, #06-04/06, Singapore 079906

Cambridge University Press is part of the University of Cambridge.

It furthers the University's mission by disseminating knowledge in the pursuit of education, learning and research at the highest international levels of excellence.

www.cambridge.org
Information on this title: www.cambridge.org/9781108411462
DOI: 10.1017/9781108303668

© Mark Eli Kalderon 2018

First published 2018
First paperback edition 2019

A catalogue record for this publication is available from the British Library

ISBN 978-1-108-41960-4 Hardback
ISBN 978-1-108-41146-2 Paperback

Cambridge University Press has no responsibility for the persistence or accuracy of URLs for external or third-party internet websites referred to in this publication, and does not guarantee that any content on such websites is, or will remain, accurate or appropriate.

I focused at intervals as the great dome loomed up through the smoke. Glares of many fires and sweeping clouds of smoke kept hiding the shape. Then a wind sprang up. Suddenly, the shining cross, dome and towers stood out like a symbol in the inferno. The scene was unbelievable. In that moment or two I released my shutter.

– Herbert Mason

Contents

Preface

The present essay is an unabashed exercise in historically informed, speculative metaphysics. Its aim is to gain insight into the nature of sensory presentation. Allow me to explain why it should be historically informed and in what sense the metaphysics developed herein is speculative.

One of the fundamental issues dividing contemporary philosophers of perception is whether perception is presentational or representational in character (see, for example, the recent collection devoted to this topic Brogaard 2014 and Campbell and Cassam 2014). To claim that perception is presentational in character is to claim that it has a presentational element irreducible to whatever intentional or representational content it may have. So conceived, the object of perception is present in the awareness afforded by the perceptual experience and is thus a constituent of that experience. Representationalists deny that perception has such an irreducible presentational element, claiming, instead, that the object of perception is exhaustively specified by its intentional or representational content. If there is indeed a presentational element to perception, then, according to the representationalist, this is because sensory presentation is either reducible to the exercise of an intentional or representational capacity or otherwise essentially involves the exercise of such a capacity (see, for example, Chalmers 2006; McDowell 2008; Searle 2015). There are two aspects of this debate. On the one hand, there are arguments on one side or the other urging that perception must be conceived in presentational or representational terms. On the other hand, there is a more positive, constructive aspect, where, taking for granted one's preferred conception, one goes on to develop detailed theoretical accounts of perceptual experience.

Representationalists have been more active in this latter task. And unsurprisingly so. For suppose one took sensory presentation to be an indispensable aspect of perceptual experience and further held, in a Butlerian spirit, that it was reducible to no other thing. What positive account could one give of sensory presentation, so conceived? Since it is irreducible, no positive account could take the form of a reduction. So no causal or counterfactual conditions on sensory representations, understood independently of perception, could be jointly necessary and sufficient for the presentation, in sensory experience, of its object. One might specify the relational features of presentation in sensory experience, but not much insight into the nature of sensory presentation is thereby gained. The tools of contemporary analytic metaphysics would seem not to leave one much to work with, at least in the present instance. So it can seem that if one maintains that perceptual experience involves an irreducible presentational element, all that one can do is press the negative point that sensory presentation, an indispensable element of perceptual experience, is reducible to no other thing.

I believe that perception has an irreducible presentational element. And yet I hoped to learn something positive about the metaphysics of sensory presentation. If there was, in fact, anything further to be learned, I could not limit myself to the tools of contemporary analytic metaphysics. The present metaphysics is historically informed, at least in part, as a result of looking for tools more adequate to the task at hand. There is a real question about how such borrowings should be understood, if they are not simply an invitation to roll back philosophical thinking about perception to some earlier period. Before we are in a position to address that question, let us first address two additional motives to look to historical material in thinking about the nature of sensory presentation.

Putnam (1993, 1994, 1999) has described the present metaphysical orthodoxy in the philosophy of mind as "Cartesianism *cum* materialism" (compare Merleau-Ponty's 1967 related charge of "pseudo-Cartesianism"). While it is easy to find dissenters to either the Cartesian or materialist elements of that orthodoxy, it is equally easy to appreciate the way in which Putnam's description is apt. That it is apt shows that, despite its technical sophistication and being informed by twenty-first-century psychology, contemporary philosophy of mind is still working within a seventeenth-century paradigm. After an initial collaboration (Hilbert and Kalderon 2000), as I continued to work on color and color perception (Kalderon 2007, 2008, 2011a, 2011b, 2011c), it became increasingly clear that I was defending an anti-modern conception of color and perception. The conception of color defended was anti-modern in that the colors were in no way secondary, but mind-independent qualities that inhere in material bodies. The conception of color perception was anti-modern in that it was not conceived as a conscious alteration of a perceiving subject, but rather as the presentation of instances of mind-independent color qualities located at a distance from the perceiver. The anti-modern metaphysics provided an additional motive to look to historical, and in particular, premodern sources. Doing so was a means of self-consciously disrupting habits of mind inculcated by the modern paradigm that has reigned for four centuries.

There is a third additional motive for the turn to historical sources, one flowing from the methodology pursued in the present essay. Given our presupposition that sensory presentation is irreducible, and leaving to one side what form a positive account of sensory presentation could take if it is not, indeed, a reduction of some sort, how are we to proceed? How can one gain insight into the nature of the irreducible presentational element of perceptual experience? My thought, not at all original, was to proceed dialectically, by considering puzzles about the nature of sensory presentation. As it happens, there are a number of historically salient such puzzles that are useful for a metaphysician proceeding dialectically to consider (for a detailed historical discussion of at least one of these, see Kalderon 2015). Moreover, many of these puzzles are premodern, though they have been obscured by the prevailing modern paradigm.

It can often happen, in the course of dialectical argument, that the insights of one's predecessors are not only preserved, but transformed. Thus, it can happen that a respected predecessor was right to hold a certain opinion, but only on an understanding as of yet unavailable to them. That is one way, at least, in which the insights of our predecessors may be transformed even as they are preserved in the course of dialectical argument. This bears on the question of how such historical borrowing is to be understood. There is no real possibility of rolling back philosophical thinking to the fifth century BC, say, just as there is no real possibility of living "the life of a Bronze Age Chief, or a Medieval Samurai," in our present historical circumstances, as Williams (1981, 140) reminds us. In deploying ancient or Scholastic concepts in a contemporary metaphysical inquiry new sense is accrued, and such borrowings become a kind of concept formation (Moore 2012, 587–8). New sense is accrued when an ancient or Scholastic concept is applied to novel problems that arise in a theoretical and historical context distinct from the one in which the concept was originally formed. Compare Bergson's (1912a) retrofitting the concepts of Stoic physics in the development of his philosophical psychology. If we are to take it at all seriously, it can only be understood as a method of concept formation. Moreover, novel concepts are what are needed if one hopes to contribute to, if not indeed effect, a Kuhnian revolution against the prevailing modern paradigm.

That the present metaphysical inquiry proceeds dialectically bears on its speculative character. In proceeding dialectically, in taking puzzles about the nature of sensory presentation as a guide to uncovering its nature, the present essay is aporetic and exploratory. Its conclusions necessarily fall short of apodeictic proof. This, at any rate, should be obvious since the conclusion of dialectical argument hardly constitutes an a priori demonstration, drawing, as it may, upon the testimony of the many and the wise, as well as any empirical evidence as may be relevant.

Self-proclaimed naturalistic metaphysicians sometimes lampoon their opponents as engaging in a priori reasoning from the armchair. But eschewing reductionism about sensory presentation while pursuing insight into its nature by proceeding dialectically, no a priori demonstration is offered. Nor indeed could there be if the ambition is to contribute to, if not indeed effect, a Kuhnian revolution. Demonstrations are only possible at the stage of normal science. Demonstrations require a stable conceptual framework, about which there is widespread and non-collusive agreement, in which to take place. Part of the present task is to disrupt just such a framework.

A more specific task provides a fourth motivation for why the present metaphysical inquiry should be historically informed. I have long been puzzled by the primordial and persistent tactile metaphors for sensory awareness, even for non-tactile modes of sensory awareness such as vision and audition. Such imagery persists even among those who would eschew any explanation of perception in terms of, or on analogy with, tactile perception. Thus, in a remarkable passage, Brian O'Shaughnessy, a careful, independent thinker, warns against taking such tactile metaphors too literally but cannot restrain himself from deploying such a metaphor in describing the contrasting conception:

> I think there is a tendency to conceive of attentive *contact* [my emphasis], which is to say of perceptual awareness, as a kind of palpable or concrete contact of the mind with its object. And in one sense of these terms, this belief is surely correct ... However, there is a tendency – or perhaps an imagery of a kind that may be at work in one's mind – to overinterpret this "concreteness," to think of it as in some way akin to, as a mental analogue of, something drawn from the realm of *things* – a palpable connection of some kind, rather as if the gaze literally reached out and touched its object. (O'Shaughnessy 2003, 183)

And M. G. F. Martin has observed that "content" is a metaphor of assimilation – to have a content is to be, in a way, its container, containment being itself a mode of assimilation, as is grasping. Moreover, Martin also notes the way in which this imagery is in tension with the theoretical role content plays in representationalist theories of perception. For surely what is contained within a perception is its object, but the content of that perception is not the object of perception. Rather, the object of that perception is what is represented by its content (Martin 1998).

I wanted to understand why contemporary philosophers apply tactile metaphors for sensory awareness unselfconsciously, indeed, unconsciously – even when such imagery ultimately fails to cohere with their espoused doctrine. One explanation, to be pursued throughout this essay, is that without reducing perception generally to sensation by contact, there is, nonetheless, a way in which tactile metaphors for sensory presentation are apt. Moreover, if tactile metaphors for perception generally are apt in the way that I shall suggest they are, then the resulting conception of perception is anti-modern, or so shall I argue. But if it is, then the unconscious tendency to apply tactile metaphors for sensory awareness, even if it is in tension with one's stated doctrine, is subject to a psychoanalytic explanation, hence rendering the present essay a psychoanalytic narrative. It is the return of the repressed. Or more specifically, the return of what has been repressed by the modern paradigm. Our unconscious use of tactile metaphors for sensory awareness is the vestigial remnant of a vivid sense of the Manifest Image of Nature and our perceptual relation to it not utterly extinguished by four centuries of modernity.

Grasping is at the center of a semantic field of tactile metaphors for sensory awareness loosely organized as modes of assimilation (Section 1.1). I attempt to understand what, if anything, makes grasping an apt metaphor for sensory awareness more generally by undertaking a phenomenological investigation into grasping or enclosure understood as a mode of haptic perception. The idea is that if we better appreciate how grasping presents itself from within haptic experience, we will be in a better position to understand what, if anything, makes grasping an apt metaphor for perception generally. Moreover, in undertaking this phenomenological investigation we shall freely draw upon empirical and historical sources. Empirical psychology has a lot to teach us about the phenomenology of haptic experience. But so does the testimony of our respected predecessors and the puzzles that arise both within and without the *endoxa*.

Moreover, there is a reason why a phenomenological investigation into haptic experience whose ultimate aim is to uncover the aptness of tactile metaphors for perception generally should take the form of a conceptual genealogy. In looking at earlier occurrences of such metaphors, when they were more strongly etched in light and shadow, one can get a better sense of what made them live for these earlier thinkers and, by extension, a better sense of the power they continue to exercise over us. At any rate, it is almost impossible to get anywhere merely by examining the unself-conscious metaphors deployed by contemporary philosophers – they are lifeless in their hands. Much better to examine earlier occurrences of these metaphors, when they were more strongly and vividly felt, to get a sense of their power and persistent aptness.

Thinking our way to the future by thinking our way through the past may strike some as hopelessly anachronistic. In my defense I only say that, here, I am following Ricoeur (2004, xvii) in exercising "the right of every reader, before whom all the books are open simultaneously."

The present use of historical material contrasts with the use of historical material in my previous book. *Form without Matter* was an essay in the philosophy of perception written in the medium of historiography. Though it was an essay in the philosophy of perception, like the ancient commentators, I primarily worked exegetically. While the present essay is historically informed in the ways that I have described, I do not, however, primarily work exegetically. In the present essay, I am driven less to understand the history of my subject matter than to speculatively resolve certain puzzles concerning it. In the present essay, then, selective historical reflection is in the service of, and subordinate to, this larger aim in speculative metaphysics. Toward this end, I have endeavored, less to interpret and exposit our predecessors systematically, than to speak to them across the ages like colleagues (see Ryle 1971, 10–11).

The present essay is an exercise in historically informed speculative metaphysics. I have explained in what sense it is speculative and in what sense it is historically informed. But in what sense is it metaphysics? Consider the central question to be pursued in the present essay: What is it for the object of perception to be present in the perceiver's experience of it? This is a metaphysical question. It concerns what it is to be something. Specifically, it concerns what it is to be present in perceptual experience. In asking what it is to be something, one asks a metaphysical question, even should the thing, whose being one is inquiring into, turn out to be mental. "But metaphysics concerns extra-mental reality!", one might object. One might, but the objection is not very cogent. Substance dualism is a metaphysical thesis. That there are two mutually exclusive kinds of substances is, straightforwardly, a metaphysical thesis. And it remains one, even when one of these kinds of substances turns out to be essentially thinking and hence mental.

The results of the present inquiry may strike analytically inclined philosophers to be more in line with continental metaphysics. And while the present essay is self-consciously a departure from the prevailing orthodoxy of analytic metaphysics, it remains true to, and is a staunch defense of, what has been a central tenet of analytic metaphysics from its inception, namely, realism. And while it is true that recent continental thinkers have recovered for themselves a form of realism, the present perceptual realism is more in line with Cook Wilson (1926) than Meillassoux (2008). Moreover, continental philosophers will quickly recognize that the present essay defends, in Heideggerian terminology, a metaphysics of presence. The present conception of sensory presentation is thus fundamentally at odds with conceptions of perception developed within the phenomenological tradition. To be honest, I care little for such categories. And in what follows I have drawn freely from a variety of sources.

Acknowledgments

Fortuitous serendipity has been all too evident in the composition of the present essay. Tempering the humility I feel in recognizing this – there, but for the hand of chance, go I – is the further recognition of just how much work must go into making such serendipitous encounters both possible and fortuitous. I owe a debt to many, both for providing occasions for such encounters and for preparing the way for them. Allow me to acknowledge some of them.

For a number of years now, I have taught a course structured around the opening remarks of C. D. Broad's (1952) "Some elementary reflections on sense-perception." The first five pages of that essay involve a comparative phenomenology of vision, audition, and touch. The class proceeds by evaluating Broad's comparative phenomenological claims in light of more recent literature about the senses. Sometimes I feel that my students got a raw deal. Not that I was neglectful in my pedagogical duty. Rather, I feel that I learned more from these class discussions than they did. For all that I have learned from them, and all the serendipitous encounters that they have helped prepare the way for, I am most grateful.

Material from the first two chapters was presented in a research seminar at UCL in 2015. I am very grateful to all who participated, especially for the many clarifications they elicited from me that resulted in considerable improvement of the text.

To Maarten Steenhagen I am grateful for one such serendipitous encounter. In *De spiritu fantastico sive de recptione specierum*, Robert Kilwardby provides a vitalist twist on the Peripatetic analogy of perception with wax receiving the impression of a seal. Specifically, Kilwardby imagines life to inhere in the wax and to be actively pressing against the seal. Reflection on Kilwardby's vitalist twist on the Peripatetic analogy forms one of the key threads throughout this book. I am very grateful to Steenhagen for bringing my attention to it. I am also grateful for his intellectual companionship.

We have discussed these and related issues over the years. Steenhagen also read some preliminary drafts of early chapters, which helped me to improve them greatly, for which I am also indebted.

Craig French also read drafts of two chapters. The level-headed clarity of his comments, and more than that, the demand that I too should sometimes display such clarity, prompted considerable improvement, and for that I am most grateful. I am also very grateful to have had the opportunity to discuss the nature of perception with French over a number of years.

I have long wondered whether extramission theories of perception, though false if interpreted as causal models of perception, might, nonetheless, express some phenomenological truth. A serendipitous encounter with Keith Allen introduced me to the research of Winer and Cottrell (1996). Allen also pointed out this research's relevance to a passage in Merleau-Ponty. This provided renewed impetus to think about the phenomenological underpinnings of extramission and Chapter 5 is the result. I am also grateful to Allen for discussions, over the years, about color and the nature of perception.

Clare Mac Cumhaill provided another serendipitous encounter in reminding me of a passage in Hans Jonas that plays a key role in Chapter 5, for which I am grateful as well. My colleague Sarah Richmond, upon encountering me in the hallway clutching a copy of Maine de Biran's *Influence de l'habitude sur la faculté de penser*, pointed out to me some relevant passages in Sartre that proved very useful and for which I am most grateful.

A not unsympathetic, if not exactly credulous, audience at the University of Glasgow to whom I presented material culled from Chapters 1 and 2 in 2014 provided much-needed feedback and prompted considerable improvement. I would especially like to thank Fiona MacPherson for her comments on that occasion.

I owe a debt of gratitude to Charles Travis for his friendship, intellectual companionship, and encouragement. His encouragement proffered at an early critical period kept me motivated, and for that, I am especially grateful. I am also indebted to Matt Soteriou, who also generously proffered encouragement at a critical period.

Mike Martin has been a friend and colleague since I first arrived at UCL. My discussions with him about the nature of perception have been invaluable. I doubt, though, that he would approve of the application of his insights, which must appear in the text as if reflected through a glass darkly. Sometimes, as I wrote, I fancied that I could hear a Humean growling somewhere. Is it wrong to give thanks when, perhaps, an apology is due?

Greenwich Park is a ten-minute walk from where I live in Blackheath. As I composed the present work, I walked through that park almost daily. In a Peripatetic fashion, much of my thinking was done on these walks. And before I even embarked upon the present work, Plotinus' *Enneads*, an inspiration to much of what follows, were read, for the most part, in the rose garden of Greenwich Park. It is perhaps unsurprising, then, that the park emerges as a minor character in the examples that I give. Let these remarks serve as both an acknowledgment and an expression of gratitude.

Finally, I would like to thank the readers for the Press who provided detailed and insightful comments. I have learned a lot from these, and I am very grateful for the spur they provided. I would also like to thank Hilary Gaskin for her help and encouragement in seeing the present essay into print.

CHAPTER I

Grasping

1.1 The Dawn of Understanding

In a justly famous scene from *2001: A Space Odyssey*, set to Richard Strauss's *Also Sprach Zarathustra*, a hominid ancestor, squatting among the skeletal remains of a tapir, reaches out and tentatively grasps a femur. It is telling that this is how Stanley Kubrick chose to dramatize the initial transformation, induced by an alien obelisk, of our hominid ancestors, that eventually gives rise to space-exploring humanity in the twenty-first century. Not only does our hominid ancestor grasp the femur, but they grasp, as well, an important application. Squatting among the skeletal remains, femur in hand, our hominid ancestor taps the bones in an exploratory manner. Each strike of the femur grows in force until finally, in a crescendo of activity, they smash the tapir's skull to pieces. Our hominid ancestor has reached a crucial insight, that an implement, such as the femur, might transform tapir into prey. Moreover, the application generalizes. The femur might also be used as a weapon against competing groups of hominids. The acquired technology thus has political consequences. What is presently important, however, is the connection between grasping and cognition. We say we have grasped a situation when we have understood it. And philosophers are prone to speak of thinkers grasping the thoughts they think. Kubrick dramatizes the connection between grasping and cognition by having our hominid ancestor's grasping the femur among the tapir's skeletal remains be the primal scene of a dawning understanding.

We have *grasped* a situation when we have understood it. We have a *grip* on it. If the understanding in question is practical, we might say that we have *matters in hand*. And we *touch upon* subjects for discussion. Nor are tactile metaphors confined to forms of higher cognition and their expression in rational discourse. They persist, as well, in our description of perceptual awareness. Not only do we speak of recognizing an object that we see as *grasping* the object present in our perceptual experience, but the presentation in experience is itself a kind of grasping. In perceiving an object we *apprehend* it. In this way, perception puts us in *contact* with its object. The tactile metaphors for perceptual awareness tend, on the whole, to be modes of assimilation, and *ingestion* is a natural variant (see Johnston 2006b; Price 1932), as when we *drink in* the scene. Thus, for example, Peter John Olivi and Jacopo Zabarella use the Latin *imbibere*, to drink in, to describe perceptual apprehension. While drinking in is a species of gustation and so not, strictly speaking, a species of touch, it does, however, involve a tactile component. Relatedly, our hominid ancestor, looking up from the tapir's remains, *takes in* the scene before them. Indeed, this metaphor is inscribed into the history of the English language – "perception" derives from the Latin *perceptio*, meaning to *take in* or *assimilate* (Burnyeat 1979, 102). If in looking up from the tapir's remains, they see the obelisk, then, in a manner of speaking common among contemporary philosophers, the obelisk is the *content* of our hominid ancestor's perception. But if the obelisk is the content of their perception, then their perception of it is its *container*. To bring something into view so that it figures in the content of perception would be to contain it within that perception. But containment itself is a mode of assimilation.

Even granting the primordial and persistent use of tactile metaphors for perception and cognition more generally, one may wonder whether grasping is really at the center of the semantic field of metaphors for sensory presentation. Grasping may involve contact, but not all contact involves grasping, not even all perceptual modes of contact. Some elements of the semantic field, such as talk of "contact," are logically independent of grasping. And this can raise the following worry. Perhaps for something to be present in sensory experience is for the perceiver to be in perceptual contact with it. If so, perhaps it is contact, and not grasping, that is the central metaphor for sensory presentation. Grasping, on this interpretation, is something further than the object of perception being presented in the perceiver's experience. Perhaps to grasp what we are in perceptual contact with is to recognize what perception presents us with.

The logical observation that occasioned this worry does not force upon us the alternative reading where contact is sensory presentation and grasping recognition (though, as we have observed, the metaphor of grasping can have such uses). That there can be perceptual contact without grasping is consistent with contact being an important component of grasping that is at the center of the semantic field. Thus, for example, Broad (1952) uses both "contact" and "prehension" for sensory presentation presumably because prehending the object of perception involves being in contact with it. Talk of contact captures the visceral immediacy of sensory presentation, its force and vivacity. Moreover, talk of contact emphasizes the existence of an external limit determined by that with which we are in contact, the experience of which, as we shall see, plays an important role in sensory presentation. Talk of grasping, on the other hand, captures other important aspects of perceptual presentation, specifically, that it is apt to think of perception as a mode of assimilation. Moreover, it will emerge that the objectivity of perception is best understood in terms of perception formally assimilating to its object in the sense that it does. In this way, the full justification for the claim that grasping is at the center of a semantic field of metaphors for sensory presentation consists in the fruits that it will bear. However, that is not all that can be said. The hypothesis that grasping is at the center of the semantic field can explain why contact is included, but the alternative hypothesis that contact is at the center of the semantic field could not explain why so many of the other metaphors are modes of assimilation.

What makes tactile metaphors for perception apt? Tactile metaphors for perceptual awareness, even for non-tactile modes of awareness such as vision and audition, are primordial and persistent. Most contemporary philosophers of perception apply them unselfconsciously, indeed, unconsciously. That they do is a testament to the power of such metaphors. Understanding the power they have over us, understanding what makes them so compelling, we may gain insight into the object of these metaphors. In understanding what makes grasping an apt metaphor for perception generally, if it is indeed one, we may gain insight into the nature of sensory presentation. Or so I suggest.

We shall begin with a phenomenological investigation into the nature of grasping, a form of haptic touch. The investigation is phenomenological in that it seeks to uncover how grasping, understood as a mode of haptic perception, presents itself from within tactile experience. It is phenomenological because the object of investigation is restricted to perceptual appearances and not because of any methodology deployed in pursuing that investigation. The investigation thus need not involve "bracketing," nor need it confine itself to the deliverances of introspection in determining the nature of haptic appearance (for discussion of the reliability of introspection, see Bayne and Spener 2010; Schwitzgebel 2008). In trying to understand how grasping, understood as a mode of haptic perception, presents itself from within tactile experience, we may avail ourselves of empirical and historical resources. Once we have a better understanding of how grasping presents itself from within tactile experience, we will be in a better position to understand why grasping also presents itself as an exemplar of sensory presentation more generally.

We may avail ourselves of empirical resources since phenomenology is something about which discoveries can be made. As Hilbert (2005) and Phillips (2012) argue, psychophysics can contribute to our understanding of perceptual phenomenology. Similarly, we might reasonably expect empirical research to reveal important aspects of the phenomenology of haptic perception. Indeed, as Fulkerson (2014) argues at length, there is much to learn about the phenomenology of haptic perception from its empirical study.

In investigating the phenomenology of haptic perception, not only may we avail ourselves of empirical resources, but we may also avail ourselves of historical resources. If I am right that our unselfconscious, indeed, unconscious, use of tactile metaphors for perception is best explained by their persistent aptness, then looking at early historical examples of these metaphors, when they were more vivid and strongly felt, promises to shed light on those aspects of the phenomenology of haptic experience that make them apt.

Grasping may be an apt metaphor for perception generally, and to that extent at least, an exemplar of sensory presentation, but it does not follow that all perception is a form of touch. One may grant that tactile metaphors for perceptual awareness are in some sense apt while eschewing any such reductive explanatory ambition. Such ambitions were rife in Greek antiquity. Thus Lindberg (1977, 39) observes that in the ancient world, "the analogy of perception by contact in the sense of touch seemed to establish to nearly everybody's satisfaction that contact was tantamount to sensation, and it was not apparent that further explanation was required." Aristotle criticizes this reductive explanatory strategy. Conceiving of nontactile modes of perceptual awareness on the model of touch will only seem explanatory insofar as touch is antecedently understood to be an unproblematic mode of perception. However, Aristotle's belaboring and not always completely resolving the *aporiai* concerning touch in *De anima* 2 11 undermines that assumption (Derrida 2005; Kalderon 2015). And if further explanation is required, then we can no longer simply assume that contact is tantamount to sensation. Nevertheless, Aristotle accepts the aptness of the metaphor. Perception, for Aristotle, remains a mode of assimilation. Aristotle defines perception as the assimilation of sensible form without the matter of the perceived particular (*De anima* 2 12 424 a 18–23, 2 5 418 a 3–6). So acceptance of the aptness of the metaphor carries with it no commitment to any such reductive explanatory ambition. Grasping may be an apt metaphor for perception, even for non-tactile modes of perceptual awareness, such as vision and audition, without perception being reduced to a form of touch. Indeed, if perception is reduced to touch, then what strikes us as tactile metaphors for perception generally would, in truth, be no metaphors at all.

1.2 Haptic Perception

Grasping is a form of haptic touch. Haptic touch involves active exploration of the tangible object. This can involve a range of different stereotypical exploratory activities often combined in sequence. The different stereotypical exploratory activities are suited to presenting different ranges of tangible qualities. Thus to discern the texture of an object the perceiver may deploy lateral movement across its surface. Holding a stone in their hand, our hominid ancestor may feel the roughness of the stone by rubbing their thumb across its surface. And its hardness may be felt by applying pressure to it. According to the taxonomy of Lederman and Klatzky (1987), grasping is a distinctive exploratory activity that they describe as "enclosure." Grasping an object allows the perceiver to discern a different range of tangible qualities. If texture is perceived by lateral motion and hardness by applying pressure, grasping or enclosure makes volume and global shape available in tactile experience. Other stereotypical exploratory activities include: "static contact" – passively resting one's hand on an externally supported object, without an effort to mold to its contours, to determine its temperature; "unsupported holding" – holding the object without external support, and without molding, to determine the object's heft or weight often involving a "weighing" motion; "contour following" – a smooth, non-repetitive tracing of the contours of the object; "part motion test" – moving a part of the object independently of the whole; and "specific function test" – moving the object in such a way as to perform various functions. Though these stereotypical exploratory activities are optimized for determining a specific range of tangible qualities, they can also determine other tangible qualities, though perhaps less well, with less tactual acuity. Thus while grasping or enclosure may present the overall shape of the object, to determine its exact shape the perceiver must use contour following. Grasping, however, like contour following, is relatively general in the range of tangible qualities it can present. Thus, grasping is itself a way of applying pressure to an object and, hence, a way of perceiving its hardness, as well as other of the object's tangible qualities such as temperature, moistness, vibration, a metallic feel, and so on. Not only are these stereotypical exploratory activities optimized to determine a specific range of tangible qualities that vary in generality, but they can also be chained together to provide the perceiver with a more complete profile of the corporeal aspects of the object under investigation.

With enclosure, Lederman and Klatzky write:

> the hand maintains simultaneous contact with as much of the envelope of the object as possible. Often one can see an effort to mold the hand more precisely to object contours. Periods of static enclosure may alternate with shifts of the object in the hand(s). (1987, 346–7)

The quoted passage brings out several important features of grasping, understood as a mode of haptic perception.

First, grasping a rigid, solid body involves the hand's maintaining simultaneous contact with as much of its overall surface as possible. Grasping is thus a kind of incorporation. Recall that what unites the various tactile metaphors for perception, even for non-tactile modes of perceptual awareness such as vision and audition, is that they tend to be modes of assimilation, and grasping exemplifies this pattern. It may not be as complete an incorporation as the variant, ingestion, but it remains a clear mode of assimilation nonetheless. In maintaining simultaneous contact with as much of its overall surface as possible, the hand assimilates to the contours of the object. As we shall see, that the grasping hand assimilates to the object grasped is a manifestation of the objectivity of that haptic perception. This is part of what makes it an apt metaphor for perceptual presentation more generally.

Second, not only does the grasping hand assimilate to the overall shape and volume of the object grasped, but, as Lederman and Klatzky (1987) observe, effort is typically exerted to mold the hand more precisely to the object's contours. So grasping or enclosure involves not only the hand's configuration in maintaining simultaneous contact with the overall surface of the object, but the force of the hand's activity as well. Not only is this force exerted in achieving the end of molding the hand more perfectly to contours of the object grasped (on the preparatory reach involved in grasping see Jones and Lederman 2006, chapter 6), but it is exerted as well in the end's achievement – maintaining simultaneous contact with the overall surface of the object requires continued effort to sustain. This is physiologically and phenomenologically significant. It is physiologically significant in that the activation of different sets of receptors is coordinated in haptic perception (see Fulkerson 2014, chapter 3, and Hatwell et al. 2003, chapter 1, for discussion). Grasping or enclosure will involve not only cutaneous activation, but also the distinct sets of activations involved in kinesthesis, motor control, and our sense of agency. Moreover, this is reflected in our phenomenology. We feel the force with which we grip the object as well as the object's overall shape and volume.

Third, there is a tendency, in grasping or enclosure, to shift the object periodically in one's hands. What explains this? Begin with Lederman and Klatzky's (1987) observation that there is a tendency for perceivers to exert effort to mold their hand more precisely to the contours of the object grasped. In grasping an object, the grasping hand in this way assimilates to the overall shape and volume of the object grasped. Consider grasping a rigid, solid body, such as a stone. In grasping a stone, our hominid ancestor extends their hand's activity; they tighten their grasp, until they can no more. Since the stone is solid, it resists penetration. Since it is rigid, it maintains its overall shape and volume even when in the hominid's grasp. Contrast the way the overall shape and volume of an elastic body, such as a sponge, deforms as it is squeezed. With the stone in its grip, the hand of our hominid ancestor assimilates to the overall shape and volume of the stone. Of course, hands are unevenly shaped and imperfectly elastic. This means that an effort to mold one's hand to a rigid, solid body thus disclosing its overall shape and volume will most likely be imperfectly realized. There may be some areas of the object's surface that the grasping hand does not conform to. Haptic perception is thus partial in something like Hilbert's (1987) sense. Perception is partial if the object of perception is not wholly present in the awareness of it afforded by perceptual experience. There may be more to the object of perception, even in its sensible aspects, than is determined in any given perception. The tendency to shift the grasped object in our hands compensates for this partial and imperfect disclosure. In shifting the object in one's hand, an area that the hand did not previously conform to may become accessible to touch. Successive grips and the manner in which the object moves in one's hands as one shifts between them may provide a better overall sense of the shape and volume of the rigid, solid body.

I have offered an explanation of the tendency, observed by Lederman and Klatzky (1987), for the perceiver to shift the object of haptic exploration periodically in their hands in terms of the partiality of haptic perception. That explanation is incomplete. Active exploration of the object of haptic investigation could only be motivated to compensate for its partial and imperfect disclosure if the perceiver has the sense, perhaps instinctive, that there is more to the corporeal nature of the object than is disclosed in their grasp. This is the allure of the tangible – the sense, or premonition, that, at any given moment, the body exceeds what is disclosed to us by touch. Our tactile sense of a body's "thingness" – its concrete particularity – consists, in part, in this allure. (Compare Harman's 2005, 141–4, discussion of allure; though, for Harman, allure carries with it, not only the suggestion of hidden depths, but inaccessibility as well.) Without this primitive sense that there are further tangible aspects of the body as of yet unfelt, the partiality of haptic perception, by itself, could not explain the tendency for perceivers to shift the object of haptic investigation periodically in their hands. The partial and imperfect character of haptic disclosure must itself be disclosed in the haptic experience that affords it.

The explanation is incomplete in another way. In periodically shifting the object in their hands to compensate for the partial and imperfect disclosure of the object grasped, the perceiver's haptic experience must exhibit perceptual constancy as well (on the importance of constancy phenomena to understanding perception, see Burge 2010; Smith 2002).

Very often, objects in the scene before us are somehow perceived to be constant or uniform or unchanging in color, shape, size, or position, even while their appearance with respect to these features somehow changes. This is a familiar and pervasive fact about perception, even if it is notoriously difficult to describe accurately let alone adequately account for. Perceptual constancy is not confined to vision. Importantly, it is exhibited in haptic perception as well. Thus, for example, our haptic experience of roughness exhibits perceptual constancy (Yoshioka et al. 2011). The texture of a stone picked up by our hominid ancestor will feel rough, and just as rough when felt with a quick motion as when felt with a slow motion, even though feeling the stone's rough texture with a quick motion does not feel the same as feeling it with a slow motion. Other forms of haptic perception exhibit perceptual constancy as well.

Grasping or enclosure, understood as a mode of haptic perception, itself exhibits perceptual constancy. Thus, the perceiver feels the constant overall shape and volume of the object even though it feels different in successive grips. What the perceiver feels in moving the object between successive grips changes throughout this process, but the object disclosed by this haptic exploration is not Protean in character. If the object were changing its overall shape and volume in the process of the perceiver's handling it, then shifting the object could be no compensation for the partial and imperfect disclosure of the object grasped. If the object were Protean, and the perceiver shifted it in their hands, then its overall shape and volume would change, and the opportunity to feel what was unfelt would be forever lost.

In grasping, understood as a mode of haptic perception, the perceiver attends only to the constant tangible qualities it presents; in the case of a rigid, solid body, the perceiver attends to its constant overall shape and volume, as well as other constant tangible qualities that grasping may disclose. Though there may be a felt difference in changing patterns of intensive sensation in handling the object (changing patterns of pressure and thermal sensation, say), haptic experience presents the constant overall shape and volume of the object. Of course, different aspects of the overall shape and volume may be present at different times, given the different ways the body is being handled. Sensory presentation being partial, the perceiver may now feel this corner and now that. But these presented aspects of the overall shape of a rigid, solid body are experienced as stable aspects of a body that retains its shape, despite the perceiver's handling, because of the self-maintaining forces at work in its constitution. So the tendency, observed by Lederman and Klatzky (1987), for the perceiver to periodically shift the object in their hands is not only explained by the partiality of haptic perception, but could only be so explained if the haptic experience this behavior gives rise to exhibits perceptual constancy. (Compare Matthen's 2015 discussion of the construction of isotropic perceptual models in active perception.)

Allow me to make two further observations about this passage, though now about issues that are merely implicit.

First, grasping is an activity and so is spread over time. It has duration. Not only does our hominid ancestor tentatively reach out and grasp the tapir's femur from among its skeletal remains – an event with duration – but its grasp must be actively maintained over a period of time. Maintaining simultaneous contact with the overall surface of a rigid body, or some non-insignificant portion of it, is a state sustained by activity. In this regard, it is like Ryle's (1949, 149) example of keeping the enemy at bay, or Kripke's (1972/1980) example of the connection between heat and molecular motion. The state thus obtains for the duration of the sustaining activity. Moreover, in coming to perceive its overall shape and volume, the perceiver may shift the object in their hand. The tactile sense of an object's overall shape or volume is disclosed by such activity. And since activity has duration, it is disclosed over time. The presentation of the overall shape and volume of an object in tactile experience is itself spread over time like the activity that discloses it. One potential lesson, then, for the metaphysics of sensory presentation, is that the object of perception may be disclosed over time, that its presentation in perceptual experience may have duration.

Second, that the grasping hand assimilates to the overall shape and volume of the object grasped is potentially epistemically significant. The full case for this will have to wait (Section 1.5 and Chapter 6.1), but we can begin to get a sense of why this might be so. A rigid, solid body has a certain overall shape and volume prior to being grasped. Moreover, it is sufficiently rigid and solid to maintain that overall shape and volume even when grasped. In making an effort to more precisely mold the hand to the contours of the rigid, solid object, the hand thus takes on, to an approximate degree, the overall shape and volume of the object grasped. That is to say, the hand takes on a certain configuration determined by the hand's anatomy, the activity of the hand, and the overall shape of the object grasped. And with the hand so configured, the shape of its interior approximates the overall shape of the object grasped. Moreover, the hand, so configured, encompasses a region of a certain volume itself determined by the hand and the volume of the object grasped. And the volume of the region that the hand encompasses approximates the volume of the object grasped. That is the point of making an effort to more precisely mold the hand to contours of the rigid object. In engaging in such haptic activity, in molding one's hand more precisely to the contours of the object, one ensures that the overall shape and volume the object had prior to being grasped, and maintained in being grasped, explains, in part, the hand's configuration in grasping the object and the force that needs to be exerted to maintain that configuration. Suppose that it is our hand's configuration in grasping and the force that needs to be exerted in maintaining that configuration that discloses the overall shape and volume of the object. If so, at least in the present instance, haptic perception is dependent, in some appropriate sense, upon proprioception, kinesthesis, our capacity for motor activity, and our sense of agency (for relevant discussion, see Fulkerson 2014; Martin 1992; O'Shaughnessy 1989, 1995; we will discuss this dependency in Chapter 2). Since the object's overall shape and volume explains the hand's configuration and force, if the object eludes the hand's grasp, then that configuration and force would not have occurred. If the object is absent, there is nothing for the hand to assimilate to. Perhaps the objectivity of grasping, understood as a mode of haptic perception, consists in the grasping hand's assimilating to the tangible qualities the object had prior to grasping.

Against this suggestion, it might be objected that, at least for certain graspings, it is possible for the object to be absent and yet the hand to be in a duplicate configuration. However, a felt difference would remain. Maintaining the hand's configuration in the absence of the object requires different muscle activity since the perceiver can no longer rely on pressing against the rigid body in maintaining that configuration. The different pattern of activation of receptors in muscles and joints will result in a felt difference. Compare leaning against a wall with making as if to lean against a wall. Sustaining that posture in the absence of the supporting wall can be difficult to do. Miming is an acquired skill. As Jacques Tati demonstrates in *Cours du Soir*, it can be taught and learned. So in the case of duplicate configuration, where the hand takes on the configuration it would have had if it were grasping the object, while the hand's configuration has been maintained in the absence of the object, there is a felt difference in the force exerted.

That the grasping hand assimilates to the contours of the object grasped is potentially epistemically significant. It is, if not the source of that haptic perception's objectivity, then its manifestation. In grasping an object, the hand assimilates to the object's contours. If in grasping an object, the hand's configuration and force disclose the object's overall shape and volume, and that configuration and force would not have occurred in the absence of the object grasped, then our tactile experience would not be as it is when we haptically perceive if that object were in fact absent. While not yet proof against a Cartesian demon, one can begin to see the potential epistemic significance of the effort exerted in more precisely molding one's hand against the contours of the object grasped. It is the means by which certain tangible qualities of an external body are disclosed in our grasp. We shall return to this issue in Section 1.5 and again in Chapter 6.1.

1.3   The Protagorean Model

We have undertaken to uncover how grasping, understood as a mode of haptic perception, presents itself from within tactile experience. The investigation is phenomenological in the sense that the object of investigation is restricted to perceptual appearances. Moreover, we have engaged in a phenomenological investigation into the nature of grasping, understood as a mode of haptic perception, in order to understand what makes grasping an apt metaphor, if it is, of perception more generally, including non-tactile modes of perception. Perhaps part of the aptness of the metaphor consists in providing a model for sensory presentation more generally. On the basis of our discussion of Lederman and Klatzky (1987), we are now in a position to sketch, to a first approximation, the contours of such a model. It is usefully compared, if only to highlight the differences, with the conception of perception that Socrates attributes to Protagoras.

In the *Theaetetus* 156 a–c, Socrates elaborates the Secret Doctrine of Protagoras by providing an account of perception as the contingent outcome of active and passive forces in conflict. Grasping as a mode of haptic perception can seem to approximate to that account. At the very least, the felt shape and volume of the object grasped is determined by conflicting forces. On the one hand, there is the force exerted in molding the hand more precisely to the contours of the rigid, solid body. On the other hand, there are the self-maintaining forces of the rigid, solid body itself. A rigid, solid body, such as a stone picked up by a hominid ancestor, is no mere sum of matter. It has a form or material structure determined by forces that are the categorical bases for its rigidity and solidity (Johnston 2006a; compare also Leibniz's and Kant's dynamical theories of matter). Haptic perception is the joint upshot of the force exerted by the grasping hand and the self-maintaining forces of the object grasped. There remains a crucial difference, however, from the account elaborated by Socrates. The overall shape and volume of the object and our haptic perception of them are not "twin births" as Protagoras maintains:

> Motion has two forms, each an infinite multitude, but distinguished by their powers, the one being active and the other passive. And through the intercourse and mutual friction of these two there comes to be an offspring infinite in multitude but always twin births, on the one hand what is perceived, on the other, the perception of it, the perception in every case being generated together with what is perceived and emerging along with it. (Plato, *Theaetetus* 156 a–b; Levett and Burnyeat in Cooper 1997, 173–4)

Aristotle's criticism of Protagoras often fits the following pattern: an important concession is made to Protagoras, only for Aristotle to argue that the concession can only be accepted on an understanding unavailable to the Protagorean (see, for example, *Metaphysica* Γ 5 1010 b 30–1011 a 2 and see Kalderon 2015, chapter 2.1.1, for discussion). In appropriating the Protagorean model, we shall be following Aristotle's lead.

Begin with the way in which haptic perception, as so far described, differs from the conception of perception that figures in the Secret Doctrine. The forces that determine the object's rigidity and solidity are sufficient to maintain the object's overall shape and volume within the hand's grasp. So the perceived tangible qualities of the external body inhere in that body prior to being perceived, whereas in the account attributed to Protagoras, the perceived object comes into being with the perceiver's perception of it. One might concede to Protagoras that the presentation of the object's overall shape and volume in tactile experience and the perceiver's feeling its overall shape and volume are, in fact, "twin births." It is at least the case that if overall shape and volume are not present in tactile experience, then they are not felt, and if they are not felt, they are not present in tactile experience, at least not in that way. But not only is this consistent with perceptual realism, it is only intelligibly sustained against the background of a realist metaphysics. If a tangible quality's presentation in tactile experience is explained, in part, by that quality inhering in the object perceived, then the object must possess this quality prior to perception. There is a connection, then, between explanatory priority and objectivity (this, I argue, is Aristotle's view, Kalderon 2015). At least with respect to grasping or enclosure, understood as a mode of haptic perception, this perceptual realism is sustained by the force of the hand's activity in conflict with the self-maintaining forces of the object grasped. At the very least, the force of the hand's activity ensures that the tangible quality determined by the object's self-maintaining forces explains the hand's configuration and force and the haptic experience these give rise to. Explaining how this may be so is the task of this chapter and the next.

The model of perception that has emerged from our phenomenology of haptic perception is realist and not at all relativist. Nevertheless, it remains apt to describe it as Protagorean, given the way that perception is the joint upshot of forces in conflict. To highlight this, consider the following. The Protagorean model, as presently understood, is neither an extramission theory nor an intramission theory. The distinction between extramission and intramission theories arises in the historiography of perception (see, for example, Lindberg 1977, 3–67). The distinction is an historian's classification of accounts of perception. Very roughly, whereas intramission theories emphasize the passive reception of the effects, from without, of the object of perception, extramission theories emphasize, instead, outer-directed activity, such as the emanation of a visual ray in Euclid's geometrical optics. This rough characterization of the distinction is incomplete, but suffices to mark the differences with the Protagorean model (a more complete characterization of extramission is given in Chapter 5). The Protagorean model is not adequately described as either extramissive or intramissive, but contains elements of both. The Protagorean model is neither extramissive nor intramissive, but is perhaps better described as interactionist (for ancient interactionism, see Squire 2016). Like the extramission theory, the Protagorean model emphasizes outer-directed activity of the perceiver in the disclosure of the object of perception. Like the intramission theory, the Protagorean model emphasizes that not only does the perceiver act, but that the perceiver is acted upon, as well. The perception of what is there, prior to perception, is the joint upshot of forces in conflict. On the Protagorean model, then, perception is determined by the interaction of the perceiver and the object perceived and is thus more aptly deemed interactionist than by either of the traditional categories of the historiography of perception.

1.4   Assimilation

So far in our discussion of grasping or enclosure, we have established at least one claim about the metaphysics of sensory presentation, that sensory presentation is of such a nature that its objects may be disclosed over time. Broad (1952) took this dynamical aspect of sensory presentation to be confined to haptic perception. This is, at best, an exaggeration. If sounds and their sources, if not their audible qualities such as pitch and timbre, are spread over time, then it is at least natural to think that their presentation in auditory experience is itself disclosed over time. Moreover, there is reason to think that the presentation in visual experience of color qualities may itself be spread over time, at least some of the time. Thus as Broackes observes:

> in order to tell what colour an object is, we may try it out in a number of different lighting environments. It is not that we are trying to get it into one single "standard" lighting condition, at which point it will, so to speak, shine in its true colours. Rather, we are looking, in the way it handles a variety of different illuminations (all of which are more or less "normal"), for its constant capacity to modify light. (1997, 215)

And similar claims connecting color perception to activity with duration have been made by Noë (2004) and Matthen (2005). Notice that perceived colors belong to a distinct ontological category than sounds and their sources. Sounds and their sources may be particulars like perceived colors, but whereas perceived colors are quality instances, sounds and their sources are events or processes. This claim is controversial. Further defense of it is given in Chapters 3 and 4. For the moment, however, let us suppose the controversial claim to be true, if only to observe a consequence of it. Suppose that sounds and their sources that we hear are events or processes whereas the colors that we see are quality instances, but that each may be disclosed over time in our perceptual experience of them. So the fact that sensory presentation is spread over time need not be a consequence of the temporal mode of being of its object, as when a quality instance is disclosed over time. Thus our phenomenological investigation into grasping understood as a mode of haptic perception has made vivid at least one claim about the metaphysics of sensory presentation, that the presence of the object of perception may be disclosed over time in perceptual experience, that sensory presentation may have duration. Moreover, this holds not only for the sensory presentation at work in haptic perception, but plausibly, as well, for the sensory presentation at work in other sensory modalities such as audition and vision.

Though a small claim about the metaphysics of sensory presentation, it has significant consequences. To take but one example, consider the claim that our ordinary experience of the natural environment is nothing more than a Grand Illusion. When our hominid ancestor turns, and looks, and sees, they are seemingly presented with a richly detailed scene of the alien obelisk set against a cloudy dawn sky. And this is true of the experience of twenty-first-century humanity as well. When we visually perceive something, we are seemingly presented with a richly detailed scene. However, empirical research into change and inattentional blindness has suggested to some psychologists and philosophers that this aspect of our phenomenology is illusory (see, for example, Blackmore et al. 1995; Simons and Chabris 1999). Our visual experience may present itself as the presentation of a richly detailed scene, but, in fact, at any given moment, we are at best visually presented with a detail of some fragment of that scene.

In at least some cases, the reasoning for the Grand Illusion hypothesis may be resisted, for it seems to presuppose that experience only presents what could be present at any given moment. But if perceptual experience may disclose its object over time, then the claim that visual perception presents a richly detailed scene is consistent with the claim that, at any given moment, visual perception at best presents a fragment of that scene, so long as the richly detailed scene is understood to be disclosed over time and not present at a moment. Some of the arguments, then, if not all of them, for the Grand Illusion hypothesis turn on denying this claim about the metaphysics of sensory presentation – that sensory presentation may be a kind of disclosure with duration. (For recent relevant discussion see, inter alia, Noë 2004; Campbell and Cassam 2014, 72–4.)

Our first claim about the metaphysics of sensory presentation involved a literal feature of grasping or enclosure. Grasping is a mode of haptic perception, and the presentation of its object is spread over time. That observation suffices to establish that sensory presentation may be a kind of disclosure with duration. Consider now another feature of grasping or enclosure that the grasping hand assimilates to the rigid, solid body in its grasp. The hand's assimilating to the overall shape and volume of the object grasped is a manifestation, if not the source, of that haptic perception's objectivity. This, I suggested, is part of what makes grasping or enclosure an apt metaphor for sensory presentation more generally. It is important to get clearer about what this assimilation amounts to, and how it may be generalized, if assimilation is genuinely part of what makes grasping an apt metaphor for sensory presentation.

Grasping, understood as a mode of haptic perception, is, like the variant metaphor, ingestion, a kind of incorporation. This can suggest that the mode of assimilation is material – that it is a taking in, or incorporation, of a material body. Thus, for example, in eating an olive, the matter of the olive is taken in and presented to the organ of taste and thereby tasted. But while some forms of sensory perception involve material assimilation such as tasting, not all do. Vision and audition involve the material assimilation of no thing. So if the assimilation at work in grasping or enclosure is part of what makes it an apt metaphor for sensory presentation generally, it must be understood in some other way.

Perhaps, the assimilation at work in grasping or enclosure is not merely material, but formal. Whereas material assimilation involves the taking in, or incorporation, of a material body, formal assimilation involves the assimilation of nothing material. Formal assimilation, instead, involves taking on the form, if not the matter, of an object, by becoming like it, at least in some respect. In grasping or enclosure, the hand formally assimilates to the contours of the object grasped. The interior of the hand thus approximates to the overall shape of the object, and the volume it encloses approximates to the object's volume. The shape of the interior of the hand is similar to the overall shape of the object, and the volume of the region it encloses is similar to the volume of that object. Perhaps, in this way, the hand assimilates the tangible form of the object grasped, by becoming like it. However, while our hand may be warmed when feeling the warmth of an object, our eyes do not become red when viewing a traditional English phone booth. Such a view, however, has been attributed to Aristotle by Slakey (1961), Sorabji (1974), and Everson (1997). I have my doubts (Kalderon 2015). Thus Theophrastus, Aristotle's student and successor at the Lyceum, in inquiring into his master's definition of perception as the assimilation of form without matter, similarly judged it absurd if it is the sense organ that is meant to become like the object of perception, and this prompted Theophrastus to understand Aristotle's definition in some other way, in a commentary now lost though reported by Priscian in *Metaphrasis* 1 3–8 and referred to by Themistius, *In De anima* 3 5 108. Regardless of how Aristotle is best interpreted, if Theophrastus is right that it is absurd that the eye becomes red in seeing a red thing, then formal assimilation can seem no better off than material assimilation in this regard.

However, this latter problem for assimilation understood formally, if not materially, may be avoided by means of a small generalization. In grasping an object, where is the overall shape and volume that you feel? If grasping is a mode of haptic perception, then surely they are in the object that you grasp. Now, where is your haptic experience of that object? In your head? That answer seems so implausible on its face that only a philosopher could believe it. If anywhere, it seems more reasonable to suppose, at least initially, that it is closer to where the overall shape and volume are felt, in your handling of the object. Perhaps in trying to come to an understanding of formal assimilation at work in grasping or enclosure that may be generalized to other sensory modalities, we focused too closely on the shape of the interior of the hand and the volume it encloses. If our haptic experience is where we handle the object grasped, perhaps the similarity obtains not only between the hand and certain tangible qualities of the object, but between the haptic experience that the hand's activity gives rise to and the tangible qualities presented in it. Haptic experience, like perceptual experience more generally, has a conscious qualitative character. Perhaps, in grasping or enclosure, understood as a mode of haptic perception, the phenomenological character of haptic experience formally assimilates to the tangible qualities presented in it. And, arguably at least, this feature, suitably qualified, is generalizable to other sensory modalities as well – that in sensory perception quite generally, the phenomenological character of perceptual experience formally assimilates to the object presented in it.

Before considering whether that generalization partly grounds the aptness of grasping or enclosure as a metaphor for sensory presentation, even for non-tactile modes of perceptual awareness such as vision and audition, let us look closer at formal assimilation at work in haptic perception. Earlier we noted that haptic perception, like perception generally, is partial. The partial character of grasping, understood as a mode of haptic perception, explained the tendency, observed by Lederman and Klatzky (1987), for the perceiver to shift the object of haptic exploration periodically in their hands. Such behavior compensates for the partial and imperfect disclosure of the overall shape and volume of the object grasped. Successive grips and the manner in which the object moves in one's hands provide a more complete profile of the corporeal aspects of the object under investigation. If the successive grips disclose different aspects of the object's overall shape and volume, then they provide something like different haptic perspectives on the object grasped.

While talk of "perspective" derives from the case of vision, a clear analog of that notion finds application in the haptic case. To the extent that
it does, then talk of "haptic perspective," while in a sense visuocentric,
is not pejoratively so (on visuocentrism in philosophy of perception, see
O'Callaghan 2007; for the critique of "occularcentrism" in twentieth-
century French thought, see Jay 1994).

To appreciate this, let us first get clearer on some salient features of
visual perspective. Our hominid ancestor, looking up from the skeletal
remains of the tapir, sees the alien obelisk. In seeing the obelisk, our hominid ancestor has a perspective on it. Their perspective occurs in a space
that encompasses the object seen, the alien obelisk. The space is extrapersonal. It is also egocentrically structured. Thus, from our hominid ancestor's perspective, there are things to the left of the alien obelisk and to the
right of it. At least for things that exist independently of our awareness of
them, such as the obelisk, multiple perspectives on it are possible. (This is
part of the reason we cannot have a perspective on a headache or a phos-
phene.) For there to be multiple perspectives on a thing, not only is it
necessary that it should exist independently of our awareness, but it should
be complex as opposed to simple. Importantly, more or less of an object
may be disclosed in the multiple perspectives on it. Perspectives can reveal
things to the perceiver's view, but they can equally obscure things. That
aspect of the alien obelisk that is presented to our hominid ancestor's perspective is hidden from view from another perspective, when viewed from
behind, say. So not only can we have multiple perspectives on things that
are independent of our awareness of them, but perspectives can reveal what
was potentially hidden from view. Compelled by curiosity, our hominid
ancestor approaches the alien obelisk and cautiously moves around it. In
so doing, the obelisk is presented to different perspectives on it adopted
by our hominid ancestor in their cursory investigation. There are better
and worse perspectives on the obelisk. Our hominid ancestor initially
approaches the obelisk to get a better view. Moreover, the obelisk appears
different when presented to these different perspectives, though our hominid ancestor can perceive the constant, unaltered obelisk that persists in
their experience of it despite these variable appearances.

All of these features find analogs in the haptic case. There will be differences, of course, but enough of a pattern may be found that warrants talk
of haptic perspectives. Just as visual perspectives occur in an egocentrically
structured space, haptic perspectives occur in an egocentrically structured
space. Though, as we shall see, while, visual perspectives occur in an extrapersonal space, haptic perspectives occur in a peripersonal space. Just as

there are multiple perspectives on complex visible objects that are independent of our visual awareness of them, there are multiple perspectives on complex tangible objects that are independent of our haptic awareness of them. Moreover, like visual perspectives, haptic perspectives may disclose aspects of a thing's corporeal nature hidden from other haptic perspectives. Just as there are better and worse perspectives on the visible features of things, there are better and worse haptic perspectives on the tangible features of the object of haptic investigation. And a perceiver's haptic perspective on the object of haptic investigation is manifest in its haptic appearance. A body will feel differently when presented to different haptic perspectives.

Suppose a rigid, solid body is irregularly shaped, then it potentially feels different in successive grips. And in the case of contour following, different paths may be followed, and at different rates, giving rise to different progressions of intensive sensation, themselves constituting different haptic perspectives on the constant contour of the object of haptic investigation. In a part motion test on a set of keys, the perceiver may pick up a single key and move it to the left or to the right. They may even lift it straight up and jiggle the keys, thus performing a specific function test. And we may pinch, squeeze, and pull on the object of haptic investigation and these distinct activities provide us with distinct haptic perspectives on that object.

Like visual perspective, haptic perspective occurs in an egocentrically structured space. However, whereas visual perspective presents visible aspects of extrapersonal space, haptic perspective presents tangible aspects of peripersonal space. (Deleuze and Guattari's 1987, chapter 14, discussion of smooth and striated space makes an interesting comparison here.) Peripersonal space is the space within which the perceiver may immediately act with their limbs. The representation of peripersonal space is thus linked with our motor capacity and our sense of agency. There is some evidence that human psychology operates with a representation of peripersonal space distinct from a representation of extrapersonal space (Halligan and Marshall 1991). Grasping, contour following, part motion, and specific function tests are all activities taking place in peripersonal space. So distinct haptic activities that constitute distinct haptic perspectives on the object under investigation occur in an egocentrically structured peripersonal space. (See, for example, Benedetti's 1985 explanation of the Aristotle Illusion – so called because it was first described by Aristotle in *Metaphysica* Δ 6 and *De Insomniis* 2 – from which Benedetti 1985, 524 concludes that "tactile stimuli are located in the body reference system according to the only available kinesthetic information, namely, the limit of the fingers' range of action.") Like visual perspectives on objects that exist independently of our visual awareness of them, there are multiple haptic perspectives on objects that exist independently of our haptic awareness of them. That is to say that there are multiple ways to interact with the object of haptic investigation in peripersonal space. Moreover, different events in peripersonal space, different haptic interactions with the external body, disclose different tangible aspects of that body. So the haptic activities occurring in an egocentrically structured peripersonal space can disclose previously hidden aspects of the object of haptic investigation. As we have seen, different stereotypical exploratory activities occurring in peripersonal space are suited to presenting different ranges of tangible qualities. Moreover, different stereotypical exploratory activities may determine the same tangible quality, though with different tactile acuity. There are thus better and worse haptic perspectives on the tangible features of things. Moreover, different haptic perspectives, different ways of interacting with the object of haptic investigation in peripersonal space, give rise to different haptic appearances of the same object. A body may be experienced as retaining its overall shape and volume throughout the perceiver's handling of it, but it feels different in different grips.

This perspectival relativity bears on our understanding of the formal assimilation at work in grasping understood as a mode of haptic perception. In haptic perception, the tangible qualities of the object are presented to the perceiver's haptic perspective on that object – the distinctive way they are handling that object in the given circumstances – and this is reflected in the conscious character of their haptic experience. So with respect to grasping or enclosure understood as a mode of haptic perception, the doctrine of formal assimilation should be understood as the claim that the phenomenological character of haptic experience formally assimilates to the tangible qualities presented to the perceiver's haptic perspective. Naïve realists and disjunctivists accept something like this view if not the Peripatetic vocabulary with which I have described it. Thus naïve realists and disjunctivists are prone to speak of the phenomenological character of perceptual experience being shaped by the object as presented to the perceiver's partial perspective (see Fish 2009; Kalderon 2011c; Martin 2004; McDowell 1998; see also Nagel's 1979 conception of perceptual experience as contrasted with Jackson 1982).

It might be objected that haptic experience formally assimilating to the tangible qualities presented in it is absurd on its face. Perhaps in grasping a cube, my hand will approximate to a cube shape, but is it really the case that my experience is cube shaped, even approximately? The claim that in seeing an English phone booth my visual experience becomes red seems even worse than the view literalists attribute to Aristotle, that in seeing the phone booth my eye becomes red. What does it even mean for an experience to be cubical or red? A point that Theophrastus also makes (Priscian, *Metaphrasis* 1.3–8). Although, something like this conclusion was embraced by William Crathorn in his commentary on Lombard's *Sentences*: "A soul seeing and intellectively cognizing color is truly colored" (*Quaestiones super librum Sententiarum* q. 1 concl. 7 Pasnau 2002, 288); thus prompting Robert Holcot to compare the soul, as Crathorn conceived of it, to a chameleon (see Pasnau 1997; Chapter 1.1 for discussion).

It is important in this regard to recognize that the posited similarity need not be exact. It is only on that assumption that the similarity involved in formal assimilation involves the sharing of qualities. But if we abandon that assumption, then there is a clear sense in which, in color vision say, in seeing the phone booth, the conscious qualitative character of my color experience depends upon and derives from the qualitative character of the color presented in that experience relative to my perspective on it in the circumstances of perception (for defense of this claim, see Kalderon 2008, 2011a, 2011c). And similarly we might say that in haptic perception, the conscious qualitative character of haptic experience depends upon and derives from the tangible qualities present in that experience relative to the perceiver's perspective on the object of haptic investigation, the distinctive way that they are handling it in the circumstances of perception.

Consider again the claim that haptic experience only formally assimilates to the tangible object it presents relative to the perceiver's haptic perspective. The perspectival relativity of formal assimilation bears on the inexactness of the similarity between experience and its object. The assimilation is formal in that, not only the shape of the interior of the hand and the region it encloses is similar to the overall shape and volume of the object, but the haptic experience, its conscious qualitative character, is similar to the tangible object at least as it is presented to the perceiver's haptic perspective. However, this does not require that the similarity be exact. The perspective relativity of formal assimilation nicely brings this out. Thus an irregularly shaped, rigid, solid body, thanks to the self-maintaining forces that constitute the categorical bases of its rigidity and solidity, maintains its overall shape and volume despite progressive handling and the successive grips with which it is held. But that same shape feels different with different grips. If the phenomenological character of haptic experience were wholly determined by the tangible qualities presented in it, then we would be hard pressed to explain why this should be so.

Earlier I claimed that the partiality of haptic perception only explained the tendency, observed by Lederman and Klatzky (1987), for the perceiver to periodically shift the object in their hands if the haptic experience this behavior gives rise to exhibits perceptual constancy. One of the philosophical challenges posed by perceptual constancy is to adequately describe and explain the phenomenology of stability and flux. In cases of perceptual constancy, a constant unaltered object of perception is presented though its appearance varies. In explaining perceptual constancy, it is not enough to determine the constant object of perception. That object continues to present itself unchanged even though its appearance may vary with a change in the perceiver's perspective or circumstances of perception. In determining only the constant object of perception, one explains the phenomenology of stability at the expense of the contribution to our phenomenology of flux (for discussion in the color case, see Cohen 2008; Hilbert 2005; perhaps Fulkerson 2014, 98, falls prey to this error in his account of haptic perceptual constancy; see Chapter 2.2). Even if, in the case of grasping or enclosure, understood as a mode of haptic perception, we attend only to the constant overall shape and volume of the object grasped, these feel differently in different successive grips. Accommodating the contribution of flux to our phenomenology of grasping or enclosure requires acknowledging that haptic presentation, like sensory presentation more generally, is perspective relative.

Haptic experience formally assimilates to its object, relative to the perceiver's haptic perspective on it, the distinctive way that they are handling that object in the circumstances of perception. Suppose that this feature of haptic perception generalizes to other modes of perception – that, in general, perceptual experience formally assimilates to its object, relative to the perceiver's partial perspective. The resulting conception of perception would be, to that extent at least, anti-modern. One fundamental feature of the early modern conception of perception is the denial of the formal assimilation of perception to its object, even relative to the perceiver's partial perspective. For at least with respect to, in Peripatetic vocabulary, the proper objects of perception, there is nothing in the external object that resembles the perceiver's perceptual experience of it. Secondary qualities are the eighteenth-century avatar of Aristotelian proper objects. And there was something like an early modern consensus that there is nothing in the external object that resembles our experience of secondary qualities. That is one of the lessons that Descartes draws, in *La Dioptrique*, from the

Stoic analogy between a perceiver and a blind man with a stick and, in the *Second Meditation*, from the wax argument. And it is a lesson preserved by Locke. Though aspects of external objects may be found to resemble our experience of their primary qualities, nothing in such objects resembles our experience of their secondary qualities. On the early modern conception of perceptual experience, there is nothing in the obelisk that resembles our hominid ancestor's idea or sensation of its blackness. And if there is nothing in the obelisk that resembles our hominid ancestor's idea or sensation of its blackness, then their perception of its blackness could not consist in their perceptual experience formally assimilating to its object, even relative to their perspective on it. There is nothing to formally assimilate to, and, hence, no formal assimilation to constitute the perception. And if secondary quality perception cannot be understood as a mode of formal assimilation, then sensory presentation, generally, cannot be understood as essentially involving the perceiver's experience formally assimilating to its object, relative to their partial perspective on it in the circumstances of perception.

1.5 Shaping

So far we have distinguished material and formal modes of assimilation, and have suggested that while grasping or enclosure, understood as a mode of haptic perception, involves material assimilation – it is a kind of incorporation – its objectivity is connected to the way in which the hand and haptic experience more generally formally assimilates to its object. Moreover, we have emphasized the way that the similarity involved in formal assimilation need not be exact so as to involve the sharing of qualities. And we have explained how the inexact similarity is related to the formal assimilation's perspectival relativity. We now turn to another important distinction. Consider Lederman's and Klatzky's (1987) claim that grasping or enclosure involves molding one's hand to the contours of the object grasped. Molding is a kind of shaping. And there are causal and constitutive senses of shaping that can be distinguished. Correspondingly, there are causal and constitutive explanations of perception's formal assimilation to its object.

So consider the way that the Nazi air campaign shaped the London skyline. The destructive impact of the bombing caused the London skyline to be shaped in a certain way. This contrasts sharply with the way that St Paul's shapes the London skyline, as Herbert Mason's iconic photograph of December 29, 1940 dramatically demonstrates. St Paul's defiantly shapes the London skyline by being part of it despite the devastating impact of the bombing campaign. Whereas the Nazi bombing shaped the London skyline in a merely causal sense, St Paul's constitutively shapes that skyline by being a part or contour of it.

The causal–constitutive distinction plays out, I believe, in the use that Aristotle makes of Plato's wax analogy from the *Theaetetus*. Plato, in the *Theaetetus*, appeals to an impression made on wax as an analogy for the operation of memory in the context of explaining how error in judgment is possible:

> We may look upon it, then, as a gift of Memory, the mother of the Muses. We make impressions upon this of everything we wish to remember among the things we have seen or heard or thought of ourselves; we hold the wax under our perceptions and thoughts and take a stamp from them, in the way in which we take the imprints of signet rings. Whatever is impressed upon the wax we remember and know so long as the image remains in the wax; whatever is obliterated or cannot be impressed, we forget and do not know. (Plato, *Theaetetus* 191 d–e; Levett and Burnyeat in Cooper 1997, 212)

In *De anima*, Aristotle uses the wax analogy, not for memory and knowledge as Plato does, but for explaining his definition of perception as the assimilation of the sensible form without the matter of the perceived particular:

> Generally, about all perception, we can say that a sense is what has the power of receiving into itself the sensible forms of things without the matter, in the way in which a piece of wax takes on the impress of a signet-ring without the iron or gold. (Aristotle, *De anima* 2 12 424 a 18–23; Smith in Barnes 1984, 42–3)

Part of the point of using Plato's wax analogy, not for memory or knowledge, but for perception is to highlight that Aristotle is assigning to perception functions that Plato assigned only to reason. (For discussion of how far Aristotle departs from Plato in drawing the distinction between perception and cognition, see Sorabji 1971, 2003.) There is a further, and for present purposes, more important way in which Aristotle departs from Plato's use of the wax analogy. There is a sense in which he takes the signet ring in the analogy more seriously than Plato. Or rather, Aristotle takes seriously, in a way that Plato does not, the distinctive discursive role of signet rings as opposed to a stylus, say. Moreover, this makes a difference to how the shaping of the wax by the ring is to be understood. Whereas Plato has in mind a causal notion of shaping, Aristotle has in mind the constitutive notion (or at least, so I argue Kalderon 2015, chapter 9). Plato's explanation of the reliability of memory crucially relies on causal features of the situation. An object's impression is the effect it has on the mind's wax. So the operation of peoples' memories may vary as to how hard or soft their mind's wax is, or how pure or impure it is, since these features causally bear on how clear an impression the object will produce and how long it may persist in the mind's wax.

If, however, we reflect on the distinctive discursive role of a signet ring over a stylus, say, this can motivate the alternative, constitutive understanding of shaping. Notice that the impression of a signet ring plays a similar role to a signature. Thus Caston writes:

> A signet produces a *sealing*, an impression that establishes the identity of its owner and consequently his authority, rights, and prerogatives. When a sealing is placed on a document, especially for legal or official use, it authorizes the claims, obligations, promises, or orders made therein. A sealing thus differs from other impressions in that it *purports to originate from a particular signet*. The wax thus receives the "golden or brazen signet" … which is representative of the office or person to whom the signet belongs. (2005, 302)

Signet rings and styli thus have distinctive discursive roles. The impression made by a stylus is not linked to its legitimate possessor – one scribe may borrow another scribe's stylus – the way an impression sealed by a signet ring is.

Taking this feature of the analogy seriously has an important consequence for how sensory impressions are individuated. Just as a forged signature is not my signature, an impression sealed by a forged or stolen ring is not the seal of the ring's legitimate possessor. Impressions are individuated by their legitimate sources. If this feature of the analogy carries over, then perceptions, conceived on the model of sealed impressions, are individuated by their objects that are their source. A perception of Castor and a perception of Pollux are different perceptions, no matter how closely the twins may resemble one another. Castor may be a perfect duplicate of Pollux, but my impression of Castor is not an impression of Pollux. If I grasp his hand, it is Castor's hand I grasp, not Pollux's. My tactile impression of Castor is not thereby a tactile impression of Pollux, even if they feel the same.

Notice that a causal understanding of sensory impressions, as merely the effects of causal shaping, does not have this consequence. If, as Hume maintained, cause and effect are contingently connected, the same effect, the same impression, could have been produced by a different cause.

Sensory impressions, understood as the effects of causal shaping, are not individuated by their causes. If sensory impressions are individuated by their objects that are their sources, they cannot be understood as merely the effects of causal shaping.

What taking seriously the distinctive discursive role of the signet ring in the wax analogy brings out is that the formal assimilation at work in haptic perception and, arguably at least, in perception more generally, might be understood, not on the model of causal shaping, but rather on the model of constitutive shaping. If sensory impressions are individuated by their objects, perhaps these objects shape sensory consciousness not causally, or at least not merely. Perhaps in being individuated by their objects, these objects constitutively shape our sensory impressions of them (for contemporary discussion of this suggestion, see Kalderon 2008, 2011a, 2011c). Recall that the assimilation at work in grasping or enclosure understood as a mode of haptic perception is formal in that, not only the shape of the interior of the hand and the region it encloses is similar to the overall shape and volume of the object grasped, but that the haptic experience, its conscious qualitative character, is similar to the tangible object at least as it is presented to the perceiver's haptic perspective. On the causal model, a haptic experience, with its conscious qualitative character, is a sensory impression caused in a perceiver with an appropriate sensibility by the object of haptic investigation. Moreover, if the causal structure of the world cooperates and the circumstances of perception are propitious, then the conscious qualitative character of the haptic experience may be like, if not exactly like, the qualitative character of the tangible object. (Locke thinks something like this about primary quality perception.) On the constitutive model, haptic experience formally assimilates to its tangible object as well. However, that object does not merely cause the perceiver to undergo a haptic experience with a certain conscious qualitative character. Rather, corporeal aspects of the object constitutively shape the perceiver's haptic experience of it. Not only does the perceiver's haptic experience formally assimilate to its tangible object relative to their haptic perspective, in the sense that the conscious qualitative character of the experience is like, if not exactly like, the qualitative character of the tangible object present in it, but the tangible quality present in their haptic experience constitutively shapes that experience. The conscious qualitative character of the haptic experience depends upon and derives from, at least in part, the tangible qualitative character the object had prior to haptic investigation. If something feels metallic, and this is a case of tactile perception, then not only is this because of its metallic feel, but something's feeling metallic is also constituted, in part, by that metallic feel. The metallic feel of the thing is felt in it and in conformity with it. That is just what it is for something to be present in tactile experience.

In grasping or enclosure, understood as a mode of haptic perception, the hand maintains simultaneous contact with as much of the overall surface of the object as possible. Grasping is a kind of incorporation, and thus a material mode of assimilation. Moreover, in grasping, the hand is so configured that it approximates to the contours of the object. Just as the shape of the interior of the hand and the region it encloses is like, if not exactly like, the overall shape and volume of the object grasped, the phenomenological character of the haptic experience, its conscious qualitative character, is like, if not exactly like the overall shape and volume presented to the perceiver's haptic perspective, the particular way they are handling the object. Moreover, the shaping involved, at least in the latter formal assimilation, is not merely causal but constitutive. The conscious qualitative character of the haptic experience is constituted, in part, by the tangible qualities presented to their haptic perspective.

While not all modes of perception involve material modes of assimilation, arguably at least, the formal assimilation of haptic experience to its object relative to the perceiver's haptic perspective generalizes to other modes of perception. The conscious qualitative character of perceptual experience is constituted, in part, by the qualitative character of the object presented to the perceiver's partial perspective. Our hominid ancestor turns, and looks, and sees the alien obelisk set against a cloudy dawn sky. The blackness of the obelisk is a constituent of their visual experience. The blackness of the obelisk is a constituent of their experience insofar as that experience involves the presentation of that blackness in the visual awareness afforded them by their experience of that scene. And since the experience of our hominid ancestor is constitutively linked to the blackness of the alien obelisk – an awful darkness in which stars may appear – the obelisk's blackness shapes the contours of their visual consciousness by being present in that consciousness. The blackness of the obelisk shapes the contours of their visual experience in the way that St Paul's defiantly shapes the London skyline, the Shard notwithstanding, simply by being present.

If this feature of grasping or enclosure, understood as a mode of haptic perception, generalizes to other modes of perception, then it is easy to see its epistemic significance. If perception involves becoming like the perceived object actually is, then it is a genuine mode of awareness. One can only perceptually assimilate what is there to be assimilated. If perceptual experience is a formal mode of assimilation understood as a kind of constitutive shaping, then one could not undergo such an experience consistent with a Cartesian demon eliminating the object of that experience. If there is no external object, then there is nothing to which the perceiver, or perhaps their experience, can assimilate to. If the phenomenological character of perception is constitutively shaped by the object presented to the perceiver's partial perspective, then we can begin to see the epistemic significance of perceptual phenomenology. If the phenomenological character of perception is constitutively shaped by the object presented to the perceiver's partial perspective, then it is the grounds for an epistemic warrant for the range of propositions whose truth turns on what is presented in that perceptual experience (see Chapter 6.2).

Earlier, in Section 1.2, I claimed that the effort exerted in more precisely molding one's hand against the contours of the object grasped was not yet proof against a Cartesian demon. How is this consistent with what is now being claimed? Notice the earlier claim was essentially a claim about the hand's formal assimilation to the object of haptic investigation in grasping or enclosure. What is distinctive about modern skepticism is that it counts the perceiver's body as an aspect of the external world and so doubts about the external world comprise the body as well. As Burnyeat (1982) argues, skeptical doubts about the existence of our bodies were not so much as entertained in the ancient world. So the felt force of one's hand in molding to the contours of the object grasped is no proof against a Cartesian demon since the hand falls within the scope of the external world and thus is cast into doubt by the demon hypothesis. (The rhetorical genius of Moore's 1903 example, "This is a hand," turns precisely on this point or, rather, precisely calls this point into question.) However, the present discussion is not about the hand's formal assimilation to the object of haptic perception, but about the formal assimilation of the haptic experience, that the hand's activity gives rise to, to the object presented in it. Haptic experience, and conscious experience more generally, is not within the purview of the skeptical doubt licensed by the demon hypothesis. But if haptic experience is constituted, even in part, by tangible aspects of an external body, then haptic experience contains within itself tangible aspects of the external body, so there is no room for the possibility of eliminating that body while leaving experience as it is. Just as the hand incorporates its object in grasping or enclosure, the haptic experience that this activity gives rise to is itself a kind of incorporation, in a different, metaphorical, and anti-Cartesian sense.

Haptic experience is a kind of incorporation, in the metaphorical sense, insofar as its formal assimilation to its object, relative to the perceiver's haptic perspective, is understood on the model of constitutive shaping. If haptic experience is, in this way, a kind of incorporation, the resulting conception of experience is anti-modern. Descartes, by contrast, models sensory experience on bodily sensations, such as tickles and pains (*Le Monde de M. Descartes ou le Traité de la Lumière*, chapter 1). Tickles and pains, as conceived by Descartes, are not incorporations of the extra-somatic so much as conscious modifications of the perceiving subject that do not resemble their external causes. What in the feather resembles the tickle that it prompts? Indeed, it is the conception of sense experience as a conscious modification of the perceiving subject that generates the possibility that the external cause of sense experience may fail to resemble it. However, if haptic experience is a kind of incorporation, in the sense that the formal assimilation of haptic experience to its object, relative to the perceiver's haptic perspective, is the result of constitutive shaping, then it is not a conscious modification of the perceiving subject, at least not in Descartes' sense. Vestigial remnants of this conception are the Cartesian core of what Putnam called "Cartesianism *cum* materialism." (For a staunch defense of this Cartesian core, see Farkas 2008.) If haptic perception must be understood in some other way, and is an exemplar of perception more generally, then this aspect of the early modern paradigm must also be rejected.

If the formal assimilation involved in haptic perception is the result of constitutive shaping, then the resulting anti-modern conception of experience does not allow for the possibility of a demon eliminating the object of the perceiver's experience while leaving that experience just as it is. Nevertheless, the anti-modern conception of experience is not, by itself, sufficient to refute skepticism. For skeptical worries may be posed in terms of non-perceptual experiences that appear from within just like the corresponding perceptual experience, consistent with perceptual experiences being constitutively shaped by their objects (Chapter 6.2).

1.6 Active Wax

I have claimed that the assimilation at work in grasping or enclosure, understood as a mode of haptic perception, is the manifestation, if not the source, of the objectivity of haptic perception. I have also claimed this is part of what makes grasping an apt metaphor for sensory presentation more generally. We are now in a position to elaborate further. Not only does the grasping hand assimilate to the contours of the object, but the perceiver's haptic experience – there where they are handling the object – assimilates to the overall shape and volume of the object as well, at least relative to their haptic perspective on it, the specific manner in which they are handling the object. But one can only assimilate to what is there to be assimilated. The objectivity of haptic perception is thereby manifested. And if this formal assimilation, understood on the model of constitutive shaping, generalizes to other modes of perception, then part of what makes grasping an apt metaphor for perception generally is our consequent understanding of perceptual objectivity. The formal assimilation of haptic experience to its object relative to the perceiver's handling of it, the constitutive shaping of the phenomenological character of that experience by the presentation of its object to the perceiver's haptic perspective, is the manifestation of the objectivity of that haptic perception. But what is its source? What explains haptic experience assimilating to its object? If we bear in mind that haptic experience is where the perceiver is handling the object, then a plausible thought is that it is the force of the hand's activity, the effort exerted in more precisely molding the hand to the contours of the object, that is the source of the hand, and consequently our haptic experience, assimilating to its object. Objective haptic perception is an experience sustained by the hand's activity.

While the assimilation of haptic experience to its object, relative to the perceiver's haptic perspective, is the manifestation of the objectivity of haptic perception, it is the force of the hand's activity that is its source. It is because the hand tightens its grip that its flexible interior surface may more precisely mold to the object's contours. Molding more precisely to the object's contours ensures that those contours explain the hand's configuration and force. And in molding more precisely to the object's contours, the haptic experience this activity gives rise to formally assimilates to its constituent object.

Robert Kilwardby provides a vitalist twist on the Peripatetic analogy that potentially sheds light on the epistemic significance of the force of the hand's activity in grasping or enclosure, understood as a mode of haptic perception. (On Kilwardby on perception, see Silva 2008, 2012; Silva and Toivanen 2010.) Kilwardby composed *De spiritu fantastico sive de recptione specierum* most likely while in Blackfriars in Oxford in the 1250s prior to being elevated to the Archbishop of Canterbury. In a remarkable passage, Kilwardby writes:

> if you place a seal before wax so that it touches it, and you assume that the wax has a life by which it turns itself towards the seal and by striking against it comes to be like it, by turning its eye upon itself it sees in itself an image of the seal. (Kilwardby *De spiritu fantastico*, 103; Broadie 1993, 94)

Kilwardby transforms the Peripatetic analogy by imagining life to inhere in the wax so that it is actively pressing against the seal and so taking its sensible form upon itself. (Kilwardby's image of active wax will be echoed by Peter John Olivi, perhaps independently of Kilwardby, in *Quaestiones in secundum librum Sententiarum*, q. 58 415–16, 506–7; q. 72 35–6.)

Kilwardby's account is motivated, in no small part, by his conviction, grounded in his reading of Augustine, that the soul cannot be acted upon by the body (*De spiritu fantastico*, 47–54; on Augustine's philosophy of mind, see O'Daly 1987; on Augustine's influence on Kilwardby, see Silva and Toivanen 2010). It is a consequence of the soul's ontological superiority over the corporeal that the latter may never act upon the former. Kilwardby tentatively accepts a Peripatetic model where, in vision, say, the perceived object acts upon the transparent medium such that its image (its likeness, in Scholastic terminology, its species) exists, in some sense, in it, and that the medium, in turn, affects the sense organ such that the image comes to, in some sense, exist in it as well (*De spiritu fantastico*, 69, 97). But how does the sensory soul receive the image that informs the sense organ, if the sense organ is precluded, by its corporeal nature, from acting upon the soul?

The vitalist twist on the Peripatetic analogy is meant to address this problem. The sensory soul pervades the sense organ, and animates it, and in so doing makes itself like the external body. So it is the sensory soul that is the efficient cause of the likeness of the body occurring in it. The sensory soul makes itself like the external body by pressing against the sense organ that it animates itself impressed with the image of the object. In actively pressing against the impressed sense organ, the soul makes within itself the image of the external body: "For in this way the sensory soul, by turning itself more attentively to its sense organ which has been informed by a sensible species, makes itself like the species, and by turning its own eye upon itself it sees that it is like the species" (*De spiritu fantastico*, 103; Broadie 1993, 94).

What does the metaphor of the sensory soul pressing against the impressed sense organ mean? Sense can be made of it in terms of Kilwardby's doctrine that the soul's use of a body is limited by the passivities of matter (*De spiritu fantastico*, 99–100). So a feather striking a tapir's skull will not break it, but a femur will, even if it is the same hominid striking the skull with equivalent musculature exertion in each instance. The difference is due to the way in which the activity of the agent is limited by the passivities of matter inhering in the body that is being used. A species inhering in a sense organ is among the passivities of matter exhibited by

that corporeal body. And Kilwardby explains the soul's assimilation of the
sensible form of the perceived object in terms of how the species inhering
in the sense organ limits the sensory soul's use of it (Kilwardby *De spiritu
fantastico*, 103).

It is not clear whether the subsequent account constitutes a genuine
reconciliation of Augustinian and Peripatetic metaphysics (for discussion of Kilwardby on perception, see Silva 2008, 2012; Silva and Toivanen
2010; Chapter 4; selections from *De spiritu fantastico* are also translated in
Knuuttila and Sihvola 2014). Regardless of Kilwardby's intent, however,
and dropping his Augustinian dualism, the hand, the mobile and elastic
instrument of haptic exploration, is the active wax in grasping or enclosure,
understood as a mode of haptic perception. It is the hand that is actively
molding itself to the object in grasping or enclosure. And it is the hand
that is thereby taking upon itself a configuration and enclosing a certain
volume determined by the overall shape and volume of the object grasped.
And it is these activities of the hand that give rise to the perceiver's haptic
experience. In making an effort to mold more precisely to the contours of
the rigid, solid body, not only does the hand assimilate to the contours of
the object grasped, but the perceiver's haptic experience – there where the
perceiver is handling the object – assimilates to the overall shape and volume of the object presented in it.

Further, I take it that it is at least part of Kilwardby's suggestion that it is
the activity of the wax and the resistance it encounters in pressing against
the seal – the passivities of matter that limits its activity – that discloses the
shape the seal had prior to perception. So if the hand is the active wax
in grasping, understood as a mode of haptic perception, then it is the
force of the hand's activity and the resistance it encounters in maintaining simultaneous contact with a non-insignificant portion of the object's
overall surface that discloses the tangible qualities the object had prior to
that haptic encounter. Kilwardby's suggestion, then – if released from the
confines of Augustinian metaphysics, if, in turn, narrowly confined to haptic presentation – is that the presentation of tangible qualities of objects
external to the perceiver's body is due, at least in part, to the activity of the
hand in grasping and the felt resistance it encounters. The hand, and haptic experience in turn, only assimilate to the tangible aspects of the rigid,
solid body thanks to the force of the hand's activity in conflict with the
self-maintaining forces that constitute the categorical bases of that body's
solidity and rigidity. At least with grasping or enclosure, understood as a
mode of haptic perception, perceptual realism is sustained by the force of
the hand's activity in conflict with the self-maintaining forces of the object

grasped. It is only in this way is it ensured that the tangible qualities determined by the self-maintaining forces of the object grasped explains the configuration and force of the grasping hand.

1.7 A Puzzle

In discussing the objectivity of grasping, understood as a mode of haptic perception, we supposed that it is our hand's configuration in grasping and the force that needs to be exerted in maintaining that configuration that discloses the overall shape and volume of the object grasped. The hand is, in this way, the active wax in haptic perception. I believe this supposition to be both plausible and true, but once it is clearly stated, a puzzle immediately arises.

Embodiment is a fundamental feature of animal existence and so a fundamental feature of the existence of primates like ourselves. So much so, that many philosophers take animality to be the key to our very identity (for a recent statement, see Snowdon 2014). An animal's awareness of its body is a mode of self-presentation. There may be more to an animal than is revealed in bodily awareness, but bodily awareness nevertheless presents corporeal aspects of the animal whose awareness it is. Bodily awareness remains a mode of self-presentation even if its disclosure of the animal whose awareness it is is partial in this way. Let bodily awareness be understood broadly enough to comprise both proprioception and kinesthesis and potentially more besides. So bodily awareness affords the perceiver with, among other things, awareness of the configuration of their limbs as well as awareness of their motion. So understood, awareness of the hand's configuration in grasping and awareness of the force that needs to be exerted in maintaining that grasp are both modes of bodily awareness. And since bodily awareness is a kind of self-presentation, so are awareness of the hand's configuration and awareness of the force exerted in maintaining it.

Our puzzle now is this. How can a mode of self-presentation disclose the presence of some other thing? After all, perceivers, in being aware of their body, in presenting only themselves, present no other thing. So how can bodily awareness be leveraged into disclosing the presence of something external to the perceiver's body? What alchemy transmutes bodily sensation into tactile perception?

Our puzzle concerns whether grasping so much as could be a mode of haptic perception. Though our interest is presently restricted to grasping as a mode of haptic perception, we can, however, get a better sense of that puzzle by considering an analogous case. So consider felt temperature.

Contrast two cases. In both cases you feel warm, and you feel warm to the same degree. But in the first case, you feel warm because of a fever, and in the second case, you feel warm because of the ambient heat. In both cases, your body is warmed. They differ only in the source of the warmth, with whether the warmth of your body is internally or externally generated. And in both cases, you feel equally warm. Nevertheless, a phenomenological difference remains. In the second case, not only do you feel warm, but you feel, as well, the warmth in the ambient air. Indeed, the warmth you feel is in conformity with the warmth felt in the ambient air. What explains this phenomenological difference? How are tangible qualities felt in something external to the perceiver's body such that the perceiver feels in conformity with such qualities?

The puzzle is not meant to underwrite skepticism about haptic perception or tactile perception more generally. We are taking for granted that in grasping a stone, say, our hominid ancestor feels the overall shape and volume of that stone. We are taking for granted that grasping is a mode of haptic perception that affords the perceiver awareness of tangible qualities that inhere in the object grasped. Our puzzle is not meant to underwrite skepticism about whether grasping is a genuine mode of haptic perception so much as to underwrite a "how-possible" question (Cassam 2007). How is it that the configuration of the hand and the force exerted in maintaining that configuration disclose the overall shape and volume of the object grasped? How is objective haptic perception so much as possible? The puzzle, then, is at best proof of an explanatory lacuna rather than proof of the impossibility of objective haptic perception.

There is an aspect of grasping or enclosure that has so far remained implicit in our discussion of it but is crucial for refining our how-possible question in such a way as to point toward an adequate solution. The perceiver, in exerting effort in more precisely molding their hand to the contours of the object grasped, encounters felt resistance to their efforts. It is because the self-maintaining forces of the body resist the hand's encroachment that the hand can assimilate to the body's contours. The forces that constitute the body's solidity ensure that the force of the grasping hand does not penetrate it. And the forces that constitute the body's rigidity ensure that it maintains its overall shape and volume despite the force of the hand's grasp. Maybe it is the hand's encounter with felt resistance – the activity of the wax limited by the passivities of matter – that discloses the tangible qualities of an external body. The suggestion, here, is not merely that the puzzle overlooked the contribution of cutaneous activation to tactile awareness, but rather with how cutaneous activation interacts with kinesthesis and bodily awareness more generally in giving rise to the experience of an external limit to the body's activity. If among the objects of bodily awareness are limits to the body's activity, a question arises whether bodily awareness is exhaustively understood as a mode of self-presentation. In presenting a limit, does not one, implicitly at least, present, as well, what lies beyond that limit? Thus, in presenting a limit to the body's activity, bodily awareness is more than a mere mode of self-presentation. (We shall return to this issue in Chapter 2.5.) While the initial formulation of the how-possible question relied on the assumption that bodily self-awareness is a mere mode of self-presentation, the refined how-possible question that will guide us from here on out dispenses with that assumption.

A. D. Smith has appropriated Fichte's term, *Anstoss*, for the way in which the experienced limitation of the body's activity can disclose sensible aspects of an external body:

> Although neither touch sensations nor the active / passive distinction suffices for perceptual consciousness, when the two are taken together we *do* find something that suffices ... Although no mere impact on a sensitive surface as such will give rise to perceptual consciousness, we certainly feel objects impacting on us from without. This fact needs to be recognized in any adequate perceptual theory. I shall name the phenomenon that is central here by the term that is at the heart of Fichte's treatment of the "external world," or the "not-self": the *Anstoss*. This phenomenon is that of a *check* or *impediment* to our active movement; an experienced obstacle to our animal striving, as when we push or pull against things. (2002, 153)

Part of what we shall learn from the refined how-possible question is that *Anstoss*, at least as Smith conceives of it, is itself subject to further explanation (elaborating that explanation is the task of the next chapter).

Influenced by Fichte, Maine de Biran applies this conception to grasping or enclosure, understood as a mode of haptic perception, thus:

> If – the object still remaining on my hand – I wish to close the hand, and if, while my fingers are folding back upon themselves, their movement is suddenly stopped by an obstacle on which they press and thwarts them, a new judgment is necessary: *this is not I*. There is a very distinct impression of solidity, of resistance, which is composed of thwarted movement, of an *effort* that I make, in which I am *active*. (Maine de Biran, *Influence de l'habitude sur la faculté de penser*, 1803; Boehm 1929, 57)

It is the experienced limit to the hand's activity, a felt resistance to touch, that discloses the presence of a material object external to the perceiver's body.

There is a long history connecting objectivity to felt resistance to touch. In the *Sophist*, Plato recasts the Gigantomachy, the struggle for political supremacy over the cosmos between the Olympian Gods and the Giants, as a metaphysical dispute. The Gods, or Friends of the Forms, insist that only imperceptible forms are most real. Against them, the Giants, the off-spring of Gaia, insist that only bodies that can be handled and offer resistance to touch are real:

> One party is trying to drag everything down to earth out of heaven and the unseen, literally grasping rocks and trees in their hands, for they lay hold upon every stock and stone and strenuously affirm that real existence belongs only to that which can be handled and offers resistance to the touch. (Plato, *Sophist* 246a; Cornford in Hamilton and Cairns 1989, 990)

For the Giants, felt resistance to touch has become a touchstone for reality. Only that which can be handled and offers resistance to touch is real. Even if one rejects the corporealist metaphysics of the Giants, one can accept that the experience that grounds their corporealist conviction is phenomenologically compelling. It would have to be to elicit such cosmic conviction. Grasping something that offers resistance to touch is a phenomenologically vivid and primitively compelling experience of what is external to us.

The phenomenologically vivid and primitively compelling experience of felt resistance to touch will underwrite the dramatic episode involving Dr. Johnson outside of a church in Harwich:

> After we came out of the church, we stood talking for some time together of Bishop Berkeley's ingenious sophistry to prove the non-existence of matter, and that every thing in the universe is merely ideal. I observed, that though we are satisfied his doctrine is not true, it is impossible to refute it. I never shall forget the alacrity with which Johnson answered, striking his foot with mighty force against a large stone, 'till he rebounded from it, "I refute it thus." This was a stout exemplification of the first truths of Pere Buffier, or the original principles of Reid and Beattie; without admitting which, we can no more argue in metaphysicks, than we can argue in mathematicks without axioms. To me it is inconceivable how Berkeley can be answered by pure reasoning. (Boswell 1935, i 471)

The reality of external matter was demonstrated in the resistance it offered to Dr Johnson's foot, which rebounded despite its mighty force. It was a demonstration not in the sense of proof, since it is inconceivable how Berkeley can be answered in pure reasoning. Moreover, what was stoutly exemplified was metaphysically axiomatic, a first truth, but proof proceeds from axioms; it does not establish them. Rather Dr Johnson's performance was a demonstration of first truths by showing or exhibiting them. (On the character of Johnson's refutation of Berkeley, see Patey 1986). Dr Johnson's demonstration, like the Giants' before him, draws its dramatic power from the phenomenologically vivid and primitively compelling experience of felt resistance to touch. And this remains true even if the dramatic power of that gesture is all but exhausted in the twentieth-century cliché of the exasperated, table-pounding realist.

Campbell, in his contribution to Campbell and Cassam (2014, 71), argues, instead, that Dr Johnson's demonstration was essentially multimodal, depending not only upon the kicking of the stone, but upon seeing it as well:

> It is important that Johnson's kicking the rock is a multimodal affair. It would not have had the same visceral impact if Johnson had rebounded off the thing while kicking it in the pitch dark. That would merely have established the presence of some force or another. (Campbell in Campbell and Cassam 2014, 71)

To be sure, Dr Johnson's performance would have no impact on his audience (Boswell, and by extension, us, as recipients of his eyewitness account) if no one saw his demonstration of a first truth or original principle. Recall, his performance is a demonstration in the sense that it showed or exhibited first truths or original principles. So the demonstration, involving Dr Johnson's activity addressed to an audience, was essentially multimodal. But it does not follow that haptic component of that demonstration merely presented some force or another.

There is more to the experience of kicking a stone in the dark than Campbell allows. For example, despite the darkness, Dr Johnson, perhaps through the reverberation of his foot, which rebounded despite its mighty force, might discern that it was stone and not a log that he was kicking. The characteristic density of stone as opposed to wood might be felt in this manner. And if it is sufficiently cold, he might feel the coldness of the stone through the leather of his boot. So it is not true that all that kicking the stone in the dark presents is some force or another. It can present as well material and thermal qualities of the object kicked.

Campbell underestimates the experience of kicking a stone in the dark in a further and more fundamental way. Not only would that experience establish the presence of some force or another, it would disclose the self-maintaining forces that constitute a rigid, solid object external to Dr Johnson's body. If Dr Johnson's exasperation merely grew with the rebounding of his foot, he might kick it again. But as exasperated as he was in the dark, Dr Johnson's haptic experience presents him with the same stone kicked twice. Each kicking of the stone constitutes distinct haptic perspectives on that object, and Dr Johnson has the capacity to haptically re-identify the stone presented to distinct haptic perspectives, distinct kickings in the dark. Notice that this would not be possible if kicking the stone in the dark merely presented some force or another. Earlier in Campbell and Cassam (2014, 26), however, and more plausibly to my mind, Campbell claimed that it was "the obstinance of the rock, its resistance to the will" that manifest its mind independence. But surely the obstinance of the rock, its resistance to the will, the effect of the rock's self-maintaining forces that reveal it to be mind-independent matter, was manifest in Dr Johnson's haptic encounter with it independently of being seen. Moreover, it would have to be, if Dr Johnson's performance is to constitute a genuine demonstration wherein a first truth or original principle is shown or exhibited to an audience. Dr Johnson's demonstration, an activity directed to an audience, may be multimodal, but the visceral impact upon the audience depends upon their sympathetically responding to what is present in Dr Johnson's haptic experience.

Campbell may be wrong about what the experience of kicking a stone in the dark may disclose, but a mystery remains as to how Dr Johnson may feel the characteristic density of a stone and its coldness in an external body, or how he may have the experience of kicking the same stone twice. That is to say, it remains a mystery how haptic perception is so much as possible. How does felt resistance to touch disclose tangible qualities inhering in external bodies prior to perception? After all, not all limitations to the body's activity are due to its interaction with external bodies. Not all passivities of matter that limit the hand's activity are external to the perceiver's body. There are internal limitations to the body's activity as well. We encounter an internal limitation to the body's activity due to fatigue or in an inability to touch one's toes. And Smith (2002, 154) gives the nice example of separating your index and middle fingers until you can no more. So not every experience of a limitation to the body's activity is due to the tangible qualities inhering in an external body prior to perception. The problem, then, is a failure of sufficiency. So how is it that in grasping or enclosure the experienced limitation to the hand's activity in molding more precisely to the contours of the object grasped discloses that object's overall shape and volume? How does the experienced limitation to the hand's activity become, in haptic perception, an experience of the tangible qualities of an external body? How is it that by means of an experienced limitation to the hand's activity tangible qualities are felt in something external to the perceiver's body and felt in conformity with those qualities?

This, then, is the refined version of our how-possible question: How is it possible for felt resistance to the hand's activity in grasping or enclosure to disclose a rigid body's overall shape and volume? How does the experience limitation to the hand's activity allow the perceiver to feel something in an external body and in conformity with it? Earlier I claimed that the refinement of our question could point toward an adequate solution. Indeed, we have all but stated it. Though perhaps that can only be appreciated once the solution is clearly in view.

CHAPTER 2

Sympathy

2.1 Haptic Metaphysics

Tactile metaphors for perception are primordial and persistent. What makes grasping an apt metaphor for perceptual awareness, even for non-tactile modes of awareness such as vision and audition? In order to answer this question, we undertook a phenomenological investigation into the nature of haptic perception. That investigation was phenomenological in that it confined itself to perceptual appearances and not because of any methodology involved. The hope was that if we better understood how grasping or enclosure, understood as a mode of haptic perception, presents itself from within haptic experience, then we would be in a better position to understand what potentially makes grasping an apt metaphor for perception generally. We discussed three claims about the metaphysics of haptic presentation:

(1) Tangible qualities of the object of haptic exploration are disclosed over time and so presentation in haptic experience has duration.
(2) Haptic perception formally assimilates to the tangible qualities presented to the perceiver's haptic perspective, understood as the distinctive way they are handling the object.
(3) The formal assimilation of haptic perception to its objects is a consequence of haptic experience being constitutively shaped by the object presented to the perceiver's haptic perspective.

Not only does the hand assimilate to the contours of the object grasped, but the haptic experience that this activity gives rise to itself formally assimilates to its object. Moreover, the formal assimilation of haptic experience to its object relative to the perceiver's haptic perspective is not merely causal, but constitutive. Haptic perception formally assimilates to its object, relative to the perceiver's haptic perspective, because that object constitutively shapes that perceptual experience. This, I suggested, was the

40

basis of haptic perception's objectivity and part of what makes it an apt metaphor for perception generally.

Beside these three metaphysical claims about haptic presentation, I also made a further explanatory suggestion about haptic perception's objectivity. Specifically, while haptic experience assimilating to its object is a manifestation of the objectivity of haptic perception, it is not its source:

(4) The presentation of tangible qualities of objects external to the perceiver's body is due, at least in part, to the activity of the hand in grasping and the resistance it encounters.

The hand, and haptic experience in turn, only assimilate to the tangible aspects of the rigid, solid body thanks to the force of the hand's activity in conflict with the self-maintaining forces that constitute the categorical bases of that body's solidity and rigidity. In engaging in such haptic activity, in molding one's hand more precisely to the contours of the body, one ensures that the overall shape and volume of the body had prior to being grasped, and maintained in being grasped, explains, in part, the hand's configuration and the force that needs to be exerted to maintain that configuration. At least with grasping or enclosure, understood as a mode of haptic perception, perceptual realism is sustained by the force of the hand's activity in conflict with the self-maintaining forces of the object grasped. In this way, the hand is the active wax of haptic perception. And the end of this activity is to ensure that the tangible quality explains, in part, the hand's configuration in grasping the object and the force that needs to be exerted to maintain that configuration, and the experience these give rise to.

However, this last insight, if it is one, gave rise to the puzzle that arose at the end of the previous chapter. That puzzle revealed no genuine incoherence in the Manifest Image of Nature. The puzzle was not meant to be the basis of skepticism about objective haptic perception so much as the basis of a how-possible question, how is objective haptic perception so much as possible? The puzzle began with haptic perception's dependence upon bodily awareness. For animals like ourselves, bodily awareness can be a mode of self-presentation even if there is more to our nature than is revealed in bodily awareness. But how can a mode of self-presentation disclose the presence of some other thing? How is it that bodily awareness is leveraged in haptic perception into disclosing the presence and tangible qualities of an external body? Perhaps bodily awareness is not merely a mode of self-presentation if it can present, as well, limits. Taking on board Kilwardby's transformed insight that the presentation of tangible qualities of an external body is due, at least in part, to the activity of the hand and the felt resistance it encounters, we refined our how-possible question: How does felt resistance to the hand's activity in grasping or enclosure disclose the overall shape and volume of an external body? After all, not every felt resistance is due to the tangible qualities of an external body. There are internal as well as external limits to the body's activity. So how does the experienced limitation to the hand's activity allow the perceiver to feel something in something external to the perceiver's body and in conformity with it?

Reflection on this puzzle or *aporia* shall be the basis for further substantive claims about the metaphysics of haptic presentation. The present chapter thus proceeds dialectically. Chief among the substantive claims to be made on this basis is the perhaps surprising claim that haptic presentation is governed by the principle of sympathy – that feeling something in another thing and in conformity with it is a kind of sympathetic disclosure. Part of what makes this claim surprising is our tendency to think of sympathy exclusively as a kind of fellow-feeling, akin to compassion or pity. However, as we shall see, sympathy, here, should not be thought of as fellow-feeling, though perhaps it is its principle.

2.2   The Dependence upon Bodily Awareness

Our puzzle began with the dependence of haptic perception upon bodily awareness. Getting clearer on the nature of that dependence should help with our puzzle's resolution.

In a chapter devoted to discussing the nature of this dependence, Fulkerson (2014; Chapter 4.6) draws the distinction between implicit and explicit experiences:

> An implicit bodily experience is one that is in the background or recessive. "Background" here can be understood as an experiential content that is not consciously attended, in the minimal sense that it does not allow its objects to be open for epistemic appraisal. Such unattended contents or experiences do not incur an additional attentional load on our conscious experiences (we can only actively attend to a limited number of items at any one time, but implicit experiences do not add to this threshold). However, they are in consciousness nonetheless, primed for attention. (2014, 90)

The object of an implicit experience is not attended to and so is not the object of epistemic appraisal. An explicit experience, by contrast, involves attending to, or actively thinking about, the object of that experience, and so that object is open to epistemic appraisal. That an object is "open for epistemic appraisal" I take to mean that it is potentially recognizable and that the perceiver, in undergoing an experience that affords explicit awareness of it, is in a position to make judgments about its presence and character should they have the relevant conceptual resources. Bracketing, for the moment, Fulkerson's use of "consciousness" and its cognates, that is how we shall understand his distinction. Why ignore Fulkerson's use of "consciousness" and its cognates? As will emerge, there is reason to think that it is not fully coherent. The quoted passage already provides a hint of this. On the one hand, there is a tendency to identify what the perceiver is conscious of with what they are attending to. On the other hand, there is the claim that implicit experiences, whose objects are unattended to, occur in consciousness. Surely, "consciousness" must receive a sense distinct from and uncoordinated with the qualifier, "conscious," on pain of incoherence. For how can implicit experiences be in consciousness, if this is understood to be what is in the range of the perceiver's attention, and be such that their objects are unattended to? Consciousness, here, must not be a matter of what falls in the range of the perceiver's attention, but must rather be a matter of what falls in the range of the perceiver's sensory experience, elements of which fall within the range of the perceiver's attention while other elements of which are merely potential objects of attention, there to be selectively attended to.

With the distinction drawn between implicit and explicit experience, we may ask whether grasping or enclosure, understood as a mode of haptic perception, depends upon an explicit bodily experience of the hand's configuration and force, or whether the presentation of the object's overall shape and volume in haptic experience merely depends upon an implicit experience of the hand's configuration and force. If the bodily experience upon which haptic perception depends is explicit, then the perceiver consciously attends to the state and activity of the body and haptic perception of the tangible qualities of an external body depends upon this explicit bodily experience. Fulkerson calls this Strong Experiential Dependence. On the hypothesis of Strong Experiential Dependence, the haptic perception involved in grasping or enclosure, an explicit experience, depends upon another explicit experience, specifically, of the hand's configuration and force.

Fulkerson (2014; Chapter 4.8) argues, instead, that the dependence is best understood in terms of what he calls Informational Bodily Dependence. Though information from processes that underlie proprioception and kinesthesis are integrated with afferent information, such as the information provided by cutaneous activation, these give rise to a

single conscious experience. The idea is that the sensitivity exhibited by
haptic perception, such as grasping or enclosure, depends upon the tactile
system drawing upon functionally distinct streams of information involved
in bodily awareness. Nevertheless, the percept that is thereby determined is
a single conscious experience, in the case of grasping or enclosure, our feeling of the overall shape and volume of the object grasped. This contrasts
with Strong Experiential Dependence where haptic experience is understood to depend upon a distinct explicit experience of the body's configuration and motion. On the alternative, haptic experience depends upon,
not an explicit, but an implicit experience of the hand's configuration and
force. Fulkerson (2014, 91) cites with approval Gallagher (2005, 137) in
this regard: "Our pre-reflexive, kinesthetic-proprioceptive experience thus
plays a role in the organization of perception, but in a way that does not
require the body itself to be a perceptual object." If we understand the
perceptual object as something that is actively attended to, then haptic
experience merely depends upon an implicit experience of the hand's configuration and force (see also Bower and Gallagher 2013).

   Put another way, according to Informational Bodily Dependence, our
capacity for haptic perception draws upon our distinct capacities for proprioception, kinesthesis, motor activity, and our sense of agency, but its
exercise is an experience that affords the perceiver awareness of the presence and tangible qualities of an object external to the perceiver's body. So
understood, Informational Bodily Dependence could not, by itself, be a
solution to our puzzle. First, while haptic perception may depend upon
the functionally distinct streams of information associated with the various forms of bodily awareness, it depends as well upon distinct afferent
information provided by cutaneous activation. So Informational Bodily
Dependence fails to provide anything like a sufficient condition for the
tangible qualities of the perceived body to be present in haptic experience. More importantly, that our capacity for bodily awareness, however
implicit, enables haptic experience to present the tangible qualities of an
external body is less an explanation than what needs explaining. Our puzzle is not completely resolved until we understand how this may be so.

   Campbell cites Huang and Pashler's (2007) distinction, in visual attention, between selecting something out from its background and character-
izing or accessing its features:

> So a property may be used to *select* the object or region. Or the property may
> be *accessed* as a property of that object or region. Selection is what makes
> the object or region visible in the first place; selection is what makes it pos-
> sible for the subject to focus on that object or region in order to ascertain

its various properties. Access is a matter of the subject making it explicit, in one way or another, just which manifold properties the object or region has. (Campbell in Campbell and Cassam 2014, 54)

Notice that the property used to select an object or region, though unattended to, may, nonetheless, contribute to the phenomenological character of the sensory experience. Should the same object or region be selected by a different property, the subsequent experience would differ in phenomenological character.

Tactile perception, like visual and auditory perception, involves grouping, segmentation, and recognition. Suppose, then, that this distinction can be drawn, not only within visual attention, but also within tactile and, specifically, haptic attention. So a property may be used to select an object or region for active attention in haptic exploration or a property may be accessed in haptic experience as a property of that object or region. With Huang and Pashler's distinction in mind, and supposing it may legitimately apply to haptic attention as well, Fulkerson's notion of an explicit experience is characterized in terms of our accessing its object – it is attended to and open for epistemic appraisal. Now suppose Campbell is right in thinking that a property may be used to select an object in visual attention but not be accessed in consciously attending to it (Campbell and Cassam 2014; Chapter 3.2). And suppose, further, that this possibility is a consequence of the distinction Huang and Pashler introduced, so that, if it holds, as well, for haptic attention, then there should be cases of selecting an object or region for haptic attention without attending to the tangible quality on the basis of which that object or region was selected. Since explicit experiences are a matter of accessing their objects, then our haptic experience of a tangible quality that selected the body or region but was not attended to would be an implicit experience of that quality.

This is the basis of a worry for a further claim Fulkerson makes about implicit experiences. There is a sense in which, for Fulkerson (2014, 91), implicit experiences are no experiences at all, and this despite his claim that they occur in consciousness. The content of an implicit experience is merely the content of a potential, that is to say, non-actual experience (Fulkerson 2014, 95). And there is an associated tendency in Fulkerson's discussion to identify conscious experience with what is attended to and accessed, with explicit experience. But if the presence of a tangible quality is the basis for the selection of an object or region in haptic exploration, and if selection is what makes the object or region tangible in the first place, then surely it contributes to the phenomenological character of the haptic experience even if it is not attended to. If that same object or region were selected on the basis of a different tangible quality, the subsequent experience would differ in phenomenological character.

Another worry is this. For Fulkerson (2014, 95), the objects of implicit awareness are there for "potential directedness." But if we can voluntarily selectively attend to something about which we are merely implicitly aware, it must be present already in our experience, however recessively and in the background, if it can thus be consciously and voluntarily selected. The objects of implicit awareness are "in consciousness" in the sense of being within the range of the perceiver's sensory experience if not within the range of their attention. So the objects of implicit awareness being there for "potential directedness" are inconsistent with our experience of them being potential and non-actual. Moreover, reflection on "potential directedness" reinforces the claim of the previous paragraph. If the object of implicit awareness can be voluntarily selectively attended to, it must make a phenomenological difference to the perceiver's experience even when unattended. The phenomenological difference the object makes to the perceiver's experience is what makes for the possibility of voluntarily selecting it for increased attention.

The worries just adumbrated have consequences for how the implicit–explicit distinction may be understood. If an explicit experience is an actual conscious experience whereas an implicit experience is merely the content of a potential, non-actual conscious experience, then the distinction does not admit of degrees. But if Fulkerson is wrong about this, if an implicit experience is of something actually present, if recessive and in the background, if the object of implicit experience falls within the range of sensory experience if not the range of explicit attention, then this raises the possibility that the implicit–explicit distinction is a matter of degree. An element present in experience would then be more or less recessive, more or less in the background. A gateway conception of attention might encourage one to deny that the implicit–explicit distinction admits of degrees. However, if attention is, instead, conceived as a modification of consciousness, then it is natural to think that consciousness may be modified in degrees. So perhaps underlying the present disagreement are different models of conscious attention (see Wu 2014, for an excellent recent discussion of attention).

The possibility raised by Huang and Pashler's distinction between selection and access concerns the implicit experience of tangible qualities of external bodies. Our present focus, however, is not on implicit experiences of external bodies, but on implicit experiences of the perceiver's body. But here too it seems implausible that my awareness of my hand's configuration and force in grasping or enclosure, understood as a mode of haptic perception, while implicit, is merely potential and, thereby, non-actual. The information drawn upon from proprioception, kinesthesis, motor activity, and our sense of agency in haptic perception makes a contribution to the phenomenological character of that experience, even if there is, as Fulkerson urges, only one conscious experience (the haptic experience) in play and not two (the haptic experience and a distinct experience of the body's state and activity). The information from bodily awareness drawn upon in the exercise of our haptic capacities specifically makes a difference to the way the object of haptic awareness is presented. As I argued in Chapter 1.6, distinct exploratory activities, distinct ways of handling the object of haptic exploration, constitute distinct haptic perspectives on that object, and this perspectival relativity is manifest in the different haptic appearances presented by the constant object of haptic exploration. It is one thing to claim that bodily awareness makes no explicit contribution to haptic experience. In grasping or enclosure, understood as a mode of haptic perception, we attend only to the object grasped and its manifest tangible qualities. But it is a further, contestable claim, that bodily awareness, however implicit, contributes nothing to the phenomenological character of the haptic experience it partly gives rise to. Bodily awareness, however implicit, contributes to the variable haptic appearances in the exercise of constant haptic perception. If the phenomenological character of haptic experience were exhausted by the constant tangible qualities attended to, then no room would be left for the contribution of flux to our haptic experience. But an adequate account of perceptual constancy must determine not only the constant object of perception, but its variable appearances as well. In grasping or enclosure, understood as a mode of haptic perception, haptic experience is the joint upshot of the force of the hand's activity and the self-maintaining forces of the object grasped. Constant tangible aspects are presented in haptic experience as the forces that constitute their categorical bases come into conflict with the force of the grasping hand. And the variable appearances of these constant tangible aspects are a phenomenological reflection of the variable activity of the hand in haptic exploration.

2.3   Against Haptic Indirect Realism

That our awareness of the hand's configuration and force is merely implicit in grasping or enclosure, understood as a mode of haptic perception, rules out at least one response to our refined how-possible question. Our question was how can an experienced limitation to the hand's activity disclose the presence and tangible qualities of an external body? And one natural suggestion might be that our puzzle merely reveals haptic presentation to be indirect. That is to say, perhaps our puzzle reveals that we have an explicit experience of the hand's configuration and force and thereby come to have an explicit experience of the overall shape and volume of the object grasped. This would be an instance of what Fulkerson described as Strong Experiential Dependence. That haptic perception depends only upon an implicit awareness of the hand's configuration and force reveals this otherwise natural suggestion to be ultimately misguided. Nevertheless, it is worth examining for the light it sheds on the challenge posed by our refined how-possible question. (For a recent sophisticated defense of tactile indirect realism, see Richardson 2013; though the way Richardson's view avoids some of the present worries makes me think she has in mind a different distinction in speaking of bodily sensation as mediating tactile perception.)

Begin with bodily sensation. Among the corporeal aspects of our nature of which we may be aware are felt limitations to our body's activity, be it in the exertion and depletion of physical force – lifting something until we can no more – or in the inability to move our limbs in a certain way. Perhaps felt resistance to the hand's activity is a bodily sensation causally coordinated with tangible qualities of the object grasped. Thus the overall shape of the object grasped causes in the perceiver a certain bodily sensation, a felt resistance to the hand's activity. Perhaps it is this felt resistance of the hand so configured that is the object of explicit awareness. We thus come to haptically experience the tangible qualities of an external body thanks to the way in which bodily sensation is causally coordinated with them. The overall shape of the external object would be mediately presented by the characteristic bodily sensations that making an effort to mold more precisely the hand to its contours gives rise to. So, on this model, we would be immediately presented with aspects of our own body's configuration and the limits to its activity and thereby mediately presented with the tangible qualities of an external body.

Recall the obstacle that prompted our refined how-possible question was a failure of sufficiency. Not all experienced limitations to the body's activities, not all passivities of matter, are due to the tangible qualities of an external body. How then do we distinguish those experienced limitations that are perceptions of external bodies from those that are not? Haptic indirect realism would provide at least a sketch of an answer. The experienced limitations of the body's activity that are involved in the perception of an external body's tangible qualities are those that are causally coordinated with them, at least in the right sort of way. This last qualification is not insignificant, as anyone who is familiar with the problem of wayward causal chains will appreciate. This is part of why this is just a sketch of an answer.

The problem for this envisioned haptic indirect realism, however, lies not with its being underdeveloped in this way, but rather with its claim that haptic perception depends upon an explicit awareness of the hand's configuration and force. Arguably at least, that awareness is merely implicit. An explicit experience of a limit to the hand's activity is, according to this indirect realism, the means by which we experience the external body. But the disclosure of an object's overall shape and volume in grasping or enclosure is not apparently mediated in this way. Grasping seems from within haptic experience to directly disclose corporeal aspects of its object. Moreover, explicitly attending to the hand's configuration and force in grasping or enclosure draws attentive resources away from the object of haptic perception. In grasping or enclosure, understood as a mode of haptic perception, we attend only to the object of haptic investigation and its manifest tangible qualities. It is because the tangible qualities of an external body are directly disclosed in haptic perception that grasping becomes, in the cosmology of the Giants, a touchstone for reality. Grasping, however, could not play this rhetorical role, if it were apparently mediated.

Phenomenologically, this seems apt. Haptic experience seems to present itself as the immediate, if partial disclosure, to the perceiver's haptic perspective, of the tangible qualities inhering in a thing external to the perceiver's body. In a way, haptic indirect realism makes the converse of Fulkerson's mistake. Whereas Fulkerson emphasizes the presence of the constant tangible object in haptic attention at the expense of its variable haptic appearance, haptic indirect realism makes these variable haptic appearances the objects of active attention. Haptic indirect realism thus involves the objectification of appearing as appearance of which Cook Wilson complained in his 1904 letter to Stout:

> And so, as *appearance* of the object, it has now to be represented not as the object but as some phenomenon caused in our consciousness by the object. Thus for the true appearance (=appearing) to us of the object is substituted through the 'objectification' of the appearing as appearance, the appearing to us of an *appearance*, the appearing of a phenomenon caused in us by the object. (*Correspondence with Stout* 1904; Cook Wilson 1926, 796)

But when we perceive by means of our grasping hand, we attend only to what is in our grasp and not to the way that it is presented in our handling of it. Our sense of our hand's configuration and force contributes only to the pre-noetic structure of haptic experience and, at best, determines the way its object is presented therein. In making our awareness of the hand's configuration and force explicit, haptic indirect realism is thus precluded.

However, if anything, precluding this haptic indirect realism only makes our how-possible question more urgent and more challenging. For how can an implicit awareness of a limit to the hand's activity directly disclose the overall shape and volume of an external body? What contribution can an awareness, however implicit, of the hand's configuration and force make to haptic perception that would not undermine its directly disclosing the constant object of haptic attention? If anything, recognition of the dependence of haptic perception upon an implicit bodily awareness can seem only to make matters worse.

2.4   Sympathy

How can an implicit awareness of a limit to the hand's activity contribute to directly disclosing the overall shape and volume of the object grasped? How does the pre-noetic structuring of haptic experience determined by this implicit awareness contribute to the presentation of its object?

When our hominid ancestor reaches out and picks up a rough-hewn stone, perhaps in preparation to skirmish with a competing group of hominids, they feel the overall shape and volume of the stone in their grasp. It is not the hand's shape, the configuration of the hand in grasping or enclosure, that they haptically perceive, though they may be aware of it, however implicitly. It is the stone's shape that is disclosed in their grasp. They feel the overall shape and volume in the stone, and its overall shape and volume are tangible qualities of the stone that their hand is felt to conform to. I shall make a suggestion that will be the basis for an answer to our refined how-possible question. Specifically, feeling tangible qualities in something external to the perceiver's body and feeling in conformity with them can fruitfully be understood as due to the operation of sympathy.

Felt resistance to touch, insofar as it is the presentation of an object external to the perceiver's body, is a sympathetic response to the force that resists the hand's activity. Recall our refined version of our how-possible question was this: How is it possible for felt resistance to the hand's activity in grasping or enclosure to disclose a rigid, solid body's overall shape and volume? If feeling tangible qualities in something external to the perceiver's body and in conformity with them is due to the operation of sympathy, then we have a basis for an answer. It is when the limit to the hand's activity is experienced as a sympathetic response to a countervailing force, as the hand's force encountering an alien force resisting it, one force in conflict with another, like it yet distinct from it, that the self-maintaining forces of the body disclose that body's presence and tangible qualities to haptic awareness.

If felt resistance is the means by which the conflicting forces are sympathetically presented in haptic experience, then in being sympathetically presented with an external body, the perceiver is naturally attending to the external body, the object of haptic perception. In haptic perception, the perceiver is explicitly aware of the object of haptic perception. Insofar as felt resistance is sympathetically presenting an external body, the perceiver's awareness of the hand's configuration and force is, by contrast, merely implicit. Indeed, actively attending to the hand's activity would erode the sympathetic presentation of what is external to the perceiver's body.

Earlier, the initial statement of the puzzle was motivated by considering the analogy of felt temperature. We contrasted two cases. In both cases, you feel warm, and you feel warm to the same degree. But in the first case, you feel warm because of a fever, and in the second case, you feel warm because of the ambient heat. There is also, importantly, a phenomenological difference between these cases. In the second case, not only do you feel warm, but you feel, as well, the warmth in the ambient air. Indeed, the warmth you feel is in conformity with the warmth felt in the ambient air. What explains the phenomenological difference is that in the second case, but not in the first, the felt warmth is a sympathetic response to the ambient heat, to the thermal properties of something external to the perceiver's body. In sympathetically responding to ambient heat, the warmth you feel becomes a way of feeling the warmth in something located outside of your body. Moreover, in sympathetically responding to ambient heat, the warmth you feel is in conformity with the warmth felt in the air. Active attention to the warmth you feel can erode the sympathetic presentation of the ambient warmth. Focus too much on the warmth you feel, and you cease to feel the warmth in the air.

Sympathetically responding to the way the body's self-maintaining forces resist the hand's grasp is a way of presenting that body and its tangible qualities. Sympathy is what makes the extra-somatic present in haptic experience. Thanks to the operation of sympathy, we experience from within what the extra-somatic is like. One obstacle to appreciating this concerns our present understanding of sympathy, where sympathy is a kind of emotional response to others, a kind of fellow-feeling, akin to compassion or pity. The notion of sympathy that is being invoked as the principle governing haptic presentation is closer to the notion at work in Stoic and neo-Platonic physics, if more abstract and not at all reliant on their vitalistic metaphysics. I believe that this more abstract principle is at work both in haptic presentation and in fellow-feeling. After all, each is a way of experiencing from within what another is like.

The present approach thus contrasts with that of Whitehead (1978). Whitehead both explains perceptual prehension partly in terms of sympathy and embraces the association with emotion:

> The primitive form of physical experience is emotional – blind emotion – received as felt elsewhere in another occasion and conformally appropriated as a subjective passion. In the language appropriate to the higher stages of experience, the primitive element is sympathy, that is, feeling the feeling in another and feeling conformally with another. The separation of the emotional experience from the presentational intuition is a high abstraction of thought. Thus the primitive experience is emotional feeling, felt in its relevance to a world beyond. The feeling is blind and the relevance is vague. (Whitehead 1978, 162–3)

Whitehead's retention of the emotional associations of sympathy led him to paradoxically portray perceptual prehension as an outgrowth of blind emotion. However, as we shall see, the principle of sympathy can be understood with sufficient generality so that it may be at work both in haptic presentation and in fellow-feeling, without reducing perceptual presentation to blind emotion. Perception may not reduce to blind emotion, but that is consistent with certain natural affective responses being made possible and, indeed, partly constituted by the operation of sympathy in haptic presentation. It would have to be, if, as Derrida (2005, chapter 4) insists, an adequate philosophy of touch must leave room for both blows and caresses (see also Wyschogrod 1981).

The proposal is that presentation in haptic perception is governed by the principle of sympathy. There are two ways to understand this.

The first proceeds synthetically. That is, beginning with elements and principles understood independently of haptic perception, one constructs the notion of the presentation of tangible qualities of external bodies in haptic experience on their basis. So, for example, one might begin with bodily sensation and "extend its reach," so to speak, via the operation of sympathy to construct a notion of the presentation of tangible qualities of external bodies. So understood, haptic presentation would be the coordination of bodily sensations with the tangible qualities of external bodies via the operation of sympathy.

The second way proceeds analytically. That is, beginning with the notion of the presentation of tangible qualities of external bodies in haptic experience, one analyzes or decomposes that notion into constituent elements that must be present and principles that must be operative if haptic perception is so much as possible. On the synthetic approach, the unity of haptic presentation is an explanandum. The unity of haptic presentation is to be explained in terms of a construction from elements and principles understood independently of haptic presentation. On the analytic approach, by contrast, the unity of haptic presentation is an explanans. It explains and renders intelligible elements and principles that must be operative if haptic presentation is so much as possible. On the analytic approach, the task, then, is to articulate the intelligible structure determined by the presupposed unity.

The synthetic approach naturally, perhaps inexorably, motivates indirect realism about haptic perception, comparable to the indirect realism that we previously rejected. So consider again our toy model where we begin with bodily sensation and extend its reach through the operation of sympathy. Bodily sensation does not involve the presentation of tangible qualities of external bodies. It is, instead, a mode of self-presentation. Thanks to the operation of sympathy, in being presented with an aspect of our corporeal nature, we are mediately presented with the tangible quality of an external body. But haptic perception is not indirect in this way. When our hominid ancestor grasps a rough-hewn stone, they feel its overall shape and volume. Moreover, the presentation of these tangible qualities in their haptic experience is not apparently mediated. Our hominid ancestor need not attend to their bodily sensations as a means of attending to the tangible qualities of external bodies, rather these are directly disclosed in haptic perception. Indeed, attending to the body and its activity draws attentive resources away from the object of tactile perception.

The problem with the synthetic approach, at least as so far developed, is twofold. First, it posits two experiences – the haptic experience and the experience of the perceiver's body – when plausibly there is only one. (These would remain two distinguishable experiences even if the experience of the perceiver's body were, in some sense, a part, or constituent, of the broader haptic experience.) And, second, the awareness of the perceiver's body is explicit rather than implicit. On the synthetic approach, the state and activity of the body are actively attended to and so are, potentially at least, the object of epistemic appraisal. Moreover, both of these features were directly involved in the subsequent indirect realism. On the alternative, analytic approach, indirect realism is simply not a possibility. One begins with an irreducible unity, the presentation of the tangible qualities of external bodies in haptic experience, and then discerns what intelligible structure it must display if it is so much as possible. (On sensory presentation being a kind of unity – a "communion" with its object – see Ardley's 1958 unjustly neglected essay.) Thus the presentation of tangible qualities of external bodies in haptic experience could not be a construction from elements and principles understood independently of haptic perception, the way they would be if indirect realism were true.

The analytic approach to sensory presentation is comparable to Frege's approach to thought, at least at certain stages of his career, on certain interpretations (see, for example, Travis 2011, essays 7 and 9). Frege begins with a unity, a truth-evaluable thought, and discerns what intelligible structure it must display. Beginning with the thought, Frege analyzes or decomposes that thought into constituent elements that must be present and principles that must be operative if that thought is to be so much as truth-evaluable (which is not to say that there is a unique such decomposition). Frege's position thus contrasts with recent discussions of the problem of the unity of the proposition (compare Gaskin 2008; King 2007; King et al. 2014; Soames 2010). The problem of the unity of the proposition simply does not arise for Frege, since he does not begin with independently understood elements and principles and tries to construct thoughts on their basis. Rather the unity of thought is explanatorily prior to the intelligible structure it must display if it is to be so much as truth-evaluable. Similarly, on the analytic approach, the unity of sensory presentation is explanatorily prior to the intelligible structure it must display if it is so much as possible.

To get a general sense of the analytic approach, consider the following plausible, if contentious example (Johnston 2007, for one, seems to deny it). Arguably at least, any notion of sensory presentation essentially involves a subject–object distinction. If an object is present in perceptual experience, then not only is there the object of perception – what is present in that experience – but there is also a perceiver that undergoes that experience – the subject to whom the object is presented. If the subject–object distinction cannot intelligibly be sustained, then the presentation of the object to the subject is not so much as possible.

If we allow for modes of self-presentation where the subject and object are the same entity, then the subject–object distinction arguably required by the presupposed unity is merely hyperintensional. So compare Plotinus' view, in the *Fifth Ennead*, that intellection, the presentation of intelligible objects, the highest form of unity short of that displayed by the hyperontic One, requires the distinction between the act of intellect and its object. Nevertheless, the Intellect apprehends only itself insofar as it is an image of the One. So the subject–object distinction required for intelligible presentation is consistent with its being a mode of self-presentation and so hyperintensional (see Gerson 1994; Chapter 3.1).

If presentation may be self-presentation, and the intelligible distinction between subject and object may be hyperintensional, then I am genuinely uncertain about Johnston's denial of the claim that presentation intelligibly requires a subject. Johnston (2007) invites us to think of ourselves as Samplers of Presence, where we access objective modes of presentations that are part of a larger reality, both accessible and inaccessible, but where our access, relative to our perspective, though ours, does not involve a subject over and above the accessed objective modes of presentations. But if the subject to whom the object is presented can be one and the same thing, then there being no subject over and above the object is not yet proof that they cannot be intelligibly distinguished. Even if there is no subject over and above the objective mode of presentation accessed from our perspective, the denial that there is no subject that accesses the objective mode of presentation is a further claim. One and the same thing, the objective mode of presentation, may be playing two roles. Just as in self-hate, where, tragically, one thing both hates and is hated, perhaps, in perception, one thing both accesses and is accessed. The present point is not to criticize Johnston, nor to defend neutral monism, but to emphasize how little may be involved in the subject–object distinction.

Intelligible presentation may be a mode of self-presentation, but Plotinus claims that the subject and object of perception must be more than hyperintensionally distinguished; they must be two things. This is a reflection of the fact that the unity presupposed in sensory presentation is a lesser unity than the unity presupposed in intelligible presentation. However, once one adopts a more naturalistic approach to embodiment than Plotinus, it is plausible to allow for forms of sensory self-presentation. Since having a fever is a condition of the body, and we are fundamentally embodied, then feeling a fever is itself a mode of self-presentation, even if there is more to one's nature than the fever one is currently suffering. (For discussion of this example and the puzzlement that results from not allowing modes of sensory self-presentation, see Yrjönsuuri 2008.) If sensory presentation is partial, and primates like ourselves are fundamentally embodied, then the sensory presentation of aspects of our corporeal nature is a kind of self-presentation even if there is more to our nature than is present in bodily awareness.

There may, however, be a sense in which Plotinus was right. The unity presupposed in sensory presentation, being partial, is a lesser unity than the unity presupposed in intelligible presentation. When the Inchoate Intellect turns, and looks, and sees only itself insofar as it is the image of the hyperontic One, thus becoming the Intellect in full actuality, this intelligibly differentiated image is wholly present in the act of intellection. An intelligible object is wholly present in the act of intellection in the way that a sensible object never is in perception since sensory presentation is invariably relative to the perceiver's partial perspective.

Notice that in proceeding analytically, the subject–object distinction is not something to overcome (a characteristically modern anxiety dramatized by Cartesian skepticism). Instead we are presupposing their unity in an episode or process of sensory presentation. There is no need to bridge the gap between subject and object since we began with their unity in haptic perception and merely discern that their distinction, potentially hyperintensional, is intelligibly required. The need to bridge the gap between the subject and object constituted by their distinction only arises if their unity is not in this way presupposed. Thus bridging the gap between subject and object by having bodily sensation be coordinated with tangible qualities of external bodies via the operation of sympathy and its attendant indirect realism only arises if their unity in perceptual presentation is not presupposed but something to be constructed from elements and principles antecedently understood.

In grasping or enclosure, the overall shape and volume of the object is directly disclosed in a perceiver's haptic encounter with it. Since I believe that perception quite generally involves an irreducible presentational element, I do not believe that the haptic presentation of the tangible qualities of external bodies could be constructed out of elements and principles understood independently of haptic perception. So I am debarred from the synthetic approach. It is, at any rate, inconsistent with our implicit awareness of the hand's configuration and force in grasping or enclosure, understood as a mode of haptic perception. Thus I proceed analytically. Presupposing the unity of haptic presentation, I try to determine the intelligible structure it must display if it is so much as possible. The claim that the presentation of tangible qualities of external bodies in haptic experience involves the operation of sympathy should be understood in this light. It is not the claim that one thing, the tangible qualities of external bodies, is mediately presented by another thing, the presentation of aspects of the subject's corporeal nature in bodily sensation. Rather, it is the claim that the presentation of tangible qualities of external bodies in haptic experience is an irreducible unity that is governed by the principle of sympathy. Feeling a tangible quality in an external body and in conformity with it just is the presentation of that quality in tactile experience and can be analytically explicated in terms of the operation of sympathy.

2.5   Sensing Limits

In grasping or enclosure, understood as a mode of haptic perception, the overall shape and volume of an external body is present in haptic experience, thanks to an implicit experience of an external limit to the hand's activity. If an experienced limit to the hand's activity discloses tangible qualities of an external body, then the idea of the experience of a limit, however implicit, must be in good order. But is it really? Within the phenomenological tradition, Derrida (2005) has expressed his doubts. Our present purpose is not to lay these doubts to rest in a way that would persuade a determined Derridean skeptic, but rather to make intelligible, at least to ourselves, what would be involved in the experience of a limit, and so, in this way, sketch a few of its features.

In a representative passage, Derrida describes an *aporia* involved in the figure of touch:

> Above all, nobody, no body, no body proper has ever touched – with a hand or through skin contact – something as abstract as a limit. Inversely, however, and that is the destiny of this figurality, all one ever does touch is a limit. To touch is to touch a limit, a surface, a border, an outline. Even if one touches an inside, "inside" of any thing whatsoever, one does it following the point, the line or surface, the borderline of a spatiality exposed to the outside, offered – precisely – on its running border, offered to contact … This surface, line or point, this limit, therefore, … finds itself to be at the same time touchable and untouchable: it is as is every limit, certainly, but also well-nigh at and to the limit, and on the exposed, or exposing, edge of an abyss, a nothing, an "unfoundable" unfathomable, seeming still less touchable, still more untouchable, if this were possible, than the limit it self of its exposition. (2005, 103–4)

There is a lot to say about this passage and how the *aporia* it describes may, if at all, *pace* Derrida, be resolved. One thing to get clearer about is the sense in which a surface, understood as a limit, is abstract. On at least one good sense of the abstract–concrete distinction, the surfaces of material bodies count as concrete – they at least exist in space and time. But notice, as well, that the surfaces of material bodies could not themselves be material. They are not themselves material parts of the bodies whose surfaces they are. Surfaces are, in Sellars' (1956, iv 23) apt phrase, bulgy two-dimensional particulars. They are two-dimensional in the sense that they lack thickness. But no material thing lacks thickness. This suggests an alternative understanding of the sense in which such limits are abstract. Whether it is sufficient to underwrite Derrida's *aporia* is another matter. And there may yet be other relevant senses in which a surface, understood as a limit, may be said to be abstract. Another thing to get clearer about is whether the limit that is said to be intangible is the same limit that we must be said to touch. Perhaps like Protagorean arguments, at least on a Peripatetic diagnosis of them, the puzzle turns on a conflation. After all, limits may be said of in many ways, and there may be different senses in which we may be said to touch a limit.

Notice, however, that the putatively intangible limit at work in this passage is a spatial boundary, the surface of the object of tactile perception. An external limit to the hand's activity is not a spatial boundary or a surface, though it may disclose these, if it is experienced as their sympathetic presentation. However, if there is a puzzle about how anything as abstract, on some suitable understanding, as the limit of a bounded body may be tangible, surely a limit to the hand's activity is even more abstract. After all, the limit to the hand's activity is intangible – like virtue, and the being of capacity more generally, as the Eleatic Visitor instructs the Giants in the *Sophist*. Bodily awareness presents corporeal aspects of the embodied perceiver, just as tactile perception presents corporeal aspects of its object. Our question is whether anything as abstract as a limit to the hand's activity so much as could be the object of bodily awareness. Thus a variant of the Eleatic Visitor's lesson raises, as well, a question about the Giant's appeal to the phenomenologically vivid and primitively compelling experience of felt resistance to touch if it is to motivate their corporealism.

What would it take to be aware of a limit to the hand's activity? Such an awareness would have to afford the subject with a contrast between the hand's present configuration and a potential configuration that extends beyond the points at which the hand's force is resisted by the self-maintaining forces of the object grasped. Such an awareness would depend upon a psychological representation of potential motor activity, a sense of how far one's grasp may extend if unimpeded. The representation of potential motor activity need only be apparent. I may have a sense that I could reach the top shelf, but trying may reveal that I was mistaken.

A sense of the contrast between the hand's present configuration and a potential configuration beyond the limit of the grasped object's boundaries may be necessary for awareness of an external limit to the hand's activity, but it is not sufficient. There is a crucial additional element involved in being aware of a limit to the hand's activity. Whenever I deliberately hold my hand in a certain configuration that is not completely outstretched, I may have a sense of potential configurations extending beyond the present one, but I do not thereby experience a limit. The relevant sense of limit involves a check or impediment to the will. So not only does an awareness of a limit to the hand's activity involve a kinesthetic representation of potential motion, but it must also draw upon our sense of agency. Not only must one have a sense of how far one's grasp may extend if unimpeded, but one must also have a sense of an impediment to one's grasp. A sense of impediment arises out of a frustration of the will in being unable to extend one's grasp further. Moreover, this second condition is related to the first. The object of the will is to extend the hand further in peripersonal space, the space of potential motor activity. The object of the will is thus represented on the kinesthetic map. The location of the hand's configuration in the space of potential motor activity is only experienced as a limit insofar as it is the frustration and not the fulfillment of the will. The frustration arises from the inability to extend the hand's activity further in peripersonal space, the object of the will being located in the space beyond which the hand may extend its activity, and this despite a sense of effort exerted in trying to obtain the object of the will – the felt force, however implicit, of the hand's activity in conflict with the self-maintaining forces of the object grasped.

A qualification is needed. This may seem unobvious if one focused exclusively and superficially on the case of grasping a rigid, solid body. But here too careful reflection reveals that something more needs to be said. For it is not as if, in grasping a rigid, solid body, one is trying to crush that body. One typically does not summon all one's strength in grasping a stone. Or consider grasping a fragile body, an abandoned chrysalis, say, or a body whose overall shape and volume can deform if sufficient pressure is applied, such as a sponge. If I want to have a sense of the chrysalis' or sponge's overall shape and volume, I must take care, in conforming to their contours, not to exert so much effort that I crush or otherwise deform what is in my grasp. Crushing or deforming the grasped object would defeat the end of that activity, to become aware of that object's overall shape and volume had prior to our grasping it.

What these cases reveal is that the impediment to the will is not purely external. Let me be unequivocal. There must be an external element to the impediment to the will insofar as this is to form the basis of the sympathetic presentation of the extra-somatic. Thus the self-maintaining forces of the object grasped are an impediment to the force of the hand's activity insofar as they conflict with it. Typically, however, we wish to sense the limit of our hand's activity in grasping a body consistent with not crushing or deforming that body. Again, crushing or deforming the grasped object would defeat the end of that activity, to become aware of that object's overall shape and volume had prior to our grasping it and sustained in our grasp. Should it be crushed or deformed, it would come to have some other overall shape and volume. Its original overall shape and volume, which we aimed to sense, would, in being destroyed, remain forever unfelt. This has the consequence that the limit to the hand's activity, while external, is not purely external. Our own ends constrain, as well, our hand's activity.

We sense a limit to the hand's activity despite a sense of effort. Sartre has objected to the posited sense of effort, at least as it arises in Maine de Biran's work:

> Either it is a thing among other things, or else it is that by which things are revealed to me. But it can not be both at the same time. Similarly I see my hand touching objects, but do not know it in its act of touching them. This is the fundamental reason why that famous "sensation of effort" of Maine de Biran does not really exist. For my hand reveals to me the resistance of objects, their hardness or softness, but not *itself.* (Sartre, *L'Être et le néant*; Barnes 1958, 304)

> The body is *lived* and not *known.* This explains why the famous "sensation of effort" by which Maine de Biran attempted to reply to Hume's challenge is a psychological myth. We never have any sensation of our effort, but neither do we have peripheral sensations from the muscles, bones, tendons, or skin, which have been suggested to replace the sensation of effort. We perceive the resistance of things. What I perceive when I want to lift this glass to my mouth is not my effort but the heaviness of the glass – that is, its resistance to entering into an instrumental complex which I have made appear in the world. (Sartre, *L'Être et le néant*; Barnes 1958, 324)

One may complain that a sense of effort need not be narrowly construed as a sensation of effort. Given certain background assumptions, the sensation of effort can sound like an oxymoron. Specifically, if sensations are the passive reception of sensory impressions, and effort involves activity, one may well wonder what a sensation of effort could be if it is not merely the passive sensory effect of active effort. But a sense of effort need not be so narrowly construed as a sensation understood as a passive sensory impression.

Setting that aside, there is a more principled issue moving Sartre, namely the distinction between a thing among other things and that by which things are revealed to me. The former are known, the latter lived. Sartre's point seems to be that the body's effort or activity is not the kind of thing that is known by perception, though perception is a way in which we can know about how things are with a thing among things. Sartre is right at least to this extent. In grasping a rough-hewn stone, the hand of our hominid ancestor discloses to them the resistance of the stone, its hardness and rigidity. In grasping or enclosure, the perceiver explicitly attends to the tangible qualities of the object of haptic exploration. The activity of the hand in grasping or enclosure, understood as a mode of haptic perception, is not itself the object of explicit awareness. If the object of explicit awareness is the object of the perceptual experience that affords such awareness, then the activity of the hand in grasping or enclosure is not perceived. Explicit awareness of the hand's activity would erode the sympathetic presentation of the corporeal aspects of the object of haptic investigation. But Sartre goes too far if he denies, as well, that we are implicitly aware of the hand's activity in grasping or enclosure. Like Fulkerson, Sartre's suggestion limits phenomenological character of tactile experience to what we are explicitly aware of in undergoing such an experience.

Derrida, too, is skeptical of the Biranian sense of effort, though for different reasons:

> What does the word *effort* ... designate, appearing as it does in this singular context ... where effort, precisely, stalls in *making an effort*. At the point where effort *meets* the limit forcing it to *exert itself* in this *effort*? (2005, 110)

But the sense of effort, however implicit, does not make its appearance solely at the point where effort stalls, at the external limit to the force of the hand's activity. Effort appearing in such a singular context would indeed be puzzling. What sort of effort would it be whose actualization is necessarily ineffectual? However, a sense of effort may intensify as one's tightening grip comes into conflict with the self-maintaining forces of body that resist it, but it was manifest, however implicitly, even in the preparatory reach.

These brief remarks would be insufficient to assuage the doubts of a determined Derridean skeptic. Fortunately, however, they were not meant for such a task. Rather, the Derridean skeptic was invoked as a foil against which to do two things: first, to make intelligible, for ourselves, what an implicit experience of an external limit would be, and second, to sketch a few of its features as exhibited in grasping or enclosure. Without providing anything like a full account, I hope I have said enough to render *prima facie* intelligible the conception of an implicit awareness of a limit to the hand's activity, the passivities of matter constraining the active wax of haptic perception, not least because it is a precondition for the sympathetic presentation of the tangible qualities of external bodies in haptic experience. For it is this impediment of the will that makes the disclosure of the extra-somatic in haptic experience possible.

Notice that the felt resistance to touch involved in grasping or enclosure, understood as a mode of haptic perception, exhibits considerably more structure than the haptic indirect realist allows (Section 2.3). In taking felt resistance to touch to be the object of active attention, there was a temptation to conceive of it as a sensory impression existing, somehow, within the mind, as a conscious modification of the perceiving subject, as the objectification of appearing as appearance, at least by Cook Wilson's lights. Think again of the ways in which that experience depends upon kinesthesia and our sense of agency. Not only does felt resistance to touch involve a sense of how far one's grasp may extend if unimpeded (and so locating the hand's present configuration in a broader space of potential motor activity), but also the frustration of the will in being able to extend that grasp no further, consistent with one's other ends, and this despite the effort exerted. This complex capacity involves the representation of potential motor activity that is not only egocentrically structured, but also teleologically structured by the will. No conception of sensory impression available to the indirect realist displays a similar structure.

Our initial puzzle about bodily awareness' contribution to haptic perception was generated by a conception of bodily awareness as a mere mode of self-presentation. However, if among the objects of bodily awareness are the limits of the body or its activity, then bodily awareness is more than a mere mode of self-presentation. As Martin (1992) argues, to be aware of the limits of the body is to be aware, *inter alia*, of a space beyond those limits. Proprioceptive awareness is thus not confined to what is within those limits. Similarly, to be aware of the limits of the body's activity, at least in the case of grasping or enclosure understood as a mode of perception, is to be aware, *inter alia*, of how far one's grasp may extend if unimpeded. It is thus to be aware of, at least, a space of potential motor activity normally accessible except for the external impediment that presently limits the body's activities. And in each case, bodily awareness being more than a mere mode of self-presentation in disclosing a limit is what allows it to play a role in perceiving what lies beyond that limit. For Martin, the sense of the limit of the body allows the perceiver to use their body to measure other bodies in contact with it. Similarly, the sense of the limit to the hand's activity allows the perceiver to sympathetically respond to the self-maintaining forces of the external body and so present that body and its tangible qualities in haptic perception. So bodily awareness is no mere mode of self-presentation, which is not to say that it does not sometimes function as such.

Let me end by emphasizing a crucial difference. Martin's (1992) conception of touch and the present conception are superficially consistent and yet fundamentally opposed. They are superficially consistent insofar as they concern apparently distinct, if related subject matters. Martin provides an account of static touch, sensation by contact, whereas I aim to account for a species of haptic touch. This consistency is superficial since it masks an explanatory difference. For Martin, static touch is fundamental and haptic touch is to be explained in terms of it, albeit temporally extended and supplemented with various forms of bodily awareness. In contrast, I am inclined to think of haptic touch as fundamental and to explain static touch as a degenerate form of haptic touch. Indeed, many of Martin's examples can be described in this way. I do not mean to settle this difference here. I only observe that this is why we focus on different limits, the limit of the body, for Martin, as opposed to the limit of the body's activity, for myself. That we focus on different limits is a manifestation of the deeper underlying disagreement about explanatory priority of static and haptic touch.

2.6   The Stoics

I observed earlier that our present conception of sympathy can be an obstacle to appreciating how feeling something in another thing and in conformity with it is itself a mode of sympathy. We all too easily understand sympathy as a kind of fellow-feeling akin to compassion and pity when, in fact, sympathy, understood as an explanatory principle, had a history prior to being proposed as the principle governing fellow-feeling. To bring this abstract explanatory principle into view, it is useful to consider a select history and not only to distance ourselves from our own presuppositions about sympathy. A consideration of a select history of this principle allows us to introduce some important claims about the operative notion of sympathy. Specifically, we shall consider sympathy as a principle of action at a distance in Stoic physics in this section and Plotinus' use of sympathy in explaining distal perception in vision and audition in the next. As we shall see, Plotinus' conception of sympathy is no mere Stoic borrowing, but there is an important explanatory contrast with the Stoic conception of sympathy, an explanatory contrast that parallels the one between the synthetic and analytic approaches, and one that I shall exploit in appropriating Plotinian sympathy in an account of haptic presentation.

According to the standard Galenic narrative, the Stoic conception of sympathy is grounded in the medical thought of the Hippocratic tradition (for doubts about this Galenic narrative, see Holmes 2015). It is easy to be impressed, as ancient medical opinion was, with how affecting a part of an animal's body may affect another part of their body without affecting the parts between (see, for example, the Hippocratic *Peri trophé* and Galen's *De locis affectis*). Consider how the Hippocratic author of *Peri trophé* understands symptoms:

> Signs: tickling, ache, rupture, mind, sweat, sediment in urine, rest, tossing, condition of the eyes, imaginations, jaundice, hiccoughs, epilepsy, blood entire, sleep, from both these and all other things in accordance with nature, and everything else of a similar nature that tends to harm or help. (Hippocratic author, *Peri trophé* 26; Jones 1957, 351)

Symptoms are understood to be signs of underlying conditions, in the case of ill health, of disturbances in parts of the animal's body without any apparent disturbance in the parts between. The nature of an animal, whether in sickness or in health, is the nature of a composite natural body whose parts are organized with reference to the function of the whole and these parts may thus sympathetically interact. Thus, in a passage that Galen never tires of citing, our Hippocratic author writes:

> Conflux one, conspiration one, all things in sympathy; all the parts as forming a whole, and severally the parts in each part, with reference to the work. (Hippocratic author, *Peri trophé* 23; Jones 1957, 351)

Thus a tickling, ache, or rupture is a sign for an underlying condition since it is the sympathetic effect of an occurrence in a complex whole.

The Stoics believed that such medical phenomena were subject to a corporeal explanation, involving sympathy as its principle. And since they conceived of the cosmos as a whole as a living being, the principle involved in that explanation, sympathy, was elevated to the status of a cosmic principle.

What, then, was the Stoics' corporeal explanation of sympathetic affection? According to the Stoics, the soul that pervades and animates a living body is composed of *pneuma*, a kind of rarified mixture of air and fire

(*Stoicorum Veterum Fragmenta* 2 773–89). The soul, while corporeal, pervades the body. It does so not by filling interstitial spaces within the body, like water absorbed by a sponge. Rather, active *pneuma* is sufficiently rarified that it can occupy the same space as the passive matter of the body it animates, the way warmth may pervade a sunbaked stone. The *pneuma* in a living body is in a state of tension. This tension in the *pneuma* gives rise to a continuous wave-like motion (*Stoicorum Veterum Fragmenta* 2 448, 450–7). Since the *pneuma* in a living body is in a state of tensional motion, affecting some part of the body will affect the living body as a whole. Moreover, and more importantly for our present purposes, when a part of a living body is affected, a similar or different affection may be transmitted via the tensional motion of the *pneuma* to another part of the body without affecting the parts between, depending upon the disposition of these parts.

The operation of sympathy was not confined to ordinary living bodies. The sensible cosmos itself was conceived to be a living being as well, though perhaps an extraordinary one, at least by our lights. The sensible cosmos was thus conceived to possess the same kind of unity as living beings. The sensible cosmos, like all living beings, has a soul that animates it, the World-Soul. The World-Soul, like all souls, is composed of *pneuma*, and the souls of ordinary living beings are, in some sense, part of the World-Soul. Like ordinary living beings, the sensible cosmos is united by an all-pervading *pneuma* in a state of tensional motion. Thus, according to Alexander of Aphrodisias, Chrysippus:

> first assumes that the whole of substance is unified by a breath (*pneuma*) which pervades it all, and by which the universe is sustained and stabilized and made interactive with itself (*sympathes ... auto*) (Alexander of Aphrodisias, *On Mixture and Growth*, 216 14–218 6; *Stoicorum Veterum Fragmenta* 2 473; Long and Sedley 1987, 48 C)

So according to Chrysippus, disparate parts of the sensible cosmos may sympathetically interact due to the all-pervasive *pneuma*. Moreover, this sympathetic interaction is part of what explains the unity of the sensible cosmos. Thus sympathy was transformed, in Stoic thought, into a cosmic principle of action at a distance.

While perhaps Posidonius is the most famous proponent of cosmic sympathy (Augustine, *Civitas Dei* 5 2), the doctrine goes back at least as far as Chrysippus and, arguably, has roots in Plato's *Timaeus* (on Stoic sympathy, see Brouwer 2015; Meyer 2009; Sambursky 1959; on the *Timaeus* and sympathy, see Emilsson 2015). Sympathy, as a principle of action at a distance, was used to explain a variety of natural phenomena, such as the influence of the moon on the tides (Sextus Empiricus, M 9 79; Cicero, *De divinatione* 2 34) and the efficacy of divination (Cicero, *De divinatione*, and Seneca, *Naturales quaestiones* 2; on how explanations of divination are a part of Stoic natural philosophy, see Struck 2007).

2.7   Plotinus

Plotinus appeals to sympathy to explain a variety of natural and psychological phenomena. Plotinus' use of sympathy has been portrayed as a Stoic borrowing (Emilsson 1988, chapter 3; Ierodiakonou 2006), but most likely its roots lie in Plato's *Timaeus* (Emilsson 2015). On that hypothesis, Plotinus' use of Stoic material is confined to elaborating what is, by his lights, essentially Platonic ideas.

There are number of differences between Plotinus' use of sympathy and the Stoic's use.

First, according to Plotinus, the soul is incorporeal and so could not be composed of *pneuma*, no matter how rarefied the admixture of fire and air. So the mechanism of tensional motion in an all-pervading *pneuma* that, on the Stoic account, explained the operation of sympathy is simply left out of Plotinus' account. Moreover, not only does Plotinus abandon the Stoic explanation of sympathy as the effect of tensional motion in an all pervading *pneuma*, but he seems to offer no alternative mechanism in its place (Emilsson 1988, 48).

This latter fact may seem like a deficit of Plotinus' account until we realize that there is a deeper issue at work, here, other than Plotinus' rejection of Stoic corporealism. As the view that Alexander of Aphrodisias attributes to Chrysippus makes clear, the all-pervading *pneuma* and its tensional motion is meant to unify the cosmos. So while both the Stoics and Plotinus take sympathy to only operate within a unity, the Stoics further hold that this unity is subject to explanation. There is, then, an important difference in explanatory priority that leads Plotinus to reject the Stoic explanation of sympathy in terms of the tensional motion of *pneuma*. It is not the corporeal character of the Stoic explanation of that unity that leads to Plotinus' rejection, so much as unity being subject to explanation at all. The hyperontic One is the fundamental principle, or *arche*, of Plotinus' metaphysics. Thus, for Plotinus, unity is an explanans, not an explanandum. That sympathy only operates within a unity is a consequence, for Plotinus, of that unity making possible the operation of sympathy. No further mechanism is specified since, by Plotinus' lights, no further mechanism is required.

This second, explanatory difference roughly corresponds to the explanatory difference between the synthetic and analytic approaches discussed earlier.

If this second explanatory difference seems odd to you, or you remain in any way incredulous, consider Bas van Fraassen's explanation of how action at a distance in a system of physical events would be an intelligible effect of global constraints on that system should there be such constraints:

> By a global constraint I mean a principle that applies to a system as a whole, and is not equivalent to any principle that applies distributively to the localized particulars or point locations in that system. As an extreme illustration, imagine a world in which the total mass is conserved, but by the happenstance that some bits of matter spontaneously appear in random locations, to balance the mass that disappears elsewhere. Here the global principle of conservation of total mass of the system is not derivable from principles that govern any proper part. (van Fraassen 1989, 3)

The system of physical events is a unified manifold, and the global constraint, applying as it does to the whole, is an aspect or manifestation of the unity of that manifold. If it is coherent that there should be such global constraints on the system of physical events, then action at a distance is a potential intelligible effect. Put another way, the operation of sympathy in a unified manifold would be explained by its unity.

While Plotinus was not the first to use sympathy to explain psychological phenomena, his application of sympathy to the psychological phenomena was broader than many of his predecessors. Thus in a remarkable anticipation of David Hume and Adam Smith, Plotinus writes:

> Indeed the argument deriving from facts opposed [to the assumption of complete separation of souls] asserts that we do share each other's experiences (*sympathein*) when we suffer with (*synalgountas*) others from seeing their pain and feel happy and relaxed [in their company] and are naturally drawn to love them. For without a sharing of experience there could not be love for this reason. (Plotinus, *If All Souls are One, Ennead* 4 9 3 1–5; Armstrong 1984, 433–5)

Sympathy involves the sharing of experiences between distinct individual souls. As in Hume's system, it is an interpersonal principle, and so underwrites a kind of action at a distance within the social sphere. So the unity of all souls – whatever, exactly, that doctrine amounts to – makes it possible for distinct individual souls to sympathetically respond to one another and so share in one another's experiences. In his explanation of sympathy in the second book of the *Treatise*, however, Hume does not himself presuppose the unity of those who sympathetically interact, and so his account is, in that respect at least, more like the Stoics' than Plotinus'.

Not only does Plotinus use sympathy to explain fellow-feeling, but he also uses sympathy to explain the operation of our distal senses, specifically, in vision and audition (see especially the treatise *On Difficulties of the Soul, iii,* or *On Sight, Ennead* 4 5 and the supplementary work, *On Sense-Perception and Memory, Ennead* 4 6). He acknowledges that he was not the first to do so. Accounts of perception in terms of sympathy can be found in Cleomedes' *Meteōra* and Epicurus' *Letter to Herodotus*. So Plotinus understands sympathy as a principle that explains a variety of natural and psychological phenomena, including perception and fellow-feeling. Plotinus thus provides an important historical precedent for the idea that sympathy can be understood with sufficient generality so that it may be at work both in perception and fellow-feeling without one reducing to the other (as in Whitehead's 1978 conception of perceptual prehension as the outgrowth of blind emotion).

The main elements of Plotinus' account of sympathy are in play in the following representative passage:

> This one universe is all bound together in shared experience (*sympathes*) and is like one living creature, and that which is far is really near, just as, in one of the individual living things, a nail or horn or finger or one of the other limbs which is not contiguous: the intermediate part leaves a gap in the experience and is not affected, but that which is not near is affected. For the like parts are not situated next to each other, but are separated by others between, but share their experiences (*sympaschonta*) because of their likeness, and it is necessary that something which is done by a part not situated beside it should reach the distant part; and since it is a living thing and all belongs to a unity nothing is so distant in space that is not close enough to the nature of the one living thing to share experience (*sympathein*). (Plotinus, *On Difficulties about the Soul ii*, or *On Sight, Ennead* 4 4 32 14–22; Armstrong 1984, 235–7)

There are a number of observations to make about this passage.

First, like the *Timaeus* and Stoic accounts, Plotinus thinks that the sensible cosmos has the unity of a living being. And since living beings are essentially ensouled, sympathy is based on the unity of the soul. So the unity of the ensouled living being is explanatorily prior to the sympathetic interaction of its parts.

Second, the effects of sympathy may be between noncontiguous parts of the living being. The distance between the parts of a living being need not be an obstacle to their sympathetic interaction. The parts of a living being that sympathetically interact may be noncontiguous, but that is consistent with contiguous parts of the living being sympathetically interacting. The point is that sympathy is a mode of affection that does not require contact between cause and effect. While Plotinus acknowledges that there is affection by contact, he also maintains, like the Stoics before him, that there are natural phenomena that can only be explained by sympathetic affection.

Third, Plotinus links the sympathetic interaction between the parts of a living being with their similarity (Emilsson 1988, 2015). In cases of sympathetic affection, one part of the unified manifold formally assimilates to a potentially noncontiguous part by becoming like it. Indeed, it is the link between sympathy and similarity that explains why a distant part may be affected without the parts between being affected. This will happen when only the distant part, but not the parts between, is suitably similar to the affecting part of the living being: "For the like parts are not situated next to each other, but are separated by others between, but share their experiences (*sympaschonta*) because of their likeness." However, as we shall see, this should be understood so as to be consistent with the unity of the soul being explanatorily prior to any likeness that may obtain between the parts of the living being that it animates.

Fourth, the similarity between the parts of the living being that may sympathetically interact must be suitably understood. Suppose that some part of the living being comes to be affected in a certain way. A potentially distant part of that same living being, because of its suitable disposition, may come to be affected in that way. Let F be this way of being affected. The potentially distant part is initially not F, but comes to be F, by sympathetically interacting with the initial part's being F. So the potentially distant part is, at the beginning of this process, only potentially like the initial part actually is. So the affected part's formal assimilation to the affecting part should be understood, in the Peripatetic fashion, in terms of the capacity to become like.

Finally, it is consistent with the account provided by this passage that there be considerable leeway in how the formal assimilation is understood. So far, we have envisioned the initial part being F and a potentially distant part becoming F as a result of their sympathetic interaction. But the operative notion of similarity might be understood more broadly than this. Perhaps because of the disposition of the parts, the initial part being F induces in a suitably disposed, potentially distant part the affect G, at least if G is somehow suitably related to F, if F and G are correlatives (in something like Aristotle's sense in the *Categoriae*), or at least not incongruous. Think, for example, of fellow-feeling. Plotinus, like Hume and Smith after him, thinks that fellow-feeling is explained by sympathy operating between individuals. One person's esteem may, due to the operation of sympathy, cause in another the sentiment of pride, as Hume contends. But the latter person's pride, even if it is like the first person's esteem in being an agreeable sentiment, is a distinct affect. Pride may, in some sense, be the appropriate response to another's esteem, and like it in being an agreeable sentiment, but it is not their esteem reduplicated so much as a correlative response. Collingwood provides a nice example. Thanks to the operation of natural sympathy, a dog will feel the terror of a rabbit. However, "terror in a rabbit will communicate itself to a pursuing dog not as terror but as a desire to kill, for a dog has the psychical 'nature' of a hunting animal" (Collingwood 1938, 231). There is another dimension along which the relevant similarity may be generalized. Even if the subsequent affect is not correlative to the initial affect, perhaps the subsequent affect may be like, if not exactly like, the affect of the initial part. There is some evidence that Plotinus himself exercised considerable leeway in understanding similarity here. The stars may affect the course of human affairs, but there is nothing in the stars that is very much like their sublunary effects. Whatever Plotinus' considered view is, the passage, as it stands, is consistent with wider and narrower interpretations of the role of similarity in the operation of sympathy.

Importantly, for our purposes, Plotinus uses sympathy to give an account of the distal senses, vision and audition (*On Difficulties about the Soul iii*, or *On Sight, Ennead* 4 5, 4 6). Though that is his avowed intent, the bulk of the discussion concerns vision, with Plotinus maintaining that a structurally similar account applies, as well, to audition. Vision and audition are distal senses. By means of them, the perceiver may become aware of the object of perception located at a distance. This is a remarkable fact, to which ancient thinkers devoted considerable ingenuity explaining. An important part of what is at issue is the nature of the causal transmission between the distal object and the sensory organs of the perceiver. If that was all that was at issue, however, it would be of antiquarian interest only. We rightly believe that we have an approximately correct account of the causal transmission in distal perception involving, in the case of vision and audition, the propagation of light and sound waves.

But, equally, part of what was at issue was not just the causal influence of objects of perception located at a distance from the perceiver, but a puzzle about their sensory presentation as well. As I emphasized at the outset, insofar as the distant object is present in our experience, we are tempted to say that we are in perceptual *contact* with it, that we *apprehend*, or *grasp*, that object. However, insofar as that object is distant, we could not be in contact with it, at least not literally. Thus Broad (1965, 33) remarks that "It is a natural, if paradoxical, way of speaking to say that seeing seems to 'bring us into *contact* with *remote* objects' and to reveal their shapes and colors." So these ancient discussions concern, as well, what sensory presentation could be if it is not, indeed, tantamount to sensation by contact. In these ancient discussions, then, issues about causal transmission and sensory presentation are intertwined, which is not to say confused. The present point is important, not only for reading Plotinus on perception, but for the use I propose to put that reading. Recall, the present historical digression is in aid of the proposal that haptic presentation may be analytically explicated in terms of the operation of sympathy.

Emilsson (1988, chapter 3) correctly emphasizes that sympathy, in Plotinus' account of vision, is meant to provide an account of how the distal object of vision affects the eyes. Thus the object of perception is the causal agent affecting the patient, the organ of perception. Since the object is distant, it cannot affect the sense organ by contact. And since, at least within the sensible cosmos, Plotinus views affection not involving contact to instead involve sympathy, it is natural for him to understand the distant object acting upon the organ of perception by means of sympathy.

The principal obstacle to this line of reasoning concerns the invalidity of the inference from the object of perception not affecting the sense organs by contact to there being no affection by contact in the causing of that perception. This line of reasoning seems to present us with a stark choice: the object affects the sense organ either by contact or by sympathetic affection. But consider just one alternative. Perhaps, as on the Peripatetic model, the object affects the sense organ only mediately, by affecting an intervening medium, which in turn affects the sense organ with which it is in contact. The Peripatetic model accepts that the distant object cannot be in contact with the perceiver's sense organ, but concludes from this, not the need to postulate a principle of action at a distance, but that causal transmission from the object of perception to the sense organ requires the existence of a suitable medium, in the case of vision, the illuminated transparent.

Plotinus is well aware of this obstacle and devotes considerable effort in criticizing accounts that postulate a medium and other alternatives. We shall not review Plotinus' critical discussion here, nor who his likely targets were (for discussion, see Emilsson 1988; Chapter 3.1). However, I shall make an observation about just one of Plotinus' objections:

> For if our perception resulted from the air being previously affected, when we looked at the object of sight we should not see it, but we should get our

perception from the air which lay close to us, just as when we are warmed. (Plotinus, *On Difficulties about the Soul iii*, or *On Sight*, *Ennead* 4 5 2 50–5; Armstrong 1984, 289)

Plotinus is claiming that if the affection of the perceiver's sense organ involves the intervention of the medium, then the perception that would result would present not some sensible aspect of the distal object, but, rather, with some sensible aspect of the intervening medium.

What is presently important is not the plausibility of Plotinus' claim (the full assessment of which would involve specifying his target and explaining his explanatory framework, something from which one may depart in varying degrees), but rather with how issues about the causal influence of the object of perception are bound up with issues about their sensory presentation. It is for this reason that I suspect that Emilsson goes too far in confining sympathy to explaining the action at a distance involved in visual perception. To be sure, sympathy provides Plotinus with such an account. But sympathy explains, as well, at least in part, how it is that we are presented with the distant visible object and not the intervening medium. That explanation, however, is never made fully explicit, which is unfortunate since we are interested in explaining sensory presentation, and not action at a distance, in terms of the principle of sympathy.

Plotinus concedes that perception would not be possible in the absence of an intermediary. But Plotinus insists that this is not because of the absence of a medium, but rather "because the sympathy of the living being with itself and of its parts with each other" would be disrupted (*On Difficulties about the Soul iii*, or *On Sight*, Ennead 4 5 3 15–19). Insofar as the observation that perception is not possible in the absence of an intermediary is meant to motivate the postulation of a medium, what reason it provides should be understood on the model of inference to the best explanation. If that is right, then the fact that Plotinus has provided an equally credible alternative explanation means that the reason for the postulation of a medium is, to that extent, undermined. But why should we prefer Plotinus' alternative? To address this, Plotinus provides the following thought experiment:

> if there was another universe, that is another living being making no contribution to the life of this one, and there was an eye "on the back of the sky," would it see that other universe at a proportionate distance? (Plotinus, *On Difficulties about the Soul iii*, or *On Sight*, *Ennead* 4 5 3 21–4; Armstrong 1984, 293)

The eye on the back of the sky is an image Plotinus derives from Plato's *Phaedrus*:

> When [the gods] go to feast at the banquet they have a steep climb to the high tier at the rim of heaven ... when the souls we call immortals reach the top, they move outward and take their stand on the high ridge of heaven, where its circular motion carries them around as they stand while they gaze upon what is outside heaven. (Plato, *Phaedrus* 247 b1–c2; Nehemas and Woodruff in Cooper 1997, 525)

Like the gods feasting at their banquet, the eye on the back of the sky is looking outward, beyond the confines of the sensible cosmos ("What is in this place is without color and without shape and without solidity," *Phaedrus* 247 c 6–7; Nehemas and Woodruff in Cooper 1997, 525). Sympathy only operates within the unity provided by the soul of a living being. Since the soul of the other living being, a sensible cosmos distinct from the one within which we reside, makes no contribution to the life of this one, understood as our sensible cosmos, the parts of that other living being cannot sympathetically affect the parts of this one. The eye on the back of the sky fails to see the other universe, a sensible cosmos, at a proportionate distance, not because of the intervening void, but because the unity that makes a sympathetic response possible does not obtain between the eye in this sensible cosmos and any of the parts in the other sensible cosmos. So the eye on the back of the sky thought experiment is meant to be a case where there is no intermediary, but sight fails, not because of the absence of a medium, but because the conditions that make possible sympathetic interaction do not obtain.

Plotinus devotes the final chapter of that treatise to elaborating the thought experiment (*On Difficulties about the Soul iii*, or *On Sight, Ennead* 4 5 8). His discussion is compact and often obscure. So a reasonable treatment of that chapter would require a close exegesis. However, I want to draw our attention to one aspect of his discussion that bears on the explanatory priority of the unity of the soul. Specifically, Plotinus denies that the similarity between the parts of the living being, their capacity to become like one another, is sufficient to explain their sympathetic interaction. So, on the view that Plotinus opposes, one part's being *F* sympathetically causes another part to become *F*, say, not because they are parts of a single ensouled living being, but because of the similarity between them, understood, in the Peripatetic fashion, as the capacity to become like. Notice that if similarity alone suffices for the operation of sympathy, then the eye on the back of the sky should be able to see, at a proportionate distance,

the visible aspects of that other sensible cosmos, if these are suitably similar to the visible aspects of the sensible cosmos within which we reside.
Plotinus, however, doubts that the visible aspects of that other cosmos
would be sufficiently similar to visible aspects of our own for a capacity to
become like to ground the eye's perception of the other sensible cosmos:

> Now the objects apprehended are apprehended in this way by being like,
> because this soul [of the universe] has made them like, so that they are not
> incongruous; so that if the active principle out there is the altogether differ-
> ent soul [of that other universe], the objects assumed to exist there would
> be in no way like the soul of our universe. (Plotinus, *On Difficulties about
> the Soul iii*, or *On Sight*, Ennead 4 5 8 26–31)

What this passage brings out is the way in which the unity of the soul is
explanatorily prior to the formal assimilation among the parts of the living being. Within a single living being, because of the unity provided by
the soul of that living being, parts that are suitably disposed to become
like may sympathetically interact. Similarity, subject to the qualifications
previously discussed, may be a condition on sympathetic affection, but
it is insufficient to explain that affection. And this is so because the soul,
the active formative principle of the living being, makes its parts like or
unlike depending upon the coherence and function of the whole. While it
remains difficult to understand why, for Plotinus, there could be no duplicate *cosmoi*, his reasoning here clearly presupposes that the unity of the
soul is explanatorily prior to the disposition of the parts of the living being
to become like one another and so sympathetically interact.

   Allow me to end this historical digression with an abstract description
of the principle of sympathy. Sympathy, as Plotinus conceives of it, is
the explanatory principle governing certain cases of formal assimilation.
Sympathy is not a principle in the sense that it possesses a content that may
be discursively articulated, such as a principle of mathematics. Sympathy is
not a discursive principle, but an explanatory principle governing certain
cases of formal assimilation. Consider, then, a unified manifold where one
part of the manifold formally assimilates to another, potentially noncontiguous part, and does so because the parts, disposed as they are, are united
in the manifold, in the way that they are. Sympathy, then, is the explanatory principle governing such cases of formal assimilation:

> *Sympathy*: A case of formal assimilation is governed by the principle of sym-
> pathy when and only when one part of a unified manifold formally assimi-
> lates to a potentially noncontiguous part of that manifold because the parts,
> disposed as they are, are united in the manifold, in the way that they are.

As we shall see in the next section, the formal assimilation of perceptual experience to its object in cases of haptic perception, while not an affection, also satisfies this abstract description. The grasping or enclosure of an object, understood as a mode of haptic perception, is a unified manifold where one part of the manifold, the perceiver's hand and the haptic experience its activity gives rise to, formally assimilates to another part of the manifold, the object grasped, and does so because the parts, disposed as they are, the hand's power of haptic activity and the object's self-maintaining forces, are united in the manifold in the way that they are, in the hand's active grasp, the joint upshot of the conflict between the force of the hand's activity and the object's self-maintaining forces. If the formal assimilation of haptic experience to its tangible object really satisfies this abstract description, then sympathy is the principle governing haptic presentation.

2.8   The Principle of Haptic Presentation

In grasping or enclosure, haptic perception is the joint upshot of forces in conflict. On the one hand, there is the force exerted in molding the hand more precisely to the contours of the rigid, solid body. On the other hand, there are the self-maintaining forces of the rigid, solid body itself. Haptic perception is the joint upshot of the force exerted by the grasping hand and the self-maintaining forces of the object grasped. In resisting the force of the hand's activity, the self-maintaining forces that constitute the body's rigidity and solidity present these qualities in haptic awareness. In resisting the hand's encroachment, the hand, and the haptic experience it gives rise to, formally assimilates to the overall shape and volume of the object grasped. And the haptic experience's assimilation to its object, relative to the perceiver's haptic perspective, is a kind of constitutive shaping. The conscious qualitative character of that experience depends upon and derives from the qualitative character of the tangible object as presented to the perceiver's haptic perspective, an event in peripersonal space, the distinctive manner in which they are handling that object in the given circumstances of perception.

Perception places us in the very heart of things. In being present in our perceptual experience, they constitutively shape that experience, at least relative to our partial perspective on things. It is for this reason that Ardley (1958) describes perception as a "communion" with its object. In an episode of perception, the perceiver is united with the object of perception. Perceptual presentation is a distinctive kind of unity. It follows that haptic presentation is itself a kind of unity and more distinctive still. So in feeling the overall shape and volume of the stone in their grasp, our hominid ancestor is united with tangible aspects of that external body.

Just as the Stoics thought that the unity of the sensible cosmos was explicable in terms of tensional motion in the all-pervading *pneuma*, the synthetic approach claims that the unity involved in haptic presentation is itself subject to further explanation. However, in proceeding analytically rather than synthetically, the unity of the perceiver and the object grasped in haptic presentation is explanatorily prior to whatever intelligible structure it must display. The analytic approach thus shares at least this much with Plotinus' account. It thus contrasts with any account that would make the unity involved in haptic presentation subject to further explanation in terms of elements and principles understood independently of haptic perception.

So far, then, we have two important features of Plotinus' account of sympathy in play, namely, that sympathy only operates within a unity and the explanatory priority of that unity. What about the role of similarity in the operation of sympathy? In Chapter 1.6, we discussed how haptic perception involves a kind of formal assimilation. We observed that the hand formally assimilates to the overall shape and volume of the object grasped in the sense that the shape of the hand's interior becomes like, if not exactly like, the shape of the object grasped, and that the volume of the region that the hand encloses becomes like, if not exactly like, the volume of the object grasped. Not only does the hand formally assimilate to the object grasped, but the experience that the grasping hand gives rise to itself becomes like, if not exactly like, the tangible object presented in it, at least relative to the perceiver's haptic perspective. Moreover, the formal assimilation of the hand, and the haptic experience that it gives rise to, should be understood, like in Plotinus' account, on the Peripatetic model. The hand, the mobile and elastic instrument of haptic perception, only approximates the overall shape and volume of the object grasped in grasping. It thus has the capacity to become like the object grasped in these respects. Similarly, the perceiver possesses the capacity for their haptic experience to become like whatever object is presented in it, relative to their haptic perspective, the distinctive manner in which they are handling that object, in the given circumstances of perception.

We saw that Plotinus' account of sympathy allows for considerable leeway in the formal assimilation it gives rise to. It is enough if the potentially noncontiguous parts of the unified manifold become like, if not exactly like. After all, there is nothing in the stars that is very much like anything sublunary and yet the sublunary may be sympathetically affected by their activity. Similarly, with respect to the formal assimilation involved in haptic presentation, if a tangible quality is present in haptic experience, then that experience is like, if not exactly like, the tangible quality present in it. Theophrastus was right to insist that not only is it absurd to suppose that the eye becomes red when seeing red, but it is even more absurd to suppose that the soul becomes red when seeing red (Priscian, *Metaphrasis* 1 3–8). What would it even mean for an experience to be red or cube-shaped? But these absurdities only follow if the similarity involved in formal assimilation is exact. In following Plotinus in allowing the parts of the unified manifold to become like, if not exactly alike, Theophrastus' *aporia* is avoided.

We saw in our discussion of the eye on the back of the sky thought experiment that Plotinus understood the unity of the sensible cosmos to be explanatorily prior to the capacity for its parts to become like or unlike one another. It is not just that the unity is not subject to further explanation, but that the unity explains, as well, the capacity of potentially non-contiguous parts of the manifold to formally assimilate to one another. It is because of the unity provided by the World-Soul that potentially distant parts of the sensible cosmos that are suitably disposed to become like or unlike may sympathetically interact. The parts of the living being are so arranged that their being suitably disposed to become like or unlike is explained by the function and coherence of the whole. A similar pattern of explanation is in play in the case of haptic perception. Recall, at least the formal assimilation at work in haptic perception was understood as a kind of constitutive shaping. Not only does the perceiver's haptic experience formally assimilate to its tangible object relative to their haptic perspective, in the sense that the conscious qualitative character of the experience is like, if not exactly like, the qualitative character of the tangible object present in it, but this formal assimilation is the effect of constitutive shaping as well. If, in grasping, the perceiver feels the overall shape and volume in the object, then not only is this because of the object's overall shape and volume, but its feeling that way is also constituted, in part, by the overall shape and volume felt. But the constitutive shaping of haptic experience by its object is a "communion" with that object – in undergoing that experience the perceiver is united, in a way, with the object of their perception. Moreover, as with Plotinus, this unity explains, in part, the similarity between the haptic experience and its tangible object. It is because the perceiver's haptic experience is united with its tangible object in haptic perception that the latter shapes the former. The formal assimilation of haptic perception to its object, at least relative to the perceiver's haptic perspective, is the effect of constitutive shaping, and thus its conscious qualitative character depends upon and derives from, at least in part, the tangible qualitative character of the object grasped.

So far, then, we have seen that five key features of Plotinus' account of sympathy are in play in the haptic case. Now let us turn to the differences. There are four of them.

First, for Plotinus, like the Stoics before him, sympathy is primarily a principle of action at a distance. One of Plotinus' innovations was the broad application of such a principle in accounting for psychological phe-nomena such as fellow-feeling and the distal senses of vision and audition. But haptic perception, and touch more generally, is not a distal sense, at least not in this way. Does this mean that a principle of sympathy is inapplicable in the haptic case? No. Rather, the application to the haptic case is a natural generalization. Consider one of Cicero' examples of Stoic sympathetic affection, the resonance of strings of a lyre (*De divinatione* 2 34, *Stoicorum veterum fragmenta* 2 1211). When some strings of a lyre are struck, others resonate. The strings, however, would resonate even if they were in contact with the strings that were struck. And if we suppose, with the Stoics, that their resonance was a result of sympathetic affection when they were at a distance, then their resonance would remain the result of sympathetic affection even when in contact. Thus, Porphyry, Plotinus' stu-dent and literary executor, writes, "It is not the case that everything which operates on another thing produces effects that it produces by contiguity and contact; in fact, even those things which operate by contiguity and contact only employ contiguity incidentally" (*Sententiae* 6; John Dillon in Brisson 2005, 796). So understood, sympathy is a principle that merely allows action at a distance. If sympathy merely allows action at a distance, then it may consistently be in operation even between bodies in contact. Such cases employ contiguity incidentally. In a way, this is the converse point of the eye on the back of the sky thought experiment. The lesson of that thought experiment was meant to be that from the absence of percep-tion in the absence of an intermediary, we should not infer that a medium is required for perceptual transmission. Similarly, from the presence of contact in some cases of resonance, we should not infer that contact is required for these resonant affections.

Sympathy may present the distal, but, more fundamentally, it presents what is different or other than oneself. And in moving from self to other, the first step is the biggest. Moreover, this remains true regardless of whether the other is in contact with the perceiver or located at a distance from them. Indeed, sympathy was invoked to distinguish cases where felt resistance to the hand's activity was due to an internal limitation (such as the inability to stretch one's index and middle finger past a certain point) from cases where the felt resistance was due to an external limitation (such as the self-maintaining forces that constitute the categorical bases of an external body's rigidity and solidity). It is because we were puzzled, in a way that Plotinus was not, about how the limitation to the hand's activity could disclose the presence and tangible qualities of an external body, that it was natural for us to appeal to sympathy to resolve such puzzlement. The first difference, then, is merely a generalization of the Plotinian account, albeit a generalization prompted by a problem that Plotinus never considered.

The second difference is a partial difference in explananda. Recall, sympathy, in Plotinus' account of perception, was meant to explain how the sense organ may be affected by a distant sensible object without the intervention of a medium. And this because, if the medium intervened, the perceiver would be presented with sensible aspects, not of the distant object, but of the intervening medium. So sympathy explained not only the action at a distance involved in distal perception, but the sensory presentation of distal objects as opposed to the intervening medium. I have retained and elaborated the explanation of sensory presentation in terms of sympathy while abandoning the explanation of action at a distance. Vision may be a distal sense, but vision science reveals no action at a distance in its operation. The present account is thus consistent with Descartes' animadversions against sympathy in *Principia philosophiae*, for there he objects only to invoking sympathy to explain the motion of natural bodies (in, for example, magnetic attraction), explicitly leaving it open that such a principle should explain psychological phenomena.

The third and fourth differences are, perhaps, more of a departure from our ancient sources. Plotinus' account, not fully described here, sympathy merely playing a role in a more complex phenomena, was intended as an alternative to the Peripatetic account, at least as he understood it. Plotinus knows well and understands Alexander of Aphrodisias' Peripatetic philosophy, but his fruitful engagement with Alexander's philosophy was nonetheless the critical engagement of a rival. The present appropriation of Plotinus' notion of sympathy in explaining the haptic presentation of an external body is not, however, a self-conscious alternative to the Peripatetic account. Rather, it is, perhaps, better understood as a neo-Platonic elaboration of what is, essentially, a Peripatetic account of perception. Specifically, insofar as the assimilation of sensible form is understood as a mode of constitutive shaping, we have retained the hylomorphic account of sensory presentation from *De anima* 2, at least on a certain interpretation of that doctrine (Kalderon 2015). Plotinian sympathy was only invoked to elaborate the intelligible structure of the haptic presentation of an external body and its tangible qualities. So unlike Plotinus' account, the present account is not an alternative to, but an elaboration of, what is, essentially, a Peripatetic account of perception.

The fourth difference is also a departure from our ancient sources. Like the Stoic account of sympathy, Plotinus' account is set in the context of a vitalistic metaphysics. However, while there may be deep, if controversial reasons for thinking that the unity that grounds the operation of sympathy is an organic unity, I propose, instead, to simply drop the vitalist metaphysics, or, at the very least, remain agnostic about it (for a contemporary, Anglophone expression of sympathy for vitalist metaphysics, see Nagel 2012). What is presently important is that it is because of the unity of the perceiver with the object grasped that the felt resistance to the force of the hand's activity is a sympathetic response to the self-maintaining forces of the object grasped. So it is the unity of the perceiver and the object grasped along with the capacity for their haptic experience to become like, if not exactly, like the tangible qualities presented in that experience, relative to the perceiver's haptic perspective, that grounds the operation of sympathy in haptic perception. I simply decline to follow the Stoics and Plotinus in explicitly conceiving of that unity to be the unity of a living being.

Despite these differences, haptic presentation, as herein understood, shares the abstract description of the operation of sympathy. Sympathy governs cases of formal assimilation where one part of a unified manifold formally assimilates to a potentially noncontiguous part of the manifold and does so because the parts, disposed as they are, are united in the manifold, in the way that they are. The grasping or enclosure of an object is a unified manifold where one part of the manifold, the perceiver's hand and the haptic experience its activity gives rise to, formally assimilates to another part of the manifold, the object grasped, and does so because the parts, disposed as they are, the hand's power of haptic activity and the object's self-maintaining forces, are united in the manifold in the way that they are, in the hand's active grasp, the joint upshot of the conflict between the force of the hand's activity and the object's self-maintaining forces. Since the formal assimilation of haptic experience to its tangible object satisfies this abstract description, sympathy must be the principle of haptic presentation.

Earlier, I mentioned how one potential obstacle to appreciating that haptic presentation is a kind of sympathetic response to an external body that is the emotional associations of our contemporary conception of sympathy. Sympathy, as we nowadays tend to conceive of it, is a kind of fellow-feeling akin to compassion or pity. The Plotinian account, however, revealed that sympathy can be understood with sufficient generality to be at work in both fellow-feeling and perception. Plotinus understood the operation of sympathy to be at work in fellow-feeling and perception as well as in a number of other natural phenomena not explicable in terms of affection by contact, at least by Plotinus' lights. Thus in analytically explicating haptic presentation in terms of the operation of sympathy we need not thereby understand haptic perception as an outgrowth of blind emotion the way Whitehead (1978, 162–3) did. Whitehead takes sympathy to be a kind of fellow-feeling and in extending its application beyond paradigmatic cases of human fellow-feeling he extends, as well, the notion of a feeling. In contrast, I have followed Plotinus in taking sympathy to be a general principle at work both in cases of fellow-feeling and perception, and without the extended notion of a feeling required by Whitehead's metaphysics.

Nevertheless, in understanding haptic presentation as the sympathetic presentation of an external body and its tangible qualities by felt resistance, the present account has the resources to distinguish blows from caresses as Derrida (2005) recommends. Our sympathetic interaction with the object of our hatred (where sympathy, here, is understood more broadly than, as we might colloquially say, feeling sympathy for them) naturally differs from our sympathetic interaction with our beloved. Our sympathetic response to contact with an enemy will naturally differ in character from our sympathetic response to contact with the beloved. And there is a natural tendency for the character of our sympathetic response to be expressed in the haptic activities that sustain them. Our anger is expressed by the blows that present an enemy, just as our love is expressed by the caresses that present the beloved. Perception may not reduce to blind emotion, but that is consistent with certain natural affective responses being made possible and, indeed, partly constituted by the operation of sympathy in haptic presentation. So without reducing haptic perception to blind emotion, in understanding haptic presentation as the sympathetic presentation of an external body and its tangible qualities, the distinction between blows and caresses is rendered intelligible, at least in principle. (In an insightful and neglected discussion of sympathy and the affective character of touch, Wyschogrod 1981 overlooks the present possibility only because she narrowly understands sympathy as fellow-feeling.)

Sympathy is the principle of haptic presentation. That principle was invoked to resolve the puzzle with which the previous chapter ended.

Recall, that puzzle was a failure of sufficiency. How, in the case of haptic perception, can felt resistance to the hand's activity disclose the presence and tangible qualities of an external body when not all limitations to the body's activity are due to external bodies? How is it possible for felt resistance to the hand's activity in grasping or enclosure to disclose a rigid, solid body's overall shape and volume? If feeling tangible qualities in something external to the perceiver's body and in conformity with them is due to the operation of sympathy, then we have a basis for an answer. It is when the limit to hand's activity is experienced as a sympathetic response to a countervailing force, as the hand's force encountering an alien force resisting it, one force in conflict with another, like it yet distinct from it, that the self-maintaining forces of the body disclose that body's presence and tangible qualities to haptic awareness.

Sympathy presents what is different or other. It thus allows us to experience from within what transpires with another and so, in a sense, to be with another. In the case of haptic perception it allows us to experience from within the tangible character of the extra-somatic. The sympathetic presentation of what is other involves an implicit presentation of self. Recall how Maine de Biran dramatizes the haptic presentation of the extra-somatic with the exclamation "This is not I." To be presented with what is other is to be presented with what is other than oneself. The presentation of self need not be explicit as is its representation in the exclamation "This is not I." The explicit presentation of what is other need only involve the implicit presentation of self. Thus haptic awareness of the extra-somatic involves bodily self-awareness. More specifically, the explicit awareness of the object grasped involves a pre-reflective implicit awareness of the hand's activity in grasping or enclosure.

If sympathy is the principle of haptic presentation, as I suggest that it must be, at least as analytically explicated, then the perceiver's experience of the hand's activity could not be explicit. Explicit awareness of the hand's configuration and force would draw attentive resources away from the object grasped. If our hominid ancestor explicitly attends to the intensive sensations involved in grasping a stone, such that these are open for epistemic appraisal, then they would no longer be attending to the stone and its tangible qualities. Moreover, this would be a consequence of sympathy being the principle of haptic presentation. In order for grasping or enclosure to directly disclose the overall shape and volume of the stone, the felt resistance to the force of the hand's activity must be experienced as a sympathetic response to the self-maintaining forces that constitute the categorical bases of the stone's rigidity and solidity. In this way they feel the rigidity and solidity in an object external to their body. Consciously attending to the hand's activity would erode the sympathetic presentation of the tangible qualities of an external body. So we could not be explicitly aware of the hand's activity in grasping or enclosure, understood as a mode of haptic perception, if sympathy were the principle of haptic presentation.

But, again, that is not to say that our hominid ancestor is unaware of their hand's activity in grasping a stone. Reflection on perceptual constancy (Sections 1.2, 1.6, 2.2) revealed that the phenomenological character of their haptic experience could not be exhausted by the object of explicit awareness. An implicit awareness of the hand's configuration and force contributes, as well, to the phenomenology of their haptic experience. Our hominid ancestor's sense of their hand's configuration and force contributes only to the pre-noetic structure of their haptic experience by determining the way its object is presented therein. So not only do they feel the overall shape and volume in the stone, but their hand is felt to conform to these tangible qualities as well. Feeling the hand to conform to the stone's rigidity and solidity may be implicit, it may be recessive and in the background, so that it does not compete for attentive resources directed toward an external body, but it contributes to the conscious qualitative character of their haptic experience by being the way in which the overall shape and volume of the stone is presented in that experience. Haptic presentation in grasping or enclosure just is feeling something in an external body and in conformity with it. And feeling something in an external body and in conformity with it just is the exercise of a sympathetic capacity.

Haptic presentation is an irreducible unity. If sensory presentation is a distinctive kind of unity, then haptic presentation is more distinctive still. What distinguishes haptic presentation, as the kind of unity it is, is the intelligible structure it displays. If sympathy is the principle of haptic presentation, then haptic presentation, the kind of unity that it is, is a mode of being with (which is not to say that it is a mode of *mitsein*, in Heidegger's sense). Feeling the overall shape and volume in the stone, and in conformity with it, is a way of being with the stone in one's grasp. Grasping or enclosure, understood as a mode of haptic perception, involves the embodied perceiver consciously being with the body in its grasp. So the mode of being with involved in haptic presentation is corporeal, a way for one body to be with another. Moreover the mode of being with involved in haptic presentation is conscious. It is a way for a particular kind of body, a conscious animate body, to be with an external body encountered in peripersonal space.

In the last chapter, I claimed that while the formal assimilation of haptic experience to its object, understood on the model of constitutive shaping, was a manifestation of the objectivity of haptic perception, it was the force of the hand's activity that was its source. In focusing exclusively on the role of sympathy in Plotinus' account of perception, we have ignored a crucial aspect of that account, one that highlights the activity of the perceiver:

> It is clear in presumably every case that when we have a perception of any-thing through the sense of sight, we look where it is and direct our gaze where the visible object is situated in a straight line from us; obviously it is there that the apprehension takes place and the soul looks outwards. (Plotinus, *On Sense-Perception and Memory, Ennead* 4 6 1 14–18; Armstrong 1984, 321)

And later, Plotinus generalizes the point:

> [The soul] speaks about things which it does not possess: this is a matter of power, not of being affected in some way but of being capable of and doing the work to which it has been assigned. This is the way, I think, in which a distinction is made by the soul between what is seen and what is heard, not if both are impressions, but if they are not by nature impressions or affections, but activities concerned with that which approaches [the soul]. (Plotinus, *On Sense-Perception and Memory, Ennead* 4 6 2 1–7; Armstrong 1984, 325)

Perception is an activity and not an affection or impression. Plotinus thus stands at the head of a historical tradition that stresses the active nature of perception and includes Augustine, Boethius, Kilwardby, Olivi, Fichte, Maine de Biran, Ravaisson, Bergson, Merleau-Ponty, and contemporary enactivists (for a partial overview of this historical tradition, see the essays in Silva and Yrjönsuuri 2014).

We may retain, from this tradition, an important insight. Specifically, we are now in a position to fully appreciate why if the formal assimila-tion of haptic experience to its object, relative to the perceiver's partial perspective, is the manifestation of the objectivity of haptic perception, being a mode of constitutive shaping, it is the force of the hand's activ-ity that is its source. Engaging in such activity ensures that the tangible qualities the body had prior to being grasped, and maintained in being grasped, explains, in part, the hand's configuration and force. The force of the hand's activity, and the felt resistance it encounters, is a precondition for sympathy's partial disclosure, relative to the perceiver's handling, of the self-maintaining forces of an external body.

It is the hand, the mobile and elastic instrument of haptic exploration, the active wax of haptic perception, whose activity must be resisted, by the passivities of matter, in order to sympathetically present the external body whose self-maintaining forces constrain that activity. The felt resistance to the hand's activity in grasping or enclosure, understood as a mode of haptic perception, is an event occurring in an egocentrically and teleologically structured peripersonal space that partly discloses corporeal aspects of the object of haptic investigation. It is partly for this reason that the perceiver's handling of the object counts as a perspective on that object, albeit a distinctively haptic perspective. The hand's activity in peripersonal space constitutes, in part, the haptic perspective to which the object is sympathetically presented. Thus the activity of the hand, of which we are merely implicitly aware, is the source, nevertheless, of the objectivity of haptic perception because it is a precondition for the sympathetic presentation of the tangible object that constitutively shapes that haptic experience.

CHAPTER 3

Sound

3.1 Moving Forward

Tactile metaphors for perception, even for non-tactile modes of awareness such as vision and audition, are primordial and persistent. In trying to understand what, if anything, makes these tactile metaphors for perceptual awareness apt, we undertook a phenomenological investigation into the nature of grasping or enclosure, understood as a mode of haptic perception. Which, if any, of the features of haptic presentation plausibly carry over to other forms of sensory presentation? Do any of the features of haptic presentation carry over to the presentation of *audibilia*?

We have already observed (Chapter 1.4) that haptic presentation is a mode of disclosure and that this may be a feature that carries over to audition. To claim that haptic presentation is a mode of disclosure is to claim that corporeal aspects of the object of haptic exploration are disclosed over time and so that presentation in haptic experience has duration. As in the haptic case, sounds are disclosed over time and so their presentation in auditory experience has duration. However, we also observed a potential asymmetry. There may be a reason sounds are disclosed over time that is not applicable in the haptic case. Whereas tangible qualities are relatively static features of things, sounds are essentially dynamic entities, not wholly present at any given moment, but unfolding through time (to be further discussed in Section 3.3). And if sounds are spread over time, their sensory presentation must also be.

We also identified two features of haptic presentation the conjunction of which might plausibly be generalized to other forms of sensory presentation. First, haptic experience formally assimilates to its object, at least relative to the perceiver's haptic perspective, the particular way that they are handling that object in the circumstances of perception, in the sense that the conscious qualitative character of the experience becomes like, if not exactly like, the tangible quality presented in it.

And second, the formal assimilation of haptic experience to its object is explained by that experience being constitutively shaped by the presentation of its object. Perhaps, perspective-relative formal assimilation as a consequence of constitutive shaping is a general feature of perception. This would explain why incorporation, unconsciously echoed by contemporary talk of content, is an apt metaphor for perception generally, even for those modes of perception that involve the material assimilation of no thing (Chapter 1.6). The proposed general thesis, then, is that the conscious qualitative character of a perceptual experience formally assimilates to its object, relative to the perceiver's partial perspective, as a result of constitutive shaping. More would have to be done to fully defend this general thesis. Among other things, that there is an analog of visual perspective in each of the sensory modalities would have to be justified. (Can we really have a perspective on an odor, say?) In this chapter and the next, I will say more about the applicability of this idea to audition at least.

But what of the other important claim about the metaphysics of haptic perception, that sympathy is the principle of haptic presentation? Does sympathy operate in other modes of sensory presentation as well? Does the sensory presentation of the extra-somatic require the operation of sympathy quite generally? It was natural to appeal to sympathy to explain how felt resistance to the hand's activity in grasping or enclosure discloses the overall shape and volume of the object grasped since we began by thinking of haptic perception in terms of the Secret Doctrine that Socrates attributes to Protagoras in the *Theaetetus*. Just as on the Protagorean model, perception is the joint upshot of forces in conflict, grasping or enclosure, understood as a mode of haptic perception, is itself naturally understood as the joint upshot of forces in conflict. On the one hand, there is the force of the activity of the grasping hand. On the other hand, there are the self-maintaining forces of the rigid, solid body. Making an effort to more precisely mold the hand to the body's contours and the resistance of the body's self-maintaining forces together give rise to an experience of that body's overall shape and volume. In trying to determine whether sympathy operates in non-haptic modes of sensory presentation, we shall need to determine whether this Protagorean model can be extended to other sensory modalities. (Kilwardby, for one, thought it did: "Two motions come together as if from opposite parts in sensing," *De spiritu fantastico* 112; Broadie 1993. Though, of course, the Protagorean model finds its expression in the reconciliation of Peripatetic and Augustinian metaphysics that it offers Kilwardby.)

Smith's (2002) discussion of *Anstoss* suggests one way one might generalize from the haptic case. Haptic perception arises from the conflict between the grasping hand and the self-maintaining forces of the rigid, solid body. Reaching out and grasping something is a clear example of voluntary intentional action. Moreover, at least in the case of haptic perception, the hand is, among other things, a sensory organ (though see Paterson 2007 for the claim that touch lacks a sensory organ). Putting these ideas together, it is the voluntary intentional movement of sensory organs that are the activities whose force comes into conflict with the perceptual object. In the visual case, then, it is the deliberate movement of the eyes in their sockets and not saccadic movement that is relevant, since the latter is involuntary and non-intentional. Smith faces some difficulties, not necessarily insuperable, with this proposal. For example, unlike other animals, humans cannot cock their ears, though we may turn toward a sound to better hear it. This is not, however, the only way to generalize from the haptic case.

Reaching out and grasping something may be a voluntary, intentional movement of a sensory organ, but insofar as it is a mode of perception, it is a psychological activity as well. Consider Cook Wilson's claim (Correspondence with Stout, 1904, 1926) that in order to feel something in an object, a rough texture say, one must feel that object, and in order to weigh something, one must weigh it. If grasping is understood analogously with feeling and weighing, then this suggests an alternative generalization. On this alternative, in order to hear something, one must listen. And in order to see, one must look. Grasping, feeling, weighing, listening, and looking, while they may or may not involve the intentional movement of sensory organs, are not themselves reducible to such movements when they do. They are, perhaps, more aptly described as a kind of psychological stance, sustained by a characteristic activity, where the perceiver opens themselves up, in a directed manner, to experiencing different aspects of the natural environment. In engaging in such activities, in directing perceptual awareness in this way, the perceiver contributes to making different aspects of the natural environment perceptually available.

"In order to hear well," Maine de Biran observes, "it is necessary to *listen*" (*Influence de l'habitude sur la faculté de penser*, Boehm 1929, 63–4). How does listening, or the activity of listening out for something, come into conflict with the objects of audition such that these may be sympathetically presented in auditory experience? We can make progress with this question by first getting clearer on the objects of audition, on what there is to listen out for and to. That task will occupy us for this chapter and the next.

There is an asymmetry between haptic and auditory perception. The tangible is the object of haptic perception. And, one might correspondingly say, the audible is the object of auditory perception. While there is a sense in which that is surely true, there is also a sense in which it is potentially misleading. Bracketing, for the moment, Peripatetic worries about the unity of the tangible, the tangible is unified in the way that the audible is not. Among *audibilia* are sounds and their sources, or so I contend. And while it is controversial how hearing sounds and hearing their sources are related, there is no similar division among the tangible.

This asymmetry, while no obstacle to understanding auditory presentation as a species of sympathetic presentation, does, however, introduce a complexity that bears on the presentation of material over this chapter and the next. I shall argue that we hear sources in, or through, the sounds they make, and that sympathy explains how this may be so. However, before we are in a position to understand the sympathetic presentation of the sources of sounds, we must have in place a certain conception of sounds. It is the task of the present chapter to articulate the relevant conception of sounds, as it turns out, a modification of The Wave Theory of sound. And it shall be the task of the subsequent chapter to explain how the sources of sound may be sympathetically presented in, or through, the sounds they make. Moreover, it will only be in that chapter that we shall be in a position to understand how listening is a necessary precondition for the sympathetic presentation of the sources of sound.

Before turning to The Wave Theory, let us first get clearer on sounds, and their sources, and their relation in our experience of them. The objects of audition are diverse in a way that the objects of haptic perception are not. We hear sounds, and their sources, and their audible qualities. How are the hearing of sounds and the hearing of sources related in auditory experience? What are the bearers of audible qualities? Are sounds and their sources, as well as their audible qualities, all that we hear? These three questions will be addressed, in turn, in the following three sections.

3.2   The Berkeley–Heidegger Continuum

If we hear, not only sounds, but their sources, how are sounds and their sources related in our auditory experience of them?

From the hill in Greenwich Park where the Royal Observatory is located, one can see the towers of the City of London across the Thames. I once witnessed the Ballardian spectacle of a flock of feral parakeets flying across this scene. These formerly domesticated tropical birds, having escaped or been released, have gone feral and their population is increasing throughout London. Bright green set against mirrored skyscrapers, the parakeets were excited and were calling loudly. I heard the sound of a calling parakeet. Did I hear, as well, the parakeet's call?

We hear sounds. Do we hear, as well, their sources? Philosophers divide on this question. And even those philosophers who maintain that we hear both sounds and their sources divide as to how we do so. Philosopher's views on these matters can be usefully represented on a continuum that ranges from Berkeley on one extreme to Heidegger on the other (see Leddington 2014 for a similar suggestion).

Berkeley, in *Three Dialogues between Hylas and Philonous*, follows Aristotle in taking sounds to be the proper objects of audition. For something to be the proper object of a given sensory modality, it must be perceptible in itself and perceptible to that sensory modality alone. That a sensory modality has a proper object does not preclude it from having other objects as well. Thus we can see motion and feel motion. Berkeley thus extends the Peripatetic account in claiming, in addition, that sounds are the sole objects of audition. We hear no other thing. In a way, this is a return to an earlier, Platonic view. Plato, in the *Theaetetus* (184 e 8–185 a 3), maintained that the perception of a given sense just is the presentation of an object available through the exercise of that capacity alone (compare as well *Republic* 5 477–8). Our auditory capacity, so conceived, just is the capacity to present its proper object, sound. So on Berkeley's view, strictly speaking, we hear sounds and not their sources. In part, Berkeley argues for this by distinguishing sounds from their sources by an application of Leibniz's Law. Sounds have auditory qualities that their sources lack, and insofar as sources lack auditory qualities they are inaudible.

The neo-Berkeleans accept that sound is the proper object of audition. They accept, as well, that the sounds are distinguished from their sources. But they deny that sound is the sole object of audition. Sources of sound that can be perceived by other sensory modalities, such as sight, and are thus common sensibles, are also the objects of audition, but only derivatively – we hear the source of a sound by hearing the sound that it generates. According to the neo-Berkeleans, Berkeley goes too far in denying that we hear the sources of sound. Berkeley mistook sound's being the direct or immediate object of audition for sound's being the sole object of audition. If we allow sources to be the indirect or mediate objects of audition, then the objects of audition include not only proper sensibles, but common sensibles as well.

So, according to the neo-Berkelean, perceivers are immediately presented with the proper object of audition, sound, and thereby mediately presented with the source of the sound, the audible activity of a body, say. Sounds are audible. Indeed, they are audible in themselves in the sense that sounds contain within themselves the power of their own audibility. *Pace* Berkeley, sources too are audible. However, the audible sources of sound are not audible in themselves, but are only audible by hearing other objects that are audible in themselves, the sounds that they generate. An explicit experience of a sound is, according to the neo-Berkeleans, the means by which we experience its source. Auditory experience affords the perceiver with an explicit awareness of a sound that mediates the perceiver's awareness of its source. The explicit experience of a sound and the experience of its source that it gives rise to are, so conceived, distinct experiences, even if the former is a part or constituent of the latter.

In "The Origin of the Work of Art," Heidegger presents an opposing view:

> We never really first perceive a throng of sensations, e.g., tones and noises, in the appearance of things … rather we hear the storm whistling in the chimney, we hear the three-motored plane, we hear the Mercedes in immediate distinction from the Volkswagen. Much closer to us than all sensations are the things themselves. We hear the door shut in the house and never hear acoustical sensations or even mere sounds. (1935/2000, 151–2)

Nothing hangs on Heidegger's apparent acceptance of the empiricist identification of sound with acoustical sensation. What is important is Heidegger's denial of the central neo-Berkelean claim, that we hear the source of a sound by attending to that sound. Rather, we hear the source without attending to its sound.

In Fulkerson's (2014) terminology, we are explicitly aware of the wind whistling in the chimney, and this explicit awareness does not depend upon an explicit awareness of the sound, for there is no such awareness. At best we are implicitly aware of that sound. However, if we are to apply that distinction to Heidegger, we must depart from Fulkerson, as I have recommended (Chapter 2.2), and claim that it admits of degrees. "Much closer to us than all sensations are the things themselves." An element present in experience can be more or less recessive, more or less in the background. And, conversely, it may be more or less in the foreground, more or less within the range of explicit awareness. Much closer to the hearer than its sound is the wind whistling in the chimney.

In undergoing an auditory experience, the source of a sound is the object of an explicit awareness that does not depend upon explicit awareness of the sound. At least in this sense is it immediately present in that experience. When we attend to our auditory experience, as Heidegger invites us to, we attend to the sources of sounds and rarely, if at all, to the sounds in distinction from their sources. In hearing the storm whistling in the chimney, the three-motored plane, the Mercedes in immediate distinction from the Volkswagen, there is no explicit experience of their sound distinct from hearing these sources. That is consistent with maintaining that hearing a source necessarily involves acoustical sensation. We may be implicitly aware of the sound in explicitly attending to its source. And yet Heidegger is clearly denying the neo-Berkelean claim that we hear the source of a sound by hearing the sound. There is one explicit experience, hearing the storm whistling in the chimney, and no distinct explicit experience of its sound, even if hearing the source involves implicit awareness of its sound. This constitutes a negative result about how to characterize aural indirection, the presentative function of sound. There is more to hearing a source by hearing its sound, in the sense required by the neo-Berkeleans, than the necessary accompaniment of the former by the latter.

Heidegger exaggerates when he claims that we never attend to acoustical sensations or mere sounds. For he goes on to maintain that we can attend to sounds in distinction from their sources only by adopting the aural equivalent of the painterly attitude:

> In order to hear a bare sound we have to listen away from things, divert our ears from them, i.e., listen abstractly. (1935/2000, 152)

Heidegger observes, however, that this is a difficult attitude to adopt.

We can get a sense of how difficult it is to adopt this attitude by considering Pierre Schaeffer's piece *Étude aux chemins de fer* (1948). Whereas traditional composition begins with an abstraction, the score, which is made concrete in playing it, *musique concrète* begins with concrete sounds and abstracts them into a composition through tape looping and sound collage. Yet, despite these distancing techniques, the material sources never completely fade from the perceived soundscape. We get a sense of the train's speed, its size, the space surrounding the tracks, as well as the space of the interior given the character of the resonance. Working in Schaeffer's studio, Karlheinz Stockhausen addressed these problems in the method of tape composition deployed in *Étude* (1952). He recorded prepared low piano strings struck with an iron bar and sliced off the heads of the recorded sounds, thus eliminating information about the attack and other material features of the source. These short, headless segments were further repeated to form the basic tones of the piece. The effect is uncanny. However, the very uncanniness is itself partly a product of the limitation, or at least a variant of it, that beset Schaeffer's earlier piece. The tones are uncanny in that they are at once strange, indeterminate, and yet famil-iar, though, enigmatically, placing them proves elusive. Indeed, at the end of his career, Schaeffer pronounced *musique concrète* a failure, claiming, perhaps ironically, to have wasted his life. Heidegger's observation was the principal obstacle – it is very difficult to listen away from things and hear bare sounds, to hear sounds without also hearing their sources. And so there are limits to the degree of abstraction that can be achieved with *musique concrète*. It is telling, in this regard, that Stockhausen abandoned tape composition for the generation of tones with sine-wave generators as he continued to explore electronic composition.

The Berkelean alternative raises an explanatory challenge to the neo-Berkeleans – to explain how we can experience a source by explicitly experiencing its sound. How is the immediate presentation of sound in auditory experience the mediate presentation of its source? The aural indi-rection, as the neo-Berkeleans conceive of it, the presentative function of sound, is unlike ordinary cases of perceiving one thing by perceiving another. One might see where the shogun's army is encamped by see-ing the smoke and steam of their cooking rice. But the shogun's army is directly perceptible – and presents a suitably terrifying aspect – in the way that the sources of sounds could not be, at least by the neo-Berkeleans' lights. What is needed is an explanation of how one can hear a source by hearing a sound. What is needed is an explanation of the presentative function of sounds, how the presentation of sound in explicit auditory awareness constitutes the mediate presentation of its source (analogous, in many ways, to the presentative function of sense data, at least accord-ing to many sense-datum theories, see, for example, Price 1932). The Heideggerian alternative is a challenge to the very possibility of such an explanation. At the very least, in undergoing an auditory experience, we do not attend to sources by attending to sounds – according to Heidegger, in normal cases, there is no sound that we are attending to. Any account of the presentative function of sound would involve the explicit experi-ence of that sound, but, according to Heidegger, there is no such expe-rience. There is just the auditory experience of the storm whistling in the chimney, of the three-motored plane, of the Mercedes in immediate distinction from the Volkswagen. Neo-Berkeleans cannot afford to be as sanguine about the Heideggerian alternative as they may be tempted to be about the Berkelean alternative. A promissory note is worth nothing in the face of an inability to repay.

Smith (2002) is an example of a contemporary philosopher who has endorsed the extreme Berkelean alternative. Though some, like Smith, continue to accept the Berkelean view that sounds are the sole objects of audition, in this chapter and the next, I propose to simply set the extreme Berkelean alternative to one side and accept that we hear, in addition to the sounds, their sources as well. Leddington (2014) and Nudds (2010) approach, at least, the other Heideggerian extreme. Neo-Berkeleanism, while well represented in the twentieth century, is perhaps not well represented in the most recent literature, but is a viable sub-current of thought for all that. Whenever I talk to philosophers, not necessarily specialists, about audition, I am inevitably asked questions that only make sense within the neo-Berkelean framework. One might object to the present taxonomy that many contemporary views fit uneasily within it. Consider one prominent example. O'Callaghan (2007, 2009) is by no means a Berkelean, nor a neo-Berkelean, but is he really on the Heideggerian end of the continuum?

O'Callaghan's is among a class of accounts that is difficult to place within the Berkeley–Heidegger continuum. They tend to endorse a distal conception of sound, a conception where sounds are located at a distance from the perceiver, at or near their source. And these distal conceptions of sound tend to be motivated by criticism of The Wave Theory. As we shall see (Chapter 3.7), many of these criticisms conflate features of sources with features of the sounds that they produce. And if that is right, the resulting conceptions of sound are themselves a product of this conflation. It is no surprise, then, that such accounts fit uneasily in the Berkeley–Heidegger continuum. In conflating features of sources with features of sounds, they obscure the distinction upon which that taxonomy is based.

3.3　The Bearers of Audible Qualities

What are the bearers of audible qualities? What are the kinds of things in which audible qualities inhere? Pitch is an audible quality. In what kind of thing does pitch inhere? I claim that the bearers or *substrata* of audible qualities are essentially dynamic entities such as events, as opposed to bodies. If the bearers of audible qualities are essentially dynamic entities, then audible qualities are qualities essentially sustained by activity.

Colors are spatially extended, at least in the sense of being instanced only by spatially extended things. We can imagine smaller and smaller things being colored, but we cannot conceive of a thing without exten-sion exhibiting color. Audible qualities are temporally extended, at least in the sense of being instanced only by temporally extended things. We can imagine hearing briefer and briefer occurrences of pitch, but we can-not conceive of a thing without duration exhibiting pitch. The tempo-ral dimension of the bearers of audible qualities is not exhausted by their having a beginning and an end. In this regard, they are no different from mortal animals. But unlike natural substances such as animals and other bodies, as well as entities of distinct ontological categories such as states, sounds have a distinctive way of being in time.

Sounds have a distinctive way of being in time. Like events, at least as the three-dimensionalist conceives of them, sounds unfold in time (see Fine 2006; though for criticism, see Hawthorne 2008; Sider 1997). Unlike states, which are wholly present whenever they obtain, sounds are not wholly present at every moment of their sounding. They are spread over the interval of time through which they unfold. So sounds have a temporal mode of being that events have. Perhaps some sounds, such as the sound of the wind, or the roar of a waterfall, are more like processes than events (Broad 1952, 4). However, that distinction is not presently relevant, and at any rate, processes, like events, are essentially dynamic entities, though perhaps in their own way.

That sounds are not wholly present at any moment of their sounding precludes them from being wholly present in auditory experience at any moment of their hearing. If we further assume that perceptual experience only presents what could be present at any given moment, then a puzzle about the very possibility of audition arises, as Prichard observes:

> We should ordinarily be said to *hear* certain noises, e.g. the sound a bell or the note of a bird. But any sound has duration, however short. If so, how can it ever be true that we apprehend by way of hearing – or more generally perceiving – can only exist at the moment of hearing, and *ex hypothesi*, at least part of the sound said to be heard is over at the moment of hearing, and strictly speaking it is *all* over. And the difficulty seems a double one. For since a sound has duration, it cannot exist at the moment of hearing, and therefore we cannot hear a present sound – for there is no such thing. And if it is over and so not existing at the moment when we are said to hear it, it cannot be *heard*. Therefore, it seems, it is impossible hear a sound. (1950b, 47)

The most straightforward way to deal with this puzzle is to abandon the principle that generates it – that perceptual experience only presents what could be present at any given moment. After all, as we have seen

(Chapter 1.4), this is the principle that was driving the Grand Illusion hypothesis. If we abandon this principle, then we may conclude that since sounds are spread over time, their sensory presentation must also be. Auditory experience unfolds with its object. We listen along with what we hear. So auditory presentation, due to the distinctive temporal nature of sound, has duration. Auditory presentation is the disclosure of a sound unfolding through its temporal interval. It discloses its object, then, over time, just like haptic presentation. However, whereas haptic perception discloses relatively static features such as texture and temperature, sounds, by contrast, are essentially dynamic entities, not wholly present at any moment of their existence, but unfolding in time.

Sounds may be particular events or processes, and so have a mode of being that suffices to distinguish them from entities belonging to other ontological categories such as bodies and states, but what of other *audibilia*? Must all audible objects unfold through time? Or is this just a feature of, in Peripatetic vocabulary, the proper objects of audition?

We hear sounds, to be sure, but we also hear their audible qualities. I can hear the sound of the parakeet's call and its pitch. Audible qualities, such as pitch, are not essentially dynamic entities unfolding through time. Rather, their mode of being is more akin to the mode of being of states. Nevertheless, sound, conceived as an essentially dynamic entity, not wholly present at any moment, but unfolding through time, is the bearer or *substratum* of audible qualities (see Aristotle, *De anima* 2 11 42231–2). It is the sound of the parakeet's call whose pitch I hear. That the bearer of an audible quality is an essentially dynamic entity is manifest in the conditions under which that quality may be instantiated. There is no instantaneous pitch since there is nothing instantaneous to instantiate it. For pitch to exist, it must persist over time. And that is because sound, a bearer of audible qualities, has duration essentially. Sounds without audible qualities would be inaudible, but audible qualities without sound would simply not be (or at least, those audible qualities that modify sounds, as opposed to other audible *substrata*, if such there be). Sound, an essentially dynamic entity, has existential and ontological priority over the audible qualities that it gives rise to. Audible qualities, while not essentially dynamic entities, are qualities that audible activity gives rise to. They are qualities of audible events or processes or phases of these.

If *audibilia* means all that we can hear, and we can hear a sound's pitch, then not all *audibilia* are essentially dynamic entities. There may be no instantaneous pitch, pitch may be a quality essentially sustained by activity, but pitch, as a quality, does not unfold through time. Of all that we hear, some of what we hear is existentially and ontologically prior to other things that we hear. The audible qualities of a sound will vary and extinguish as the sound's activity varies and extinguishes. Sounds are existentially and ontologically prior to their audible qualities because sounds are the bearers or *substrata* of audible qualities. At best, then, the claim should be that the existentially and ontologically prior *substrata* of audible qualities are essentially dynamic entities, not wholly present at any moment, but unfolding through time. So conceived, audible qualities would be qualities essentially sustained by activity.

Kulvicki (2008) has argued that the bearers of audible qualities are not events, but bodies. Like Aristotle, *De anima* 2 11 42231–2, Kulvicki accepts that an audible quality has a bearer or *substratum*. Being quality instances, they must inhere in something upon which they existentially and ontologically depend. However, unlike Aristotle, he denies that sound is the bearer of audible qualities. Audible qualities inhere in bodies, but these bodies are not themselves sounds. Rather, they are ordinary material substances. Instead, sounds are the audible qualities that inhere in these bodies and are manifest in their audible activity. Thus, like Pasnau (1999b) and Leddington (2014), Kulvicki endorses a broadly Lockean metaphysics of sound. However, it is not the Lockean metaphysics of sound that is our present focus, but whether bodies are bearers of audible qualities.

Bodies have resonant modes determined by their material structure. Because of their resonant modes, bodies are disposed to vibrate at certain natural frequencies when "thwacked." According to Kulvicki (2008), the sound a body has, an audible quality of it, is the stable disposition to vibrate when thwacked. Just as the energy of the illuminant reveals the colors of things to sight, the energy of thwacking reveals the sounds of things to hearing. And just as bodies retain their colors even when unilluminated, bodies retain their sound even when unthwacked. The stable disposition to vibrate when thwacked is a sound that a body has. Not every sound that a thing makes is a sound that a thing has. Stereo speakers when thwacked produce a dull thud, but when played they can make a wide variety of sounds.

Why think that sounds are qualities of material bodies that are associated with their natural frequencies? Kulvicki (2008) provides an argument from perceptual constancy that, while not conclusive, is meant to speak strongly in favor of his view. Kulvicki draws our attention to an interesting feature of speech perception, our ability to recognize voices. A speaker's voice will vary in pitch, timbre, and so on, as they speak. And yet despite these variable auditory appearances, we seem to be presented with a constant voice in our experience of their speech. This is due, in part, to the resonant modes of the special parts of the speaker involved in speech production, such as their vocal cords and nasal cavities. And this is just the kind of auditory constancy one would expect if the sounds that we hear were stable dispositions of objects to vibrate in response to being thwacked.

We have our voices. At least as we ordinarily speak. But do we have them, as well, in Kulvicki's extraordinary sense? Or are they sounds that we make but do not have? The sound of a stereo speaker playing is a sound that it makes but does not have. I suspect that a person's voice is more like the sound of a stereo speaker playing than the sound that it makes when thwacked. Through a series of unfortunate events, I have firsthand experience of what I sound like when thwacked. I can attest it sounds nothing like my voice. Like a stereo speaker, I produce a dull thud when thwacked. When playing, a stereo speaker produces the sounds that it makes but does not have by an internal activity driving the vibration of special parts of it. When speaking, I produce the sounds that I do by an internal activity driving the vibration of special parts of myself. Are these not sounds that I make but do not have? If the sound of my voice is something that I make but do not have, then its being the constant element in an auditory experience provides no reason for thinking that sounds are stable dispositions to vibrate when thwacked since these are sounds that bodies were meant to have rather than make. However, even should the argument from perceptual constancy fail in this way, sounds may yet be stable dispositions of bodies to vibrate when thwacked.

Kulvicki is right to emphasize that auditory experience can disclose the stable dispositions of bodies to vibrate at their natural frequencies and so auditorily manifest, albeit partially and imperfectly, material properties of those bodies. But in hearing that, is what we hear a sound or its source? Suppose that we hear sounds and their sources. And suppose that the sources that we hear are sound-generating events. A body's participation, if not the body itself, is part of the audible structure of that event. And those aspects of the body relevant to its participation in the event are reflected, partially and imperfectly, in its audible structure. Stable dispositions of bodies to vibrate at their natural frequencies given their resonant modes as determined by their material structure are aspects of bodies relevant to their participation in audible activities, such as being thwacked. When Dr. Johnson, outside of the church in Harwich, kicked the stone, his boot rebounding despite its mighty force, the stone was well and truly thwacked. Doubtless, it could be heard as well as felt. And Dr. Johnston could hear, as well as feel, that it was a stone, and not a log, that he was kicking. He could hear his boot kicking a stone as opposed to a log because their different resonant modes are relevant to their participation in audible activities such as being kicked. Kulvicki is right to emphasize that auditory experience can disclose the stable dispositions of bodies to vibrate at their natural frequencies and so auditorily manifest, albeit partially and imperfectly, material properties of these bodies. But he was wrong to suggest that this requires bodies to be the bearers of audible qualities. (We shall revisit this issue when discussing O'Callaghan's argument from timbre in Section 3.7.)

3.4   The Extent of the Audible

We hear sounds and their sources. These are essentially dynamic entities, not wholly present at any given moment, but unfolding through time. Sounds and their sources have audible qualities, qualities essentially sustained by activity. Are sounds and their sources, as well as their audible qualities, really all that we can hear?

According to Broad (1952, 4), we ordinarily speak of hearing bodies. So when Big Ben strikes the time, and is in earshot, we may say that we can hear Big Ben. However, Broad concedes little in acknowledging this point of usage since he also observes that it takes but a little pressure to convince "the plainest of plain men" that "hearing Big Ben" is shorthand for hearing the striking of Big Ben. If we accept Broad's suggestion, then we only hear Big Ben insofar as it is a participant in a sound-generating event or process. And when we do, what we strictly speaking hear is Big Ben's striking and not Big Ben, that is, not the body, but an event the body participates in that is the cause of the propagation of the patterned disturbance. We hear not the body in a condition of activity, but the activity of the body. It is not clear that Broad thinks that even Big Ben's striking is an object of audition. "Hearing Big Ben" is meant to be equivalent to "hearing such and such a noise and taking it to be coming from Big Ben." But taking the sound that one hears to be generated in an event in which Big Ben participates may be a cognitive, rather than a perceptual, activity or stance. Let us set aside any doubts that Broad may have entertained, and accept, with Heidegger, that we hear not only the sound of Big Ben's striking but we hear, as well, Big Ben's striking. The view we will have arrived at is one according to which we hear sounds and their sources.

Sounds are events or processes, and their sources that we hear are the events and processes that generate those sounds. Do sources have audible qualities? Berkeley denied that they did. Only the sounds that they produce have audible qualities. And if sources lack audible qualities, then they are inaudible. Or so Berkeley contends. If sources, *pace* Berkeley, have audible qualities, then they are existentially and ontologically prior to the audible qualities for which they are bearers or *substrata*. Moreover, sources, being sound-generating events or processes, are essentially dynamic entities. Such a view would be a step closer to vindicating the general claim that among *audibilia*, the bearers or *substrata* of audible qualities have the distinctive temporal mode of being of events or processes. Full vindication would require further assurance that sounds and their sources alone have this status.

Allow me to elaborate on sources and their hearing and engage in speculation about a hypothetical sense in which we may be said to hear bodies consistent with the principle, if true, that audition only presents bearers of audible qualities with the distinctive temporal mode of being of events or processes.

First, the elaboration. It concerns the sources of sound. In the foregoing discussion, for convenience, I have silently substituted a philosophically motivated precisification for the ordinary notion. Specifically, sources were claimed to be sound-generating events or processes. While it is true that the ordinary notion of a source is a causal notion, we also speak of objects or bodies being the sources of sound. We do so presumably because these bodies possess the causal power to engage in an activity that is a sound-generating event or process. Thus Casati and colleagues (2013) speak of event sources and thing sources. In effect the precisification identifies sources with the body's activity that generates a sound. The prima facie plausibility of this is abetted in a philosophical milieu where a broadly Humean metaphysics, with its focus on regularities among events, remains widely influential. For the broadly Humean framework encourages the conclusion that sources are events from the recognition that sources are causal. However, the precisification of the ordinary notion was not motivated by a Humean metaphysics. I believe that we should accept the Eleatic Visitor's teaching and acknowledge the being of capacity. (After all, it would be impious to deny the existence of virtue.) But once we do, we can see how sources may be, at once, bodies and causal. Bodies may be the sources of sound by possessing the causal power to sound, to engage in a sound-generating activity. The precisification was not motivated by an adherence to a broadly Humean metaphysics, but rather had a phenomenological motivation. Specifically, we are presently interested in the sources that we can be said to hear. The sources that we can be said to hear may be a narrower class than what may ordinarily be described as a source. Big Ben is a source of sound. But we don't hear Big Ben, at least not strictly speaking. We hear Big Ben's striking. What we hear, strictly speaking, is not the body, but the body's sound-generating activity.

Both sounds and the sources that we hear are like events or processes in that they are not wholly present at every moment of their occurrence. The speculation, intimated earlier, is that perhaps this is a general feature of the bearers of audible qualities present in audition. Perhaps for a bearer of an audible quality to be present in auditory experience it must have a particular temporal mode of being, it must unfold through time. This would preclude, by their very nature, entities such as bodies from being present in auditory experience. First, by hypothesis, bodies lack the requisite temporal mode of being of *substrata* of audible qualities. And second, bodies do not inhere in essentially dynamic entities the way that audible qualities do. But if what is present in auditory experience is either essentially dynamic or an audible quality that the essentially dynamic *substratum* gives rise to, then bodies are not present in auditory experience. Earlier we noted Broad's helpful suggestion that perhaps "hearing Big Ben" is elliptical for hearing Big Ben's striking.

As plausible as this may be, a worry may still persist. One of the uses to which audition may be put is to track a body's progress through the natural environment. We can listen to an animal's approach, say. And it might be thought that we are attending to the animal in audition in listening to them. Moreover, it might seem insufficient for the body to be attended to that an event in which that body participates is present in auditory experience. Not every part of a visible body is seen, so why assume that every participant of an audible event is heard? How can we listen out for bodies even though they are precluded from being present in auditory experience?

Bodies may not be present in auditory experience, but perhaps they figure in auditory experience in another way, if not as the intentional object of experience, then something very much like it. Bodies are, on the speculative hypothesis that we are entertaining, not present in auditory experience. Thus bodies are absent in auditory experience. And yet we can attend to bodies in audition. How could this be?

Aristotle uses this kind of puzzle or *aporia* about presence in absence to argue for, as we might put it, the intentional character of memory (*De memoria et reminiscentia* 45025–4511, for discussion, see Sorabji 2004). The Peripatetic response to the puzzle is to straightforwardly accept the claim of absence and reinterpret what purported to be a presentation instead as a kind of re-presentation. When one remembers Corsicus, in his absence

one contemplates a *phantasma* caused by a previous perception of Corsicus
and one conceives of the *phantasma* as a likeness and reminder of Corsicus
as he was perceived. How might the Peripatetic response, so abstractly
described, be applied to the perceptual case of attending to bodies in
audition?

One obstacle to straightforwardly applying the Peripatetic response to
the perceptual case of attending to bodies in audition is this: memory and
imagination are plausibly the primitive intentional capacities in our cognitive economy in the way that perception could not be, *pace* Burge (2010), if
perception essentially involves an irreducible presentational element. And
if our perceptual capacities are not intentional, but a necessary precondition for the possession of intentional capacities, then how would the
Peripatetic response apply to the perceptual case of attending to bodies in
audition?

Perhaps what is present in auditory experience may, nevertheless, constitute a natural image of what is absent. That is, perhaps we can understand
hearing the body's sound-generating activity as providing the listener with
a dynamic aural image of the body otherwise absent in audition. It is an
image, indeed, as I have suggested, a natural image, like a fossil or a foot-
print (for a recent general discussion of images, see Kulvicki 2014). But
unlike paradigmatic images, it is not a visual image, but an aural image
(for the denial that there so much as could be such a thing, see Martin
2012). And while visual images are static, aural images, if such there be,
would be dynamic as befitting their aural character. Hearing Big Ben's
striking, while not the presentation of Big Ben in auditory experience,
would nevertheless provide the listener with a dynamic aural image of Big
Ben. We do not so much as hear Big Ben in a condition of activity as we
hear Big Ben in its audible activity. In order for this to be so, the auditory
presentation of a sound-generating event must involve at least the partial
disclosure of the event's participants. Audition partially discloses an event's
participant by presenting it as a participant of the audible event. It is the
body's participation in the event, and not the body per se, that is part of
the event's audible structure. The disclosure of such audible structure is
partial. Only those aspects of the body that are manifest in its participation in the audible event are disclosed, and perhaps only some of those.
Furthermore, there is no guarantee that if a perceiver hears an event, they
hear each of its participants, if any. But that is consistent with audition,
in certain circumstances of perception, partially disclosing at least some of
the participants in the unfolding audible event. It is only if we can hear
Big Ben's participation in its striking that we can use that hearing to attend

to Big Ben. Only if we can hear Big Ben's participation can that hearing provide us with a dynamic aural image of Big Ben and its activities that we exploit in attending to Big Ben in audition.

Before turning, in the next section, to The Wave Theory of sound, allow me to summarize the discussion so far. We hear sounds, and their sources, and their audible qualities. Perhaps we hear sources by hearing the sounds that they make, as the neo-Berkeleans contend. In the next chapter, however, I shall argue, instead, for the Heideggerian alternative. We can attend to the sources of sound without first attending to the sounds that they generate. Sounds and their sources are essentially dynamic entities, not wholly present at any given moment, but unfolding through their temporal interval. Sounds and their sources, essentially dynamic entities, are the bearers or *substrata* of audible qualities. Audible qualities are qualities essentially sustained by activity. The only bearers of audible qualities present in auditory experience are essentially dynamic entities. Bodies are not, in this sense, essentially dynamic entities and so are not present in our auditory experience. Though absent in auditory experience, we may, nonetheless, attend to bodies in audition, when an audible sound-generating event in which they participate presents a dynamic aural image of them.

3.5   The Wave Theory

An ancient tradition identifies sound with motion. Plato and Aristotle claimed that sound is a motion in a medium. In the cosmology of the *Timaeus* (67 a–c), sound is percussion in the air and the hearing of that sound is the movement it causes through the ears of the perceiver. For Aristotle, sound is motion in a medium, be it air or water (*De anima* 2 8 420 a 8–11, 420 b 11, *De sensu* 447 a 1–2; though see O'Callaghan 2007, 60–1 for an alternative interpretation; see also Johnstone 2013). But the hearing of the sound, while it may involve the sound's acting upon the ears, the organs of audition, is no mere alteration but the exercise of a capacity (*De anima* 2 5). Though sounds involve the motion of a medium, Aristotle does not conceive of sound as propagating through the medium. When a solid, smooth object, such as a piece of bronze, is struck, it causes the medium, the air, say, to move in a single, continuous mass (*De anima* 2 8 419 b 33–420 a 2). The medium is a unity that communicates the movement of the distal body to the ear of the perceiver. Think of the way movement may be communicated through a single, continuous mass such as a stick. One may poke with a stick, without the poke propagating through the stick. Aristotle derives this conception of a medium as a continuous unity from

Plato's account of perception in the *Timaeus* (see Lindberg 1977, chapter 1; the Stoic stick analogy, reported by Alexander of Aphrodisias, *De anima* 130 14, also plausibly traces to this source).

Aristotle's Platonically inspired conception of a medium as a continuous unity shows that conceiving of sound as motion in a medium is not yet to conceive of successive motion through a medium in the way suggested by talk of propagation. However, this conception of a medium as a continuous unity did not long persist. Conceptions of sound as motion in a medium were common in the Middle Ages, if variously developed (Pasnau 2000). Roger Bacon's doctrine of the multiplication of the species provides one model for sonic propagation. An object will cause a species, an image or likeness of it, to inhere, in some sense, in the medium adjacent to it. Moreover, species successively inhere in parts of the medium, each time causing the species to inhere in an adjacent part. This has the consequence that species are continuously generated along rectilinear rays that proceed in all directions, if unobstructed, from every point on the surface of a body. Influenced by al-Kindī and Robert Grosseteste, Bacon's doctrine was modeled on the propagation of light:

> For light of its very nature diffuses itself in every direction in such a way that a point of light will produce instantaneously a sphere of light of any size whatsoever, unless some opaque object stands in the way. (Grosseteste, *De Luce*; Riedl 1942, 10)

It might naturally be thought that the multiplication of the species itself provides a model for sonic propagation. On that model, audible species successively inhere in adjacent parts of the medium such that they are continuously generated, at least for the duration of their sounding, in rectilinear rays in all directions, if unobstructed, from their source.

Bacon, however, denies that there are audible species (*De multiplicatione specierum* 1 2). A species inhering in a part of the medium will cause a species to inhere in the adjacent part that is similar to it, if weaker. Species cause species. But sounds do not cause sounds and, hence, are not species. A vibration in one part of the medium produces a sound, and it will cause the adjacent part of the medium to vibrate as well. And the vibration of the adjacent part will itself produce a sound. This sound is similar, if weaker, than the sound produced by the previous vibration. And like the propagation of species, the propagation of sound occurs along a rectilinear path. But notice, that whereas vibrations cause vibrations, sounds do not cause sounds. Sounds, for Bacon, are epiphenomenal effects of the propagation of vibrations. Species are causally implicated in their propagation in a way that sounds could not be.

In *Perspectiva* I 9 4, Bacon provides an additional argument. This argument depends on the way in which species are said to propagate. The propagation of the species does not involve locomotion, but the generation of the species multiplied in the medium. Species are not bodies and so are not subject to locomotion, understood as a change to a body's location over time. The propagation of the species is rather the successive inherence of a form in different parts of the medium along a rectilinear path. In this way they contrast with sounds:

> For sound involves a motion by which the parts of the thing struck are displaced from their natural position, with and ensuing motion of vibration and a motion of rarefaction in every direction … as is evident from [Aristotle's] *On the Soul*, book 2. (Bacon, *Perspectiva* I 9 4 290–4; Lindberg 1996, 143)

Bacon's arguments raise important questions that we shall have to address (Section 3.7). Do sound waves travel? Or is the propagation of a sound wave the successive inherence of a wave form in different parts of the dense and elastic medium?

For present purposes, we shall understand The Wave Theory as identifying sound with a certain kind of event, akin to the motion of rarefaction in every direction posited by Bacon. Specifically, according to The Wave Theory, sound is the propagation, in every direction, of a patterned disturbance – longitudinal pressure waves that vary in amplitude and frequency – through a dense and elastic medium such as air or water (for contemporary defenses of The Wave Theory, though this is not their primary aim, see O'Shaughnessy 2009 and Sorensen 2009). The longitudinal pressure waves that vary in amplitude and frequency are a kind of rarefaction. They are, after all, compression waves. Moreover, as on the *Perspectiva* account, the rarefaction propagates in every direction. Notice, on The Wave Theory, as herein understood, the sound event is not the patterned disturbance in a dense and elastic medium so much as it is the propagation of a patterned disturbance through that medium.

Among events, sounds have a distinctive temporal character. According to O'Shaughnessy (2009), sounds have a "double duration," the way other events, such as the alteration of a body's color, do not. When I hear the call of a feral parakeet, my hearing of the sound that it produces has a certain duration. Suppose I heard the parakeet's call from its onset, so that I heard the whole of the call. But notice, on The Wave Theory, the sound does not cease to exist at that moment. At a later moment, as the patterned disturbance continues to propagate in the dense and elastic medium, another perceiver, situated further from the parakeet than me, may subsequently hear that same parakeet's call. The first duration is determined by the length of the patterned disturbance and the speed at which it is traveling. It is the duration of a potential hearing of the sound. The second duration is determined by how long the patterned disturbance propagates, and the speed at which it does, before completely eroding due to the resistance offered by the dense and elastic medium as well as other potential obstructers such as dampening and interference.

The Wave Theory, so understood, is usefully contrasted with two contemporary alternatives. Each identifies sounds with events. They differ only as to which event sounds are to be identified with. Whereas on The Wave Theory, the event is the propagation of the patterned disturbance through a dense and elastic medium, according to Casati and Dokic (1994, 2014), sounds are the events that would cause a patterned disturbance to propagate through a medium should there be one, and, according to O'Callaghan (2007, 2009), sounds are the causing of the pattern disturbance to propagate through a medium. On The Wave Theory, the sound event, in a perfectly elastic medium, and ignoring its density and other potential obstructers, may be envisioned as an ever-expanding sphere, the patterned disturbance propagating in every direction from its source, as on the Baconian model (Sorensen 2009). It is like an expanding ripple caused by a drop in an otherwise calm body of water, except that the sound event occurs in three dimensions, not two, and so takes the form of a sphere rather than a circle. In contrast, for Casati and Dokic as well as for O'Callaghan, the sound event exhibits no such structure. For Casati and Dokic, it is the striking, bowing, grinding, vibrating, resonating – whatever kind of event involving the material source sufficient to propagate a patterned disturbance through a dense and elastic medium, should there be one. And for O'Callaghan, it is not these, but the related event of their causing a patterned disturbance to propagate through a medium.

These alternatives are usefully understood in terms of their contrasting verdicts concerning Berkeley's question whether there could be sound in a vacuum (on Berkeley's argument from vacuums, see Pasnau 1999b). Whereas on The Wave Theory, the existence of sound depends upon a medium in which that event transpires, according to Casati and Dokic (1994, 2014), sound is existentially independent of a medium. An event involving a material source may be sufficient to cause the propagation of a patterned disturbance through a dense and elastic medium and may yet occur in the absence of such a medium. The existential independence of sound allows for sound in a vacuum in the way The Wave Theory could not. Nor are sounds existentially independent from the medium as O'Callaghan (2007, 2009) conceives of them. If there is no medium, there is no causing of a patterned disturbance to propagate through it.

"In space no one can hear you scream." Our alternatives provide contrasting interpretations of the tagline for the 1979 movie *Aliens*. According to Casati and Dokic (1994, 2014), in space no one can hear you scream because the sound of your scream is perceptually inaccessible in a vacuum. A dense and elastic medium merely contributes to the perceptual accessibility of the sound and not to its existence. According to The Wave Theory, by contrast, in space no one can hear you scream since screaming produces no sound in a vacuum. Sounds existentially depend upon a dense and elastic medium through which the patterned disturbance may propagate, and in space, there is no such medium. Similarly, for O'Callaghan (2007, 2009), sounds existentially depend upon a dense and elastic medium through which the patterned disturbance may propagate. Only if such a medium exists can there be an event that is the causing of a patterned disturbance to propagate through a medium. The Wave Theory differs from O'Callaghan's account in the structure it attributes to the sound event. The propagation of the patterned disturbance in every direction from its source constitutes an ever-expanding sphere. In contrast, the causing of the propagation of the patterned disturbance itself displays no such structure.

The Wave Theory, on the present understanding, is an idealized refinement of a traditional view. It represents a metaphysical genus, or class of views, insofar as it admits of further refinements. Are sound events, as The Wave Theory conceives of them, plausibly the objects of audition?

Traditionally, the phenomenology of auditory experience was thought to support The Wave Theory, or at least some version of it. There are, of course, contemporary dissenters. Some, at least, of their more important concerns shall be addressed in Section 3.7. But for now, let us focus on why the phenomenology of auditory experience was traditionally thought to favor The Wave Theory in the first place. It was traditionally thought that our auditory experience presents an emanative phenomenology. Within auditory experience, sounds appear to emanate from their sources. Specifically, sounds are heard to come from their sources. And, at least in the context of The Wave Theory, it is natural to understand this as the phenomenological reflection, in auditory experience, of the direction of the propagation of the patterned disturbance. If it is, then an emanative phenomenology, should it prove veridical, potentially contributes to the fitness of the animal since the direction of the propagation of the patterned disturbance carries important information about the location of its source.

Hearing the approach of another can be of vital concern, be it predator or prey.

In "Some Elementary Reflections on Sense-Perception," Broad (1952) provides a careful description of the emanative phenomenology of audition, by contrasting the hearing of sounds with the seeing of colors. Colors are seen to inhere in the surfaces of bodies in a spatial region located at a distance from the perceiver. Most events lack color despite involving colored participants. Brexit isn't literally red, white, and blue. Even in the rare case of a colored event such as a flash or an explosion, the color of the flash, say, is seen confined to the remote spatial region of its occurrence. Hearing sounds is crucially different, in this regard, from seeing colors:

> But the noise is not literally heard as the occurrence of a certain sound-quality within a limited region remote from the percipient's body. It certainly is not heard as having any shape or size. It seems to be heard as coming to one from a certain direction, and it seems to be thought of as pervading with various degrees of intensity the whole of an indefinitely large region surrounding the centre from which it emanates. (Broad 1952, 5)

In this passage, Broad not only makes clear the sense in which a sound is heard to emanate from its source, but he also connects this aspect of auditory phenomenology with a thesis in the metaphysics of sound. For suppose that this emanative phenomenology of auditory experience were determined by an aspect of what it presents, then the sounds that we hear would involve a propagation, in every direction, from the source, of a patterned disturbance that can vary as it travels through a dense and imperfectly elastic medium. That is to say, Broad is explicitly linking the emanative phenomenology of auditory experience, if veridical, with The Wave Theory. Broad (1952), however, should not be read as necessarily endorsing The Wave Theory here. The description of the emanative phenomenology of auditory experience is part of a larger task of specifying the phenomenological differences between vision, audition, and touch, phenomenological differences ultimately belied by the common causal mechanisms that underlie all of our sensory capacities.

As we observed, Broad's claim that auditory experience has an emanative phenomenology has been challenged. I shall take up such challenges in Section 3.7. But for now, for the sake of argument, suppose that audition does, in fact, have an emanative phenomenology. Sounds would have to be, at the very least, events or processes if this aspect of the phenomenology audition is veridical. And this would rule out sounds belonging to some other ontological category. Sounds, for example, could not be sensible qualities as the Lockean conceives of them. Static features like qualities could not, by themselves at least, explain the dynamic structure of sounds being heard to emanate from their sources. If sounds are qualities located in a spatial region remote from the perceiver, at or near their source, then the phenomenological distinction that Broad draws between vision and audition collapses. So not only does the emanative phenomenology of auditory experience favor The Wave Theory over other accounts of the sound event, but it favors, as well, thinking of sounds as events or processes rather than belonging to some other ontological category.

The Wave Theory not only coheres with, and would explain well, the emanative phenomenology of auditory experience, if veridical, but it would explain, as well, ordinary practices of identifying and re-identifying sound. Ordinarily, we allow that two perceivers located at different distances from a material source may hear the same sound, though at different times, and though their experience of that sound may differ. The sound may be louder for the perceiver located nearer the source, for example. And so the experience of the sound for the perceiver located near and far may differ, and yet it is the same sound that they hear.

When invited to envision the sound event, as The Wave Theory conceives of it, as an ever expanding sphere, we were invited, as well, to make certain idealizations, that the medium through which the patterned disturbance propagates is perfectly elastic and that its density made no difference to the propagation of the patterned disturbance. Of course, the air and water through which we normally hear sounds are dense and imperfectly elastic. Moreover, complex sonic environments with multiple active sources of sound will typically contain other obstructers, such as competing noise, dampening, and resonant interference. And that is presently relevant. For that means that the patterned disturbance will erode as it propagates through the imperfectly elastic medium. In Bacon's terminology, it becomes weaker. As it loses energy, it will become, not only less loud, but fine detail of the top end will be lost early on and perhaps only the bass will persist the furthest.

That the two perceivers, located at different distances from the source, hear the sound at different times is due to the different distances that the patterned disturbance had to propagate from the source to reach them. And that the auditory experience of the two perceivers differs in character is due, in part, to the erosion of the patterned disturbance as it propagated through a dense and imperfectly elastic medium. Nevertheless, they can be said to hear the same sound since sound, on The Wave Theory, is not identified with a patterned disturbance, but with the propagation of a patterned disturbance through an elastic medium. If sound were identified with a patterned disturbance, then since the patterned disturbance differed in the auditory stimulation of the two perceivers, they would be hearing different sounds. But if sound were, instead, identified with a propagation of a patterned disturbance through an elastic medium, the two perceivers may be said to hear the same sound even if they are hearing it at different stages of its career, different phases of the sound event.

Our ordinary practice of identifying and re-identifying sounds also treats them as particulars that may be qualitatively identical if numerically distinct (Nudds 2009, 70). Thus there may be two particulars, each a sound, that are, nonetheless, alike auditorily. This presupposes that sounds are bearers, or *substrata*, of audible qualities. The numerically distinct sounds are qualitatively identical since they instantiate the same audible qualities. But this could only be so if sounds are among the bearers of audible qualities. If sounds are bearers or *substrata* of audible qualities, as Aristotle contends, *De anima* 2 11 422 b 31–2, then sounds could not themselves be qualities as the Lockean contends. Should this aspect of our ordinary practice of identifying and re-identifying sounds prove valid, then sounds are not themselves audible qualities, as Locke contends, but their bearers or *substrata*.

3.6   Auditory Perspective

According to our ordinary practice of identifying and re-identifying sound, two perceivers located at different distances from a material source may hear the same sound at different times, though their experience of that sound may differ. How are we to understand this? Is this a matter of their having different auditory perspectives on the same sound? Recall how different visual or haptic perspectives on the same object can give rise to different visual or haptic appearances (Chapter 1.4). Or consider the following, related case. If the former case involved intersubjective variation in auditory experience, the present case involves intra-subjective variation in auditory experience. Suppose that the perceiver is in the presence of a continual sound, the roar of a waterfall, say. As they approach the waterfall, their auditory experience changes. Does the perceiver gain a new perspective on that sound by approaching its source? Smith (2002, 135) denies that this is a difference in perspective if that involves potentially disclosing previously hidden aspects of the sensible object. We saw this feature at work in haptic perspective (Chapter 1.4). Specifically, the haptic activities, the distinctive ways the perceiver is handling the object, occurring in an egocentrically and teleologically structured peripersonal space, can disclose previously hidden corporeal aspects of the object of haptic investigation and are, to that extent, partial perspectives on that object.

Should we accept Smith's denial that auditory perception potentially discloses previously hidden aspects of sound? At least part of the difference between hearing the waterfall from afar and hearing it nearby is due to the erosion of the patterned disturbance, continually generated by the waterfall, as it propagates through a dense and imperfectly elastic medium. There are at least two ways to use this observation to undermine Smith's denial. The first way couples that observation with the claim that since the patterned disturbance carries material information about its source, some of that information, at least, is lost as the patterned disturbance erodes. Suppose the perceiver initially hears the sound but at such a distance that they are unable to recognize it as the sound of a waterfall. As they approach the sound, at some point, if circumstances are propitious, they can recognize the material source of the sound. The difficulty with the first way is that it is not inconsistent with Smith's denial. All that has been claimed is that auditory perception may disclose previously hidden aspects of the material source of the sound, but Smith only denies that auditory perception may disclose previously hidden aspects, not of the material source of the sound, but of the sound itself. The second way of developing the observation avoids this difficulty. With the erosion of the patterned disturbance in a dense and imperfectly elastic medium, not only is information about the material source lost, but so are audible features of the sound itself, or at least audible features of the sound possessed at a certain stage of its career. At a certain distance, one may no longer hear the fine play of overtones in a sound, say. As we shall see, Smith himself provides an example of hearing a previously hidden aspect of a sound, though he does not, himself, recognize it as such.

Smith denies that hearing a sound at different distances from its source affords the perceiver with distinct auditory perspectives on that sound if a perspective potentially discloses a previously hidden aspect of the sound. Smith, however, does not himself accept the antecedent of that conditional. Following Husserl and Merleau-Ponty, Smith suggests, instead, that it is sufficient for the notion of perspective to get a grip that there are better or worse perspectives on the given object. And Smith accepts that there are better or worse perspectives in hearing a sound:

> We can discover how loud a distant sound really is, or how hot a fire really is, by moving closer to them. If we want to hear the ticking of a pocket-watch

"properly," we put it close to our ear; we behave very differently when it is a matter of hearing a cannon fire. (2002, 135)

While I agree with everything claimed in this passage, I fail to see how the contrast between a conception of a perspective as potentially disclosing a previously hidden aspect and a conception of a perspective as affording a better or worse perspective can be coherently maintained, at least as Smith apparently understands that contrast. Consider Smith's first example, discovering how loud a distant sound really is. Approaching a waterfall, one eventually reaches a position from which one can hear just how loud that waterfall really is. That is to say, it is plausible that what makes hearing the sound of the waterfall from that position a better perspective is precisely that it discloses a previously hidden aspect of the sound, the relative intensity of its loudness. Similarly, it is plausible that what makes feeling the radiant heat of a fire from a certain position a better perspective than a position located further from the fire is that it discloses just how hot the fire really is. And while I agree that placing a pocket-watch close to the ear is the "proper" way to listen to its ticking, I suspect that this is because the perceiver is in a position to hear the workings of the watch's mechanism, in which case what is disclosed in the "proper" perspective is the material source of the sound. One only hears the watch ticking, understood as the sound of the watch, if one hears the watch ticking, understood as the workings of the watch's mechanism.

Complicating matters, better and worse are said of in many ways. Specifically, whether a position from which a perceiver may hear a sound affords the perceiver with a better or worse perspective on that sound depends upon what is practically at stake in describing the perspective as better or worse. That is to say, it may be an occasion-sensitive matter in Travis' (2008) sense. Smith's own examples suggest as much: "If we want to hear the ticking of a pocket-watch 'properly,' we put it close to our ear; we behave very differently when it is a matter of hearing a cannon fire." Allow me to offer an example of my own. I own an otherwise fine recording of an Anthony Braxton solo performance marred only by the ill-judged positioning of the microphone. The microphone picked up the clacking of the keys while Braxton played his instrument, thus partially obscuring the sound of that playing. One moral might be that one shouldn't stand close enough to the saxophone to hear the clacking of its keys. Sound aesthetic advice. But suppose one is moved, not by aesthetic, but by academic concerns. A student of Braxton's playing might gain insight into Braxton's technique by hearing the clacking of the keys. So whether a given position counts as affording the perceiver with a better or worse perspective on the audible events unfolding in the perceiver's environment depends upon the practical point and interest in evaluating that perspective.

The position from which a perceiver may hear the sound of a distant source may provide a better or worse perspective, where better and worse is said of in many ways. Sometimes, for certain practical purposes, what makes a perspective better is that it potentially discloses previously hidden aspects of a sound, be it the delicate play of overtones or just how loud that sound really is. Sometimes what makes a perspective better is that it potentially discloses a previously hidden aspect of the source, as when the watch is close enough to hear the workings of its mechanism.

Audition provides the perceiver with a partial perspective on the audible events and processes unfolding in the natural environment. Like visual and haptic perspective, auditory perspective is not only partial, but occurs in an egocentrically structured space. Sometimes it is difficult to make out the direction of a sound. Sometimes hearing a sound provides us with only a general sense of its direction. Still, it is possible for us to hear a sound from behind, or to the left. Like vision, and unlike haptic touch, audible events are heard to transpire in an egocentrically structured extrapersonal space. Some of the distal events that we hear lie far beyond the limits of peripersonal space, the space within which we may immediately act with our limbs. However, audition lacks vision's rectilinear directionality. Unlike vision, audition affords the perceiver 360 degree awareness of extrapersonal space.

3.7   Phenomenological Objections

According to Pasnau (1999b), if The Wave Theory were true, then auditory experience would be illusory. Pasnau claims that we do not hear sounds pervading a volume, at least not normally, rather we hear sounds as located at their sources:

> We do not hear sounds as being in the air; we hear them as being at the place where they are generated. Listening to the birds outside your window, the students outside your door, the cars going down your street, in the vast majority of cases you will perceive those sounds as being located at the place where they originate. At least, you will hear those sounds as being located somewhere in the distance, in a certain general direction. But if sounds are in the air, as the standard view holds, then the cries of birds and of students are all around you. This is not how it seems (except perhaps in special cases …). (1999b, 311)

Other recent writers who have made similar claims about the distal character of experienced sound include Casati and Dokic (1994) and O'Callaghan (2007).

Auditory experience, so conceived, lacks the emanative phenomenology that Broad (1952) contrasts with the phenomenology of color vision. Rather, sounds are heard to be confined to the remote spatial region of their origin. Indeed, Pasnau (1999b) understands the distal senses of vision and audition, at least, as being on a par. And since Pasnau follows Locke in treating sounds as sensible qualities (though see Pasnau 2009), he is led to conceive of auditory experience as affording the perceiver with awareness of auditory qualities confined to the remote spatial region of their source. In this way is the analogy of audition with vision, *pace* Broad, completely reinstated (see also Kulvicki 2008).

Allow me to make a brief digression to highlight an important point of disagreement. Despite O'Callaghan's (2009) emphasis on Pasnau's (1999b) commitment to a Lockean metaphysics of sound, it is incidental to the aim of that paper, which is concerned, instead, with whether sound qualities inhere in the medium or in the distal source. That question, or a version of it, can be posed without assuming the Lockean metaphysics: Is sound located in the medium or at or near its source? Though incidental to the aim of the paper, the Lockean metaphysics of sound was not unmotivated. Rather, Pasnau is moved by the idea that sensible objects belong to a common ontological category. This is a monism of the sensible. Specifically, Pasnau seems attracted to a monism of at least the objects of the distal senses (as does Kulvicki 2008). And since colors are conceived to be qualities, sounds must also be. Later, Pasnau (2009) abandons the Lockean metaphysics of sound, coming to conceive of sounds as particular events. However, given the monism of the sensible, and the dynamic aspects of the physics of color generation, Pasnau suggests that colors might themselves be events, the event of color. Allow me to register a disagreement, though without offering a reason, it is perhaps merely the expression of a difference in intellectual temperament. The disagreement concerns less Pasnau's Heraclitean metaphysics of color, than the role that the monism of the sensible plays in motivating it.

Rather than thinking of sensible objects as belonging to a common ontological category, I am impressed by the heterogeneity of the sensible. Far from adhering to the monism of the sensible, on Austinian grounds, I am attracted to a pluralism of the sensible. Just consider the diversity of *visibilia* alone. We see opaque natural bodies such as Moore's (1903) blue bead or Price's (1932) red tomato, but we also see translucent volumes, flashes, reflections, mirror images, rainbows, mirages, shadows, holes. Perhaps as Sorensen (2004, 2008, 2009) suggests, we can see darkness and hear silence. And all these sensible objects seem to be of diverse categories and degrees of being. I raise the issue without pursuing it. The important point is whether there is unity or diversity in the metaphysics of sensible objects would be relevant to the kind of explanatory role they could play.

Pasnau's argument that sounds are heard to be at or near their sources raises a couple of questions. The first question concerns the metaphysical commitments of The Wave Theory. If, according to The Wave Theory, sounds have locations, where are the sounds, so conceived, located? After all, only if sounds, as The Wave Theory conceives of them, could not be located at their sources is there an alleged conflict, according to Pasnau, with the phenomenology of auditory experience. The second question concerns the phenomenology of auditory experience. In cases where perceivers genuinely hear something in the distance, are what they hear sounds or some other audible object?

Begin with the second question, about the phenomenology of auditory experience, first. (Discussion of the location of sound according to The Wave Theory will be postponed until we discuss O'Callaghan's 2007, 2009 objection to the purported emanative phenomenology of auditory experience.) When one listens to the birds outside one's window, the students outside one's door, and the cars going down one's street, what is it that one is listening to? A flat-footed answer would be, well, birds, students, and cars, or at least their audible activities. But birds, students, and cars, or at least their activities, while audible, are not themselves sounds, but their sources, at least potentially. But the claim that the source of a sound is heard to be confined to a spatial region remote from the perceiver is not inconsistent with the sound it generates pervading the surrounding medium. Pasnau moves too quickly from cases involving hearing a distal source to concluding that the sound itself is heard to be remote from the perceiver. Once we allow that we hear not only sounds, but their sources, a question naturally arises whether the audibly distal object that we hear is the sound or merely its source (see O'Shaughnessy 2009, 123, for a development of this worry).

A similar issue affects Pasnau's discussion of the precedence effect:

> Even when there is a significant reverberation in a room, we do not hear it as such, as long as the reverberation comes to the ear between 1 and 35 milliseconds after the initial wave enters the ear. In such cases, we hear the sound as being located at its initial source. Although the reverberation affects the perceived loudness and quality of the sound, it does not enter

into our perception of its location. (If the reverberation arrived more slowly than 35 milliseconds later, we would hear an echo. If it were faster than 1 millisecond we would hear the sound as centered between the source and the point of reverberation.) This is known as the *precedence effect*. On the standard view, this effect has to be described as a defect in the system. For if the object of hearing is sound, and if sound is a quality belonging to the surrounding air rather than to its source, then the precedence effect would serve to filter out information about sound. The precedence effect, in other words, would stand in the way of accurate detection of sound. Yet this seems absurd, which points to another reason for giving up the standard view of sound. (1999b, 312–13)

Once we allow that we hear not only sounds, but their sources, then Pasnau's reasoning is undone from the beginning. If the object of hearing is the source of the sound, and the function of the auditory system is to afford the perceiver with auditory awareness of distal sources (see Chapter 4.2 for further discussion), then there is nothing particularly mysterious about the precedence effect.

Another criticism of The Wave Theory that potentially conflates sounds with their sources is O'Callaghan's (2007, 89) argument from timbre. O'Callaghan argues that auditory constancies concerning timbre favor thinking of the sounds that we hear as the causing of the propagation of a patterned disturbance, as opposed to the propagation of the patterned disturbance, as The Wave Theory contends. Drawing on the work of Handel (1995), O'Callaghan argues that timbre depends, at least in part, upon features of the source and the characteristic manner in which it disturbs the medium. If timbre were an audible quality of sound, then this would favor thinking of sound as the causing of the propagation of a patterned disturbance. Timbre is an audible quality, to be sure, but is it best thought of as an audible quality of sound? The conclusion that O'Callaghan draws from Handel's research – that timbre depends, at least in part, upon features of the source and the characteristic manner in which it disturbs the medium – suggests, instead, that timbre is better understood as an audible quality of the sound's source, the sound-generating event or process. If we hear, not only sounds, but their sources, then sources, *pace* Berkeley, have auditory qualities. If sources have audible qualities, then perhaps the distal sound-generating event involving a material body as a participant is the bearer or *substratum* of heard timbre. Timbre, so conceived, is an audible quality of sound-generating events or processes that partially disclose material properties of their participants that are relevant to the generation of sound. On this conception, O'Callaghan's claim that timbre favors thinking of sounds as the causing of the propagation of a patterned disturbance conflates sounds with their sources.

In an intellectual context, such as our own, where it is controversial what sounds are, how plausible is it to rely on the distinction between sounds and their sources? After all, if sounds are up for grabs, isn't the distinction between sounds and their sources up for grabs as well? And if it is, then the present criticisms of Pasnau and O'Callaghan, relying as they do upon that distinction, are, for that reason, unpersuasive. Or so goes the present worry. What ought not to be controversial is that there are sound-generating events and processes. While it may be controversial whether sound-generating events and processes are audible, some Berkeleans such as Smith (2002) deny it, it should be uncontroversial that such events and processes exist. Which events and processes they are will depend, of course, upon what sounds are since these events and processes are the causes of sound, but it should be uncontroversial that there are such sources. But even allowing that the identification of an event or process as the cause of sound will depend upon the controversial issue of what sounds are, there are still things that we can conclude about sources, for example, that they can be at a distance from the perceiver, and that they have audible qualities if heard. Moreover, these conclusions about sources, if warranted, together with the claim that sources are audible, might legitimately ground the lines of criticism presently pursued.

Pasnau (1999b, section 6) claims that The Wave Theory invites us to envision sounds as filling the air around us. But if all sounds fill the air around us, then we should hear them pervading the dense and imperfectly elastic medium through which they propagate. But in fact it is quite rare to experience sound as pervading a volume: "Perhaps this is how we experience loud music in a disco, or a jack-hammer in a narrow street" (Pasnau 1999b, 312). But these are exceptional cases. Does The Wave Theory have the consequence that sounds fill the air around us in a sense that is inconsistent with our auditory experience? In his description of the emanative phenomenology of audition, Broad seemed to suggest that sounds fill the air. How are we to understand this? Two senses of audibility can be distinguished, and when they are, The Wave Theory can be seen to be consistent with our auditory experience, despite Pasnau's doubts.

Pasnau claims that most sounds do not audibly fill the medium. So filling the medium must be something audibly accessible. Consider a brief sound, a single call of a feral parakeet, say, as opposed to the continuous sound of a waterfall. According to The Wave Theory, the sound of the parakeet is the propagation, in every direction, of a patterned disturbance through a medium, in the present instance, the dense and imperfectly elastic air. In one clear sense, the only audible aspect of this complex event is the patterned disturbance as it is through some interval of time. The outer boundary of the sphere, the narrow band that is the patterned disturbance, is audible in the sense of being a potential proximal cause of the auditory experience of the sound. So while the complex event may be envisioned as a growing sphere, since the sound is brief, the only audible aspect of the sound is at the moving boundary of the sphere, the narrow band that is the patterned disturbance. After all, if a perceiver is placed within the sphere between the source of the sound and the narrow band at the sphere's outer boundary, they are no longer in a position to hear the call of the feral parakeet.

In one clear sense that may be so, but there are other, relevant senses of audibility. So, if circumstances are propitious, in hearing the feral parakeet's call, we can hear the direction of the sound's propagation. We may even have a sense of how far off the source is. So aspects of the complex sound event are in another relevant sense audible and in this sense are not merely confined to the patterned disturbance at the outer boundary of the sphere. Nor are these exceptional cases, like loud music in a disco, or the sound of a jack-hammer in a narrow street. The Wave Theory, as herein described, is only committed to sounds being heard to fill the air in this latter sense. In this sense, something is audible if it is heard in hearing a sound. Of course, even on the first sense of audible, understood as a potential proximal cause of the perception of the sound, a continuous sound, such as the roar of a waterfall, will audibly fill the air – the continuously produced patterned disturbances will pervade the space between the perceiver and the waterfall. But as Pasnau observes, and The Wave Theory predicts, these are exceptional cases, like loud music in a disco, or the sound of a jack-hammer in a narrow street.

O'Callaghan (2007; Chapter 3.4) criticizes The Wave Theory by attempting to undermine its phenomenological motivations. The Wave Theory is motivated, in no small part, by the purported emanative phenomenology of auditory experience. Thus sounds are heard to come from their sources. O'Callaghan (2007, 2009) argues that, at least on a certain understanding of what hearing a sound coming from its source could be, sounds are not heard to come from their sources, and thus that auditory experience lacks the emanative phenomenology that would motivate The Wave Theory, if veridical.

How are we to understand hearing a sound coming from its source? O'Callaghan writes:

> It might be that sounds are heard to come from a particular place by being heard first to be at that place, and then to be at successively closer intermediate locations. But this is not the case with ordinary hearing. Sounds are not heard to travel through the air as scientists have taught us that waves do. (2007, 34)

And O'Callaghan likens hearing a sound coming from its source to hearing a sonic missile. Audible emanation or propagation of a sound from its source is being modeled on a specific kind of change, the locomotion of a body. Locomotion is a change in location over time. So locomotion is a species of change that pertains only to those entities, paradigmatically bodies, that possess location.

I concede that, on this understanding of what it is to hear a sound coming from its source, ordinary auditory experience lacks an emanative phenomenology. Hearing a sound coming from its source is not analogous with the locomotion of an audible body. However, that is not the only available understanding of hearing a sound coming from its source. Perhaps the audible emanation or propagation of sound is better modeled on a different kind of change.

Prichard denies that waves and sounds, being what they are, are subject to locomotion. Only bodies move, and waves and sounds are not bodies:

> But ... I also made the same remark (viz. that only a body could move) to a mathematician here. What was in my mind was that it is mere inaccuracy to say that a wave could move, and that where people talk of a wave as moving, say with the velocity of a foot, or a mile, or 150,000 miles, a second, the real movement consisted of the oscillations of certain particles, each of which took place a little later than a neighboring oscillation.

> He scoffed for quite a different reason. He said that you could illustrate a movement by a noise – that, for example, if an explosion occurred in the middle of Oxford the noise would spread outwards, being heard at different times by people at varying distances from the centre, so that at one moment the noise was at one place and that a little later it was somewhere else, and in the interval it had moved from one place to the other.

> Now, of course, it was not in dispute that in the process imagined people in different places each heard a noise at a rather different time. The only question was, 'Was the succession of noises a movement?', and I think that on considering the matter you will have to allow that it was not, and that what happened was that he, being certain of the noises, and wanting to limit the term 'movement' to something he was certain of, used the term 'movement' to designate the succession of noises, implying that this was the real thing of

which we were both talking. But if this is what happened, then he was using the term 'movement' in a sense of his own, and in saying that in the imagined case he was certain of a movement, he was being certain of something other than the opposite of what I was certain of. (1950a, 99)

(*Caveat Lector*. Burnyeat 1995, 430 n. 29, appendix, lampoons Aristotle for making similar claims by citing Prichard echoing them here. I argue, that at least in this instance, Burnyeat is hoisted by his own petard, Kalderon 2015; Chapter 3.2.)

Prichard's point about wave movement can be put this way. Consider a wave propagating through a liquid mass. At any given moment, the liquid mass has a certain spatial configuration, and the wave form is instanced in a certain part of the liquid mass. At a later moment, the liquid mass will have a different spatial configuration, and the wave form will be instanced in a different part of the liquid mass. Prichard's point is that it is not the wave form that is moving in coming to be instanced in differently located parts of the liquid mass. Rather, the liquid mass is moving, or at least its parts, "the oscillation of certain particles," with the effect that the wave form is progressively instantiated. The wave's propagation is not a body's locomotion, but the generation of the wave form multiplied in the medium. A change of state and travel are different (*De sensu* 6 44628).

I want to take up Prichard's suggestion that the propagation of patterned disturbance through an elastic medium should not be understood on the model of locomotion. At any rate, The Wave Theory, as herein described, naturally suggests an alternative model based not on locomotion, but on growth. After all, on The Wave Theory, the sound event was envisioned as an ever expanding sphere. Growth, like locomotion, has direction. The emanative phenomenology of auditory experience, our hearing sounds as coming from their sources, is the partial disclosure, in audition, of the direction of the growth of the sound event. As we shall see, the growth of the sound event is consistent with the propagation of the patterned disturbance being the generation of a wave form multiplied in the medium, and that the sound event has a dynamic principle of unity that suffices to distinguish it from the motion of the local parts of the informed medium.

In cases of growth, the parts of the whole may be in motion, without growth reducing to such motion, but that does not mean that the whole is in motion, at least not in the specific sense of locomotion, a change in location over time. It is not in general true that motion in the parts of the whole involves motion, understood as locomotion, of the whole. So consider a perfect sphere rotating on a central axis. Since it is rotating, its parts are in motion. Indeed they are in motion in the specific sense that the parts of the sphere are changing their location over time. However, the sphere, while moving in some sense – it is, after all, rotating – is not moving in the specific sense of locomotion. If the location of the sphere is the bounded spatial region occupied by that body, then though its parts are moving in rotating, it is rotating in place, and so not changing its location over time. Similarly, while growth may involve the motion of the parts of a whole, without reducing to such motion, there is a sense in which a whole may grow without changing its location. In which case growth and travel are distinct.

In the 1966 film *Fantastic Voyage*, a submarine, *The Proteus*, and its crew, consisting of a surgical team, the skipper, and a security agent, are miniaturized and injected into the blood stream of a defecting Russian scientist who has suffered a blood clot in the brain, an injury sustained in his escape. Their mission is to destroy the blood clot, inoperable by conventional means. Eventually, the surviving crew emerges from the tear duct of the patient and return to their normal size in the medical laboratory. The surviving crew, in returning to their normal size, grows. Wearily, and dramatically, they are standing in place. While their boundaries may be moving in returning to normal size – their boundaries are changing location over time throughout this process – the crew themselves are not engaged in locomotion. They are standing in place.

As should be evident from the Prichard passage cited earlier, a qualification is needed. Specifically, it is not the claim that the crew are standing in place that needs qualification, but that their boundaries are moving. Initially this might seem unproblematic since their boundaries are located and their locations are changing over time. However, as Derrida (2005, 103–4) reminds us, boundaries are abstract, on some understanding of that notion. They are at least immaterial. And as Prichard (1950a) reminds us, the only material things that are moving are the parts of the bodies of the crew members. I believe that there is a way to retain talk of the movement of boundaries consistent with Prichard's insight. Aristotle distinguishes two ways in which something may move:

> There are two senses in which anything may be moved either indirectly, owing to something other than itself, or directly, owing to itself. Things are indirectly moved which are moved as being contained in something which is moved, e.g. sailors, for they are moved in a different sense from that in which the ship is moved; the ship is directly moved, they are indirectly moved, because they are in a moving vessel. (*De anima* I 3 406 a 3–8; Smith in Barnes 1984, 9)

Perhaps in cases of growth, without growth reducing to motion, what directly moves, as Prichard insists, are parts of bodies, and what indirectly moves are their boundaries. The change in the location of their boundaries, an indirect motion, is consequent upon the direct motion of the parts of the bodies. Whereas an appropriate body may be said to contain within itself the power of locomotion, a boundary – an abstraction from the body – does not contain within itself the power to change its location over time. Its motion is at best indirect, consequent upon the direct motion of other things. Let a boundary be said to bind the body whose boundary it is. Then, echoing Witt (1995, 174), we may say: "Here the relationship is not one of parts to wholes, or contents to containers, but rather" one of binding of bodies.

Typically, at least for rigid bodies, at least some of the time, their location can be understood as the spatial region encompassed by their boundaries. However, what the example of the surviving crew of *The Proteus* reveals is that this principle fails of bodies generally. If the locations of the surviving crew members are the spatial regions encompassed by their boundaries, then since their boundaries are moving, at least indirectly, so must the crew. But the crew is standing in place. This last judgment must involve a different understanding of what it is for a person to be located where they are.

Being a rigid, solid body may be sufficient, in certain practical circumstances, to locate that body within the spatial region encompassed by its stable and determinate boundaries. But not all bodies possess stable and determinate boundaries. "Where and what exactly is the surface of a cat?" asks Austin (1962, lecture 9). Even so, in cases where an entity possesses location but lacks stable and determinate boundaries, its location must be understood in terms other than the space encompassed by its stable and determinate boundaries, for it lacks such boundaries.

So far we have been discussing the location of bodies, but what of events? At least some events have locations. Battles are named after the locations where they transpired, or at least significant sites nearby. Duke William II's victory over Harold Godwinson in 1066 took place northwest of Hastings. And, sometimes at least, the locations of events and processes can change even as they occur, which is not to say that events and processes are themselves the subjects of change. The fight erupted in the bar and spilled out into the street. The conga line began in the dining room and wound its way into the living room.

According to the Lemmon (1967) criterion, events are individuated by the spatiotemporal regions of their occurrence. Suppose, for the sake of argument, that events always involve the activities of bodies that are their participants. (I doubt very much that this principle is true on Nietzschean, and, ultimately, Heraclitean, grounds – there is no lightning that flashes, just the activity, the flashing, *Zur Genealogie der Moral* 1 13.) Finite bodies are generated and destroyed, and while they exist, they occupy space, so we can envision their careers as spacetime worms. Now consider the segment of a spacetime worm bounded by the beginning and end of an event of which it is a participant. By the Lemmon criterion, the event itself is individuated by the mereological sum of the segments of the spacetime worms of its participants. If accepted, it would follow that events are located, indeed in the spatial region of their occurrence understood as the total space occupied by their participants at any given moment of the event's occurrence. However, as Davidson observes, one can accept that events are spatiotemporal particulars, without accepting the Lemmon criterion. "An explosion is an event to which we find no difficulty in assigning a location, although again we may be baffled by a request to describe the total area" (1969, 304). Even if we accept that events are located where they occur, the location of an event may be said of in many ways. It may be an occasion-sensitive matter what counts as the location of an event.

Where is the sound event? An answer may depend upon what is practically at stake in asking the question. On one natural understanding of the location of a sound, sounds are where we hear them. On that understanding, sounds are located at the intersection of the hearer and the propagation of the patterned disturbance. That understanding emphasizes the actualization of sound in hearing (compare *De anima* 3 2 426 a 2–20). So on some occasions at least, sounds may be said to be located where we hear them, and it is natural to do so when the actualization of sound by hearing is practically salient in the given circumstances. On many occasions, locating a sound where it is heard is both natural and serviceable. On other occasions, governed by different practical concerns, the location of a sound may be understood in a different way.

On occasions where a perceiver-dependent location of a sound would be inappropriate, and given that the sound event, as conceived by The Wave Theory, lacks stable boundaries (they are in constant indirect motion), we might locate the sound event at its epicenter, the point from which the patterned disturbance is propagating in every direction, at its source. That the boundaries of the sound event are in constant indirect motion would suffice for bafflement at a request to describe its total area. And given the neat symmetry of the event, its boundaries are moving in every direction from its source, it is natural to assign its location at the point of origin (compare Sorenson's 2009, 138–9, discussion of the location of earthquakes). If we locate the sound event at its source, being the epicenter of audible activity, listening to the birds outside your window, the students outside your door, the cars going down your street, the sounds you hear would, on that understanding, be located at the place where they originate. Sounds being located at their sources, at least on this understanding, is, in this way, *pace* Pasnau (1999b), consistent with The Wave Theory (see O'Shaughnessy 2009, 123, for a partial anticipation of this point). Not only does the occasion-sensitivity of sound undermine Pasnau's objection, but it undermines, as well, a recent metaphysical taxonomy of sound as distal, medial, and proximate (Casati and Dokic 2014). If the location of sound is an occasion-sensitive matter, then a metaphysical taxonomy based on the location of sound is, to that extent, vitiated.

According to The Wave Theory, as developed herein, the propagation of a patterned disturbance, in every direction, through a dense and elastic medium is the progressive instantiation of a wave form, a kind of dynamic in-formation, realized by the motion of the local parts of the medium, "the oscillation of certain particles." Though the sound event may be said to have location, the propagation of the patterned disturbance through a dense and elastic medium is not best modeled on the locomotion of a body, like a sonic missile. As O'Callaghan (2007, 2009) observes, that is not how auditory experience presents sound as coming from its source. Since the patterned disturbance at the boundary of the sound event is indirectly moving in every direction, thus determining, under certain idealizations, an ever expanding sphere, the propagation of a patterned disturbance is better modeled on growth rather than locomotion. Sounds are heard to come from their sources in the sense that the direction of the propagation of the patterned disturbance in the growth of the sound event is disclosed in auditory experience. On that model, there are certain natural alternative understandings of the location of a sound event. Locating the sound event in the space encompassed by stable and determinate boundaries is not possible since these are in constant indirect motion. On certain occasions, for certain practical purposes, sounds may be said to be where we hear them. On other occasions, for other purposes, sounds may be said to be located at their epicenter, at or near their sources. And each alternative is consistent with the sound event being the propagation, in every direction, of a patterned disturbance through a dense and imperfectly elastic medium understood as the progressive instantiation of a wave form realized by the motion of the local parts of the medium.

As a dynamic in-formation, the sound event has a kind of unity irreducible to the motion of the local parts of the in-formed medium. Conceiving of the propagation of sound on the model of the locomotion of a body – a sonic missile – mistakes the unity of the sound event for the unity of a body. Sound events may lack the unity of a body. After all, events and bodies have different modes of being. But sound events nevertheless possess sufficient unity to distinguish them from the in-formed medium that they existentially depend upon. It is a dynamic unity as befitting the double duration and spatial mutation of sound. Though the motion involved in the dynamic unity is at best indirect, being the progressive instantiation of a wave form, it is the force with which it propagates in every direction that explains the growth of the sound event. While the sound event may be realized by the motion of the local parts of the medium, "the oscillation of certain particles," it is the force of its propagation, communicated from one part to the next, that determines the dynamic in-formation. The sound event is realized by the motion of the local parts of the medium without reducing to such motion because of its dynamic unity, the force with which it grows in the dense and imperfectly elastic medium (on dynamic principles of unity, see Johnston 2006a). And it is the direction of this force that is disclosed, more or less clearly, in the emanative phenomenology of auditory experience. What Prichard's mathematician was certain about was the unity of sound. In misconceiving the unity of a sound as the unity of a body, he was misled into thinking that sounds travel like missiles. But in conceiving of the unity of the sound, or at least its principle, as the force of the dynamic in-formation, sounds do not so much as travel as they grow.

We hear sounds. We also hear sources. What is the relation between the sounds that we hear and their audible sources? Is our awareness of the sources of sound mediated in the way that the neo-Berkeleans suggest? Or is Heidegger right in insisting that we can attend to the sources of sound without first attending to the sounds that they generate? In the next chapter I shall argue for the Heideggerian alternative. In hearing the call of the feral parakeet I am explicitly aware of the parakeet's call and only implicitly aware of its sound. I do not, then, attend to the parakeet's call by attending to its sound. Rather, we hear the sources of sound through, or in, the sounds they generate. And, as we shall see, the principle of sympathy explains how this may be so.

CHAPTER 4

Sources

4.1 The Heideggerian Alternative

On one understanding, the source of a sound may be a body that possesses the power of sounding, that is, the power to engage in a sound-generating activity, a thing source in the terminology of Casati, Bona, and Dokic (2013). On another understanding, the source of a sound is simply the sound-generating activity, the event or process that generates the sound, an event source. Indeed, there may be sound-generating events or processes not involving the activity of bodies (though for the most part we shall ignore this possibility). Audible sources, the sources disclosed in auditory experience, are sound-generating events or processes. It is the audible activities of bodies, or at least sound-generating events or processes, that we hear and not the bodies themselves (though perhaps we may attend to these on the supposition that their audible activities constitute a dynamic aural image of them, Chapter 3.4). We hear sounds, and we hear their sources. What role do sounds play in affording the perceiver with auditory awareness of their sources?

The neo-Berkelean has an answer, ready to hand, that many find nearly irresistible. We hear the sources of sound by hearing the sounds they generate. We hear a body's audible activity by hearing the sound that activity generates. Hearing sounds affords the perceiver with auditory awareness of their sources since the immediate presentation of the sound in auditory experience constitutes, in a manner yet to be explained, the mediate presentation of its source.

I do not accept the neo-Berkelean answer. I believe that its central claims are at odds with the phenomenology of auditory experience. Instead, I shall refine and elaborate a Heideggerian account of the role that sounds play in affording the perceiver with auditory awareness of their distal sources (see Leddington 2014 for a different defense of the Heideggerian alternative and the replies by O'Callaghan 2014 and Nudds 2014). We do not hear sources by hearing their sounds as the neo-Berkelean would have it. Rather we hear the sources of sound directly. In cases where a perceiver can hear the source of a sound, the call of a feral parakeet, say, they are explicitly aware of the call and only implicitly aware of its sound. The application of Fulkerson's (2014) distinction between explicit and implicit awareness to Heidegger's (1935/2000) observation about audition is the first of the refinements. There is a sense in which we hear a source through, or in (Leddington 2014), the sound it produces. The sound they hear is a perceptual medium through which the audible activities of distal bodies are disclosed. And sympathy is the principle that makes possible the presentation of sources in auditory experience through the perceptual medium of sound. On the refined and elaborated Heideggerian account, the role of sounds in affording the perceiver with auditory awareness of distal sources is limited to being an audible media through which, or in which, their sources may be heard.

4.2   The Function of Audition

Begin with two claims recently defended by Nudds:

(1) The function of auditory perception is to afford the perceiver with awareness of the distal sources of sound.
(2) In hearing a sound in a complex sonic environment with multiple active sources of sound, that the sound that the perceiver hears is segmented from all that they hear is due, in part, to their auditory system identifying its source.

Concerning the first claim, Nudds writes:

> It is uncontroversial to suggest that auditory perception tells us about the sources of sounds as well as about sounds. The suggestion that I am going to develop is that the function of auditory perception is to tell us about the sources of sounds – that perceiving the sources of sounds is what auditory perception is for and that what sounds we hear we hear as a consequence of the particular way auditory perception functions to tell us about the sources of sounds. (2010, 284)

The function of auditory perception is to afford the perceiver with awareness of the distal sources of sound. This is a teleological claim. The end of auditory perception, that for the sake of which perceivers are equipped with audition, is the presentation, in audition, of distal events and processes in the natural environment. It is also an explanatory claim. The operation of audition adequate to its function constitutes an explanatorily relevant kind. It is also objective. The operation of audition adequate to its function constitutes an explanatorily relevant kind independently of whether anyone accepts that it does. Moreover, this objective, teleological, explanatory claim seems naturalistically acceptable. It is, at any rate, overwhelmingly plausible to suppose that an animal's ability to hear distal events and processes in the natural environment contributes to its fitness. And if that is right, that the function of audition is to present distal events and processes in the natural environment is plausibly determined by evolutionary pressures.

Nudds' claim about the function of audition generates a tension within the Peripatetic framework. Consider the following two claims about the proper sensibles:

(1) Proper sensibles are perceptible to one sensory modality alone (for example, one can see colors, but not hear, smell, taste, or touch them).
(2) Proper sensibles are the final cause of perception (for example, sight is for the sake of seeing colors in the light and the luminous in the dark).

The difficulty is that, at least in the case of audition, these two claims cannot be true together.

Consider the second claim first, that the proper sensibles are the final cause of perception. The proper object of sight is the visible (*De anima* 2 7 418 b 27) and there are two kinds of *visibilia*, color that is visible in light and the luminous, such as bioluminescence or starlight, visible only in the dark (*De anima* 2 7 419 a 1–7; the nice example of starlight is due to Philoponus *In de anima* 347 11). If sight is for the sake of seeing colors in the light and the luminous in the dark (*Metaphysica* Θ 8 1050 a 10), then is audition for the sake of hearing sounds? Nudds denies this, claiming, instead, that the function of audition is to afford the perceiver with awareness of distal events in the natural environment. Suppose, then, that audition is for the sake of hearing distal sources. Arguably it is that in which audition's selective advantage lies. Hearing sounds would be incidental to audition, so conceived, at least relative to its end, even if one can only ever hear sources through, or in, the sounds they generate. The difficulty is that the final cause, the distal sources, are perceptible to more than one sense alone. Thus one might hear one of London's feral parakeets calling as one sees that parakeet calling. So there is no one thing that is audible yet perceptible to no other sensory modality and that for the sake of which we possess audition. (1) and (2) are generalizations that fail for the case of audition if we accept Nudds' claim. Perhaps sounds are audible and perceptible to one sense alone and so would make (1) true, but (2) would fail – audition is not for the sake of hearing sounds, but their sources. The audible sources of sound would make (2) true, but (1) would fail – audible sources may be available to more than one sense.

That (1) and (2) fail to be jointly true of audition signals the breakdown of the guiding explanatory framework of *De anima* 2:

> It is necessary for the student of these forms of soul first to find a definition of each, expressive of what it is, and then to investigate its derivative properties, &c. But if we are to express what each is, viz. what the thinking power is, or the perceptive, or the nutritive, we must go farther back and first give an account of thinking or perceiving; for activities and actions are prior in definition to potentialities. If so, and if, still prior to them, we should have reflected on their correlative objects, then for the same reason we must first determine about them, i.e. about food and the objects of perception and thought. (Aristotle, *De anima* 2 4 415 a 14–22; Smith in Barnes 1984, 26)

Aristotle's explanatory strategy has two parts.

First, Aristotle proposes to explain perceptual capacities in terms of what they are the capacity for, perceiving. Specifically, perceptual activity is prior in account to the potential for such activity, the relevant perceptual capacity. Possessing a capacity is a way for things to be, and what it is to be that way depends upon what it is to be its exercise. So possessing audition is a way for at least animals to be, and what it is to be that way depends upon what it is to hear. Thus, if capacities are powers or potentialities, as Aristotle conceives of them, then they ontologically depend upon what they are the potential for. (On ontological dependence, see Fine 1995. On this reading of priority in account, see Peramatzis 2011. For a contemporary defense of this claim, see Kalderon forthcoming.)

Second, perceptual activities, the exercise of our perceptual capacities, are themselves partly explained in terms of their correlative objects. It will emerge that, at least with respect to perception, Aristotle means, more specifically, proper objects, understood as sensible objects perceptible in themselves and perceptible to that sense alone. So what it is to hear depends upon the presentation, in auditory experience, of the proper object of audition, sound. Crucially, that is consistent with auditory experience presenting more than just sound.

Thinking of perceptual capacities as individuated by that for the sake of which they are a potential for allows Aristotle to think that there are exercises of our perceptual capacities that are not the presentation of the proper sensibles, notably, when they are the presentation of common or incidental sensibles. And more besides – the difference between proper objects such as color and sound are perceptible as well. In this way, Aristotle broadens the domain of the perceptible (Sorabji 1971, 2003). Sight may enable a perceiver to see colors in the light and the luminous in the dark, but it enables the perceiver to see other *visibilia* such as motion, a common sensible. But the presentation of motion in sight is incidental to its operation. Sight is for the sake of seeing colors in the light and the luminous in the dark. But, even liberalizing the domain of the perceptible as Plato conceives of it, in continuing to understand the presentation of proper sensibles as that for the sake of which a perceiver possesses the relevant perceptual capacity, Aristotle cleaves too closely to the Platonic tradition undone by audition whose function is to afford the perceiver awareness of distal events and processes in the natural environment that are perceptually available to other sensory modalities, such as a storm whistling in the chimney or the call of a feral parakeet. One may feel the storm whistling in the chimney and see the parakeet calling.

The case of audition undermines the second part of Aristotle's explanatory strategy, but not the first. Nothing about audition's function is inconsistent with perceptual activity being prior in account to the capacity for such activity, that perceptual capacities are individuated by what they are the potential for, and so ontologically depend upon their proper exercise. Rather, Nudds' claim is a challenge to the second part of Aristotle's explanatory strategy, inherited from Plato, if liberalized, that perceptual activities are, in turn, to be explained in terms of the presentation of their proper objects. Moreover, nothing about audition's function is inconsistent with the exercise of a perceptual capacity being explained in terms of the objects that they present. It is not the claim that perceptual activities are explained in terms of their correlative objects that is the difficulty here. It is the restriction of correlative objects, in terms of which perceptual activities are explained, to proper objects that is the source of the difficulty. For at least with respect to an animal's capacity for audition, that power is not for the presentation of objects disclosed through the exercise of that power alone, but for the presentation of objects potentially disclosed through the exercise of other sensory powers and typically in concert with them.

4.3   Sources and the Discrimination of Sound

Audition is for the sake of hearing the sources of sounds, understood as sound-generating events or processes. If audition is for the sake of hearing, not sounds, but their sources, then hearing sound is incidental to audition, relative to its end, even if one can only ever hear sources through, or in, the sounds they generate. Perhaps, in certain contexts, one may even say that one hears a source by hearing its sound, but only in a sense unavailable to the neo-Berkelean (Nudds sometimes writes this way). In Peripatetic terminology, this is an instance of hypothetical necessity (*Physica* 2 9; for useful discussion, see Charles 1988). The necessity is hypothetical since the end of audition, to hear the sources of sounds, is presupposed. Given the end of audition, to hear the distal sources of sounds, it is necessary to hear the sounds that they generate.

Recall, according to the neo-Berkelean, sounds are distinguished from their sources in auditory experience in that only the former are the immediate objects of audition and that we hear the latter by hearing the former. For the neo-Berkelean, the preposition "by" is a placeholder for the presentative function of sounds, their presenting their sources in presenting themselves in audition. What is this presentative function? One of the lessons we learned from Heidegger was that there is more to the presentative function of sound than the sources we hear being necessarily accompanied, in audition, by their sounds, since sounds may lack this presentative function and remain a necessary accompaniment of the sources that we hear. Moreover, the mediate presentation of sources by the immediate presentation of their sounds is unlike more ordinary cases of perceiving one thing by perceiving another, so in what does this extraordinary case consist? Typically, neo-Berkeleans are no more forthcoming than sense-datum theorists were in giving an account of this presentative function.

According to the neo-Berkelean, sounds are the immediate objects of audition in something like the following sense. Sounds are audible. Moreover, sounds are audible in themselves. Sounds are audible in themselves in the sense that they contain within themselves the power of their own audibility. So one can hear a sound without hearing any other thing. In hearing a sound, auditory experience affords the perceiver with explicit awareness of that sound independently of hearing any other thing. In this sense are they at least among the immediate objects of audition. Though, of course, neo-Berkeleans typically follow Berkeley in maintaining, as well, that sounds are the only immediate objects of audition. Sounds alone have within themselves the power of their own audibility, even if neo-Berkeleans do not go so far as Berkeley in maintaining that sounds are the sole objects of audition. *Pace* Berkeley, sources too are audible. However, they are not audible in themselves. They do not contain within themselves the power of their own audibility, but are only audible by hearing other objects that are audible in themselves, namely the sounds that they generate. In this sense are they the mediate objects of audition.

So understood, sound could not be the immediate object of audition. Bracket, for the moment, worries about the, as of yet, unexplained presentative function of sound in auditory experience. Focus, instead, on the prior claim that sounds are audible in themselves, that sounds contain within themselves the power of their own audibility with the implication that hearing a sound does not require hearing any other audible object. Nudds' second claim, if true, suffices to establish that sounds are not audible in themselves in the way that the neo-Berkelean requires. Specifically, Nudds claims that in hearing a sound in a complex sonic environment with multiple active sources of sound, the sound the perceiver hears is segmented from all that they hear due, in part, to their auditory system identifying its source. And, as we shall see, that is inconsistent with sounds being audible in themselves. If anything, something like the reverse is true. In such circumstances, sounds are audible, but not audible in themselves, but audible only insofar as one hears the sources that generate them. There is then, I shall suggest, a sense in which sounds are better thought of as audible media through which, or in which, sources may be heard. At the very least, if sounds were audible media, in the intended sense, they would be audible, but not audible in themselves, but owing their audibility to other things – the sources heard through, or in, the sounds.

Audition, like vision and tactile perception, involves grouping, segmentation, and recognition (Bregman 1990). When, upon the hill in Greenwich Park near the Royal Observatory, I witnessed the Ballardian spectacle of feral parakeets traversing the mirrored towers of the City of London, the call of the feral parakeet was not all that I heard. I could hear, as well, the trees rustling in the light breeze, the occasional shouts of children playing, people conversing, a bicycle braking, dogs barking. Like most public spaces, Greenwich Park is a complex sonic environment with multiple active sources of sound, and the call of the feral parakeet was not all that there was to hear. The patterned disturbance reaching my ears was not solely caused by the parakeet's calling. And yet I could hear it clearly.

A patterned disturbance, occurring in a given temporal interval, can be analyzed into frequency components, component sine waves of a given frequency and amplitude. When longitudinal pressure waves superimpose, their frequency components additively combine to produce a new complex pressure wave. Given the detected frequency components of the complex pressure wave are not solely caused by the call of the feral parakeet, how does my auditory system afford me the capacity to hear the sound of the feral parakeet? The auditory system would need to somehow group together the frequency components that constitute the sound of the feral parakeet's call.

According to Nudds (2009, 2010), the auditory system groups frequency components by exploiting clues as to the likely source of the sound. There are a variety of different such clues, and many can be dominated by other clues.

Some clues are synchronic. That is, sometimes frequency components occurring at a time are related in such a way that it is unlikely that they are the products of distinct sources. For example, the vibration of a material object will determine frequency components of the patterned disturbance that are harmonically related to a fundamental frequency. So there is a tendency for the auditory system to group together frequency components at a time that are harmonically related since it is unlikely that they are produced by distinct sources.

Some clues are diachronic. That is, sometimes frequency components occurring over time are related in such a way that it is unlikely that they are the products of distinct sources. Thus, for example, the frequency components of a sound produced by a source will have the same onset time, and they will change over time in similar ways. So there is a tendency for the auditory system to group together frequency components that are diachronically related in important ways since it is unlikely that they are produced by distinct sources.

Nudds (2009, 74) observes that while the clues discussed so far are "bottom-up" or stimulus-driven groupings, there are as well "top-down" groupings, especially of sequences of frequency components. The idea is that certain frequency components are grouped together because they fit together to form a pattern recognized by the auditory system to likely be produced by a single source. Thus, for example, one might hear a bottle bouncing, as opposed to breaking, and this is likely to be due to such a top-down grouping. See Bregman's (1990, chapter 4) discussion of what he calls schema-based segregation and integration.

Notice how the clues to grouping together frequency components constituting a heard sound are all based on features of its material source. Thus, for example, the size of an object will determine the lowest frequency at which it will vibrate. This allows us to hear that one object dropped is larger than another object that is also dropped. How exactly the auditory system extracts information about the material source and what information it extracts from the grouped frequency components is presently not well understood.

However, exactly, the auditory system performs this feat, the important point is that in a sonically complex environment with multiple active sources of sound, an individual sound is segmented from all that is heard, in part, by identifying its source. If a likely source is not identified by the auditory system, then the frequency components will not be grouped together and the sound will not be segmented from all that is heard. If in hearing the products of multiple active sources of sound, none of the sources are discriminated, all that would be heard is a kind of undifferentiated noise. Hearing the sources of sound lends intelligibility to what is heard. The audible accessibility of the source intelligibly differentiates, in auditory experience, the sound it generates.

At least, then, in ordinary cases of hearing ecological sound, the sound is segmented from all that is heard only by virtue of the auditory system identifying its source. In such cases, sounds are not, in fact, audible in themselves. It is not possible to hear the sound segmented from all that is heard in and of itself quite apart from hearing anything else. In such cases, one hears the sound only insofar as one hears the event or process that generates the sound, only insofar as one hears its audible source. At least in sonically complex environments with multiple active sources of sound, sounds are not audible in themselves; they do not contain within themselves the power of their own audibility, but are only audible insofar as one hears their sources as well.

The neo-Berkeleans share with Berkeley the conviction that sounds are audible in themselves. They depart from Berkeley in maintaining that we hear, in addition to sounds, their sources. These latter are not audible in themselves, but are only audible insofar as we hear their sounds. But the sounds we hear in sonically complex environments are not audible in themselves as the neo-Berkelean conceives of them. Nor, in such circumstances, is there an explicit experience of sound had independently of hearing anything else. So there is no explicit experience of sound to mediately present its source as the neo-Berkelean requires.

I do not claim that we always hear sounds by hearing the sources that produce them. I claim only that in a sonically complex environment with multiple active sources of sound, we hear these sounds by hearing their sources. One case is sufficient to defeat the neo-Berkelean claim that sounds, in general, are audible in themselves. Since I do not claim that we always hear sounds by hearing their sources, it is thus consistent with the present argument that there be cases where sounds are heard while their sources remain inaudible. Perhaps in listening to stereo speakers, we hear the sounds they make and not their source. After all, if you can hear the speaker when playing – say, if the cone is torn or it somehow rattles – then it is a bad speaker.

4.4 Sympathy and Auditory Presentation

Sounds need not be audible in themselves. Rather, in some cases at least, they are more like audible media. What does it mean to describe sounds as perceptual media? Perceptual media need not be thought of as physical media, the movement of whose local parts, "the oscillation of certain particles," realizes the progressive instantiation of a wave form. While the idea of physical media merely answers to the demands of being a causal intermediary, the idea of perceptual media answers to the demands of perceptual accessibility. So consider the following. Just as illumination makes the visible perceptually accessible, sound makes the activities of distal bodies perceptually accessible. Without illumination, the colors of distal bodies remain unseen; without sound, the activities of distal bodies remain unheard. (Absent the ring of Gyges, *Republic* 2 359 a–360 d, becoming invisible is not possible for us, but becoming inaudible is easy enough – simply stop moving.) One sees through, or in, illuminated media, such as air or water, and thereby perceives the colors of distal bodies arrayed in the natural environment. One hears through, or in, audible media, the sound, and thereby perceives the activities of distal bodies arrayed in the natural environment.

By means of the propagation of light waves, the visible aspects of distal bodies are seen. By means of the propagation, in every direction, of the patterned disturbance through a dense and imperfectly elastic medium, that is, by means of sound, the audible activities of distal bodies are heard.

Sound, like the illuminant, is perceptible. Moreover, sound, like the illuminant, is perceptible in a certain way. Concerning the perception of the illuminant, Hilbert writes:

> Do we see how an object is illuminated or do we see the illumination itself? On phenomenological grounds the first option seems better to me. What we see as changing with the illumination is an aspect of the object itself, not the light source or the space surrounding the object. (2005, 150–1)

One sees the character of the illumination by seeing the way objects are illuminated. When viewing a brightly lit pantry, one sees the brightness of the pantry by seeing the brightly lit objects arranged in it. So the illuminant is visible, though not visible in itself, but owes its visibility to the objects that it illuminates. (For a comparison with Aristotle's definition of transparency, *De anima* 2 7 418 b 4–6, see Kalderon 2015, 41–2.)

Like the illuminant, sound is perceptible, though perceptible in a certain way. In cases where one hears a sound and its source, one hears the character of a sound by hearing the activities of its distal source. (Think of how difficult it is to describe ecological sound without describing audible aspects of its source.) In such cases, sound is audible, though not audible in itself, but owes its audibility to the distal source that it discloses.

Bregman describes a game that provides a useful analogy:

> The game is this. Your friend digs two narrow channels up from the side of the lake. Each is a few feet long and a few inches wide and they are spaced a few feet apart. Halfway up each one, your friend stretches a handkerchief and fastens it to the side of the channel. As waves reach the side of the lake they travel up the channels and cause the two handkerchiefs to go into motion. You are allowed to look only at the handkerchiefs and from their motions to answer a series of questions: How many boats are there on the lake and where are they? Which is the most powerful one? Which is the closer? Is the wind blowing? Has any large object been dropped suddenly into the lake? Solving this problem seems impossible, but it is a strict analogy to the problem faced by our auditory systems. The lake represents the lake of air that surrounds us. The two channels are our two ear canals, and the handkerchiefs are our ear drums. The only information that the auditory system has available to it, or ever will have, is the vibrations of these two ear drums. Yet it seems able to answer questions very like the ones that were asked by the side of the lake: How many people are talking? Which one is louder, or closer? Is there a machine humming in the background? (1990, 5–6)

One striking aspect of Bregman's analogy is how it presupposes that the function of the auditory system is to afford awareness of distal events and processes in the natural environment. The game is to figure out how such awareness is afforded by sensitivity to proximal perturbations in the surrounding medium, be it air or water. The proximal perturbations in the surrounding medium, the patterned disturbances impinging upon the perceiver, while there to be sensed, considered in and of themselves, are relatively unimportant features of the natural environment. Indeed, in Bregman's proposed game, he takes such sensitivity for granted. What is important is not the sensitivity to proximal perturbations in the medium, but sensitivity to the information they carry about distal events and processes in the natural environment, for it is in virtue of this latter sensitivity that the auditory system affords the perceiver with auditory awareness of the distal environment.

The ear channels the longitudinal pressure waves into its canal where they come into conflict with the tympanic membrane. The potential pattern of activation of local receptors constitutes the sensitivity to such proximal perturbations. As Bregman's analogy brings out, the task of the auditory system is to somehow extract information about the distal sources of the proximal perturbations. Nevertheless, quite apart from this central role, the end of audition, to afford the perceiver with auditory awareness of the distal environment, the proximal perturbations, the force of the patterned disturbance coming into conflict with the tympanic membrane, are there to be sensed, even if, as Heidegger insists, they are rarely if at all attended to, in familiar every day instances of hearing ecological sound.

Suppose, hypothetically, there could be an auditory experience that arose from this sensitivity to proximal perturbations, quite apart from what information they could provide about distal sources, so that the experience was confined to only what was proximately impinging upon the perceiver. Perhaps auditory experience upon first regaining consciousness may approximate what we are presently supposing. And perhaps the earliest forms of audition, in the evolution of animals with auditory capacities, were similar. What would be experienced would be a kind of undifferentiated noise. Upon first coming to consciousness, the perceiver hears a sound, but cannot make out its source. As things come into focus for the perceiver, they come to hear the source of the sound. In hearing the sound, there is a marked increase in the intelligibility of what is heard. Even in the case where the patterned disturbance was produced by a single source, there is a difference in audible intelligibility between hearing the sound as produced by that audible source and hearing the sound and being unaware of its source. What is heard is no longer mere noise, but the storm whistling in the chimney or the call of a feral parakeet, say.

But even hearing a noise, like the case of grasping or enclosure, understood as a mode of haptic perception, would involve the presentation of something extra-somatic. The longitudinal pressure waves may be impinging upon the perceiver, but they are extra-somatic for all that. This hypothetical limited auditory experience is no mere auditory sensation, but a mode of auditory perception, the presentation, in auditory experience, of an extra-somatic event or process. And like the case of grasping or enclosure, understood as a mode of haptic perception, it is sympathy that makes the presentation in conscious experience of the extra-somatic possible. The force of the propagation of the patterned disturbance comes into conflict with the force of the tympanic membrane and this gives rise to the hypothetical limited auditory experience. Moreover, this limited auditory experience is no mere auditory sensation, a conscious modification of the perceiving subject brought about by impingement from without, but the perception of extra-somatic events or processes. Even supposing that the impingement of proximal perturbations occasioned in the perceiver intensive auditory sensation, such sensation is only the presentation of this noise insofar as it is experienced as a sympathetic response to an extra-somatic event. Sympathy is what makes for this difference. The hypothetical limited experience that auditory sensitivity to proximal perturbations gives rise to involves the sympathetic presentation of those perturbations.

One important difference between this hypothetical limited form of auditory experience and grasping or enclosure, understood as a mode of haptic perception, is the relative passivity of the former compared to the latter. In the conflict between the force of the propagation of the sound, the dynamic principle of unity of the sound event, and the countervailing force determined by the tension and elasticity of the tympanic membrane, the former acts upon the latter and the latter merely resists the former insofar as it can (there are limits, of course, one can blow an ear drum). In grasping or enclosure, understood as a mode of haptic perception, by contrast, the hand, unlike the tympanic membrane, is active. Indeed, it is the active wax of haptic perception.

The limited auditory experience is hypothetical, even if actual auditory experiences, such as those undergone when coming to consciousness, may approximate it. However, when we consider more ordinary cases of auditory perception, such as hearing the storm whistling in the chimney, the three-motored plane, the Mercedes in immediate distinction from the Volkswagen, not only does sympathy play an expanded role in the presentation, in audition, of the activities of distal bodies, but, moreover, this sympathetic presentation is made possible by the perceiver listening out for distal events or processes, thus reinstating the analogy with haptic perception.

The perceiver hears the distal source in the sound that it generates. Moreover the perceiver hears in conformity with the sound that the distal source generates. And it is the principle of sympathy that governs the disclosure, over time, of the distal sound-generating events and processes.

The perceiver hears the distal source in the sound that it generates. On one construal of Bregman's analogy, perhaps not the only one, hearing the sources of sound through, or in, the sounds that they generate is not unlike the quasi-visual perception induced by Bach-y-Rita's tactile-visual substitution system (for an overview, see Bach-y Rita and Kercel 2002). Bach-y-Rita's tactile-visual substitution system involved a head-mounted camera wired to electrodes attached to the perceiver's body. The idea was to map the visual information captured by the camera onto a pattern of tactile activations. Perceivers that were able to control the camera by "looking" around could, within a day, make quasi-visual reports about the number, size, and relative distance of objects arrayed in their environments. At this point, perceivers were explicitly aware, in a quasi-visual mode of awareness, of distal objects in the natural environment and merely implicitly aware of any tactile sensation. In contrast, at the beginning of this procedure, when the apparatus was first mounted and used, the perceiver was only explicitly aware of the electrodes' stimulation. Their experience only came to quasi-visually present distal objects and their spatial properties when they learned to sympathetically respond to the electrodes' stimulation. In so doing, they learn to "see" distal objects through, or in, what they feel. Moreover, if sympathy is indeed the principle governing this quasi-visual presentation, then that would explain the pattern of attention described earlier. If the perceiver, having mastered the tactile-visual substitution system, were to explicitly attend to the electrodes' stimulation, this would erode the sympathetic presentation of the distal objects and their spatial properties. Similarly, in hearing a distal event or process, such as hearing the storm whistling in the chimney, the three-motored plane, the Mercedes in immediate distinction from the Volkswagen, the perceiver is explicitly aware of the source and only implicitly aware of the sound it generates. They hear the source through, or in, the sound it generates. Moreover, if sympathy were the principle of the disclosure, in audition, of distal events and processes, this would explain this pattern of attention. If the perceiver could indeed listen away from the source, listen abstractly, and attend only to the sound it generates, this would erode the sympathetic presentation of the distal source.

The perceiver hears in conformity with the sound that the distal source generates. In hearing distal events and processes in the natural environment, the perceiver is explicitly aware of these sources. However, reflection on perceptual constancy reveals that the phenomenological character of auditory experience is not exhausted by the object of explicit awareness. An implicit awareness of the sound they generate contributes, as well, to the phenomenology of the perceiver's auditory experience. Specifically, an implicit awareness of sound contributes to the way in which the explicit object of the auditory experience is presented therein. So consider approaching a continuous source of sound, such as a waterfall. The waterfall, heard from different distances, sounds different. Heard from afar, the waterfall sounds quieter than it does when heard from nearby. As the perceiver approaches the waterfall, the sound of waterfall increases in volume. But throughout the perceiver's approach, the perceiver hears the constant

flowing of the waterfall. The flowing of the waterfall is not experienced as
getting louder so much as the perceiver is getting in a better position to
hear just how loud the waterfall really is. The flowing of the waterfall, the
constant object of explicit auditory awareness, is not experienced as changing in the way that it would have to if it were in fact getting louder, only
its auditory appearance is changing with a change in auditory perspective.
The flowing of the waterfall, the object of explicit awareness and the constant element in the phenomenology of stability and flux, sounds different
when heard from different auditory perspectives. Hearing the sound of the
waterfall, from a given auditory perspective, may be implicit, it may be
recessive and in the background, so that it does not compete for attentive
resources directed toward the flowing of the waterfall, but it contributes to
the conscious character of the perceiver's auditory experience by being the
way in which the distal process is presented in that experience. The auditory disclosure of a distal source just is hearing that source in the sound
that it generates and hearing in conformity with that sound. And that just
is the exercise of a sympathetic capacity.

   In sympathetically disclosing the distal sources of sound, auditory experience is constitutively shaped by the distal events and processes that it
discloses. The conscious character of hearing a watch ticking is constituted,
in part, by the audible ticking of the watch. And the conscious character of
hearing the call of a feral parakeet is constituted, in part, by the feral parakeet's call. What it is like for the perceiver to hear the ticking of the watch
depends upon and derives from what the ticking of the watch is like – how
loud it is, its distinctive timbre, what the mechanism sounds like. And
what it is like for the perceiver to hear the call of the feral parakeet depends
upon and derives from what the call of the parakeet is like – how loud it is,
its distinctive timbre, its sharpness and urgency. Moreover, what it is like
for the perceiver to hear these events and processes depends, as well, upon
the perceiver's perspective. There are better and worse perspectives, even
if better and worse is said of in many ways. Auditory experience formally
assimilates to its object, relative to the perceiver's partial perspective, as a
consequence of being constitutively shaped by that object as presented to
that perspective, a constitutive shaping made possible by the sympathetic
presentation of that object in auditory experience. Constitutive shaping
of auditory experience by its object is a "communion" with that object –
in undergoing that experience the perceiver is united, in a way, with the
object of their perception. Moreover, as with Plotinus (Chapter 2.8), this
unity explains in part, the similarity between the auditory experience and
its audible object. The formal assimilation of auditory perception to its

object, at least relative to the perceiver's auditory perspective, is the effect of constitutive shaping, and thus its conscious character depends upon and derives from, at least in part, the audible character of the object heard.

Recall, we are generalizing from Plotinus in taking the unity of auditory presentation to be explanatorily prior to the operation of sympathy (Chapter 2.8). Auditory presentation of distal sources is not being constructed from elements and principles understood independently of their auditory presentation, rather the unity of the perceiver and the distal events and processes is presupposed, and sympathy merely analytically explicates the intelligible structure of this presupposed unity. Not only does sympathy only operate within a unity, but that unity is reducible to no other thing.

Auditory presentation is an irreducible unity. If sensory presentation is a distinctive kind of unity, a "communion" with its object, then auditory presentation is more distinctive still. Insofar as auditory presentation, like haptic presentation, is governed by the principle of sympathy, it is a mode of being with. Hearing the call of the feral parakeet is a way of being with that bird at least insofar as it is engaged in audible activity. Whereas haptic presentation is corporeal, it is a way for a conscious animate body to be with another body, auditory presentation, while involving a conscious animate body, is not completely corporeal, since it involves a conscious animate body, the perceiver, being with an event or process (which may or may not involve bodies as participants). Distal bodies are never present in auditory experience *qua* bodies, but only as audible participants of an unfolding audible event or process. Auditory presentation, like haptic presentation, is a kind of disclosure with duration. However, whereas the *substrata* of audible qualities are not wholly present at any given moment, the objects of haptic perception may be, as when one feels relatively static features of bodies such as their texture or temperature. The *substrata* of audible qualities, on the other hand, are essentially dynamic entities not wholly present at any given moment. They unfold through the temporal interval of their sounding. If heard, they are disclosed, in audition, over time. In hearing something, we listen along with it.

4.5 Listening

Let us return to the Protagorean model (Chapter 1.2) and the challenges it faces in applying to audition (Chapter 3.1). According to the Protagorean model, perception is the joint upshot of forces in conflict. Grasping or enclosure, understood as a mode of haptic perception, is itself naturally understood on this model. On the one hand, there is the force of the activity of the grasping hand. On the other hand, there are the self-maintaining forces of the rigid, solid body. Making an effort to more precisely mold the hand to the body's contours and the resistance of the self-maintaining forces that determine that body's rigidity and solidity together give rise to an experience of that body's overall shape and volume.

Can auditory perception be understood on the Protagorean model, as the joint upshot of forces in conflict? Consider, again, the hypothetical auditory experience whose content is limited only to the proximal perturbations in the local medium. On the one hand, there is the force of the tympanic membrane, determined by its tension and elasticity. On the other hand, there is the force with which the patterned disturbance propagates in the dense and elastic medium, the dynamic principle of unity of the sound event. The force of the patterned disturbance coming into conflict with the force of the tympanic membrane gives rise to the perception of an extra-somatic event, the proximal perturbations, the force of the sound event impinging upon the perceiver, even if it is only heard as a mere noise.

In the previous section, we noted a crucial dis-analogy with the case of grasping or enclosure, understood as a mode of haptic perception. Specifically, the present application of the Protagorean model to the hypothetical limited auditory experience is entirely passive. The force of the growth of the sound event acts upon the tympanic membrane, causing a pattern of local activations that give rise, after subsequent processing, to an auditory perception. In contrast, the hand, in grasping or enclosure, understood as a mode of haptic perception, is not merely acted upon by the object grasped, but actively grasps that object. The hand actively assimilates to its object. The hand is, in this way, the active wax of haptic perception.

I believe that there is a conception of listening more active than the passive power of the tympanic membrane to receive stimulation, and that this more active conception of listening will partially restore the analogy with grasping. We may distinguish three moments in grasping an object. First there is the preparatory reach, a reaching out for an object. This may be done with the end of grasping some particular object or the end may simply be to grasp what there is to grasp. The second moment is enclosure. This involves the hand's maintaining simultaneous contact with as much of its overall surface as possible. The third moment sustains this enclosure. It is not as if, once an object is grasped, no more effort is required. If the activity of the hand relaxes, the object will slip from its grasp. So not only is activity required to enclose the object in the hand's grasp, but it is also required to sustain that grasp. These three moments shall find parallels in the advertised active conception of listening. First, just as a perceiver may reach out, they may listen out as well. They may be listening out for something in particular or just to hear what there is to hear. In listening out, should the perceiver come to audibly attend to something, they listen to it. Moreover, listening is required to sustain that audible attention. Should the perceiver listen away, selectively attending to some other audible event in a sonically complex environment, they would cease to listen to what they were initially listening to. But before I explain further the advertised active conception of listening, allow me to briefly discuss an important, historically salient variant of the present difficulty.

"In order to hear well," Maine de Biran observes, "it is necessary to *listen*" (*Influence de l'habitude sur la faculté de penser*; Boehm 1929, 63–4). Listening – like grasping, feeling weighing, and looking – is active. It is something that the perceiver does. Grasping, feeling, weighing, looking, and listening are not voluntary intentional movements, though they may involve these. Rather, each is a kind of psychological stance, sustained by a characteristic activity, where the perceiver opens themselves up, in a directed manner, to experiencing different aspects of the natural environment.

Listening, for Maine de Biran, is "the putting into action the muscles destined to communicate different degrees of tension to the membrane of the tympanum, etc" (Boehm 1929, 64). Maine de Biran is engaging in speculative anatomy, here, that is to say, he is relying on a convenient empirical falsehood. Just as muscles attached to the eye can expand or contract the pupil in order to better see, Maine de Biran's thought is that muscles attached to the tympanic membrane tighten or loosen it in order to better hear. However, the efforts involved in such motor activity are "imperceptible" and "do not manifest themselves at all as expressions of the will" (Boehm 1929, 64). Compare the distinction that Smith (2002) draws between saccadic eye movement and deliberately moving the eye in its socket. The former is involuntary and so does not manifest itself as the expression of the will the way the latter does. How, then, is the analogy with haptic perception sustained?

Maine de Biran provides a providential response:

> But nature herself has taken care to supplement these faults; she has restored equilibrium by associating in the most intimate way her passive impressions with the activity of an organ essentially motor. (*Influence de l'habitude sur la faculté de penser*; Boehm 1929, 63–4)

The "organ essentially motor" is, more specifically, the vocal organ. Through the effects of natural sympathy rendered insensible by habit, the vocal organ engages in a kind of subvocalized echoing of heard sound. So sounds impinging upon the perceiver cause passive auditory impressions, and the vocal organ "repeats them, imitates them, turns them back, if one might say so, towards their source, and afterwards makes these fleeting modifications enter the sphere of the individual's activity, establishes them and incorporates them there" (Boehm 1929, 64). It is the habitual sympathetic activity of the vocal organ, echoing the auditory character of the passive impression caused by the sound, that presents the sound to consciousness. Moreover, the presentation in auditory experience of sound is described as a kind of incorporation, an image at the center of the semantic field of metaphors loosely organized as modes of assimilation (Chapter 1.1). With this active echoing of passive impressions, Maine de Biran claims to restore the analogy with haptic touch.

It is easy to be suspicious of this providential natural supplement (for criticism, see Derrida 2005, chapter 7). However, if confined to the special case of speech perception, the natural supplement is more plausible. Indeed, Maine de Biran's principal example is following along under our breath in hearing the song or speech of another. The natural supplement is charitably understood as an overgeneralization from the special case of speech perception, on a particular understanding of speech perception, where our capacity to perceive speech draws upon our capacity to produce speech (compare Bergson 1912a, chapter 2; Liberman and Mattingly 1985; Mole 2009).

What motivated the Biranian doubling of passive impression with vocal activity was the thought that to fully restore the analogy with haptic touch an actual activity must be found. The temptation to overgeneralize from the special case of speech perception may be avoided if we relax this demand. Perhaps, listening is a psychological stance sustained by the potential for activity that will make for a better or worse perspective from which the audible object may be heard. Thus, for example, our hominid ancestor, in hunting tapir, may pause to listen out for movement in the bush. In listening out for movement, our hominid ancestor may be prepared to turn in the direction of the heard movement, to better attend, in audition, to such movement. They are prepared to turn, and listen, and hear. While many forms of listening involve actual activity on the part of the perceiver, listening, understood as a psychological stance, may be sustained by the potential for such activity.

This last claim needs qualification. It is not the bare possibility of the perceiver responding in ways that will alter their auditory perspective to better hear what there is to be heard that sustains the relevant psychological stance. In one sense, that much is possible even should the perceiver be unconscious. In another sense, being unconscious, it is not possible for them to respond in an appropriate way to auditory stimuli. Not only must the perceiver be conscious, in order for it to be possible, in the relevant sense, for them to engage in the relevant activity, but more stringently still, the psychological stance must be sustained by the preparedness to act in these ways should the circumstances warrant it, given the practical ends in play in those circumstances. That the relevant sense of potential activity involves the preparedness to act is more stringent still since the preparedness to act would involve changes to the perceiver not present when a perceiver, though conscious, is not so prepared.

With this qualification in place, the analogy with haptic touch is partially, if not fully restored. Grasping or enclosure, understood as a mode of haptic perception, is sustained by the activity of the hand, while listening merely requires a preparedness to act in auditorily relevant ways. Nevertheless listening, the psychological stance, sustained by a characteristic activity, where the perceiver opens themselves up, in a directed manner, to auditorily experience distal events and processes occurring in the natural environment, is itself an activity. Listening is something that the perceiver does. Listening is a kind of listening out for, an outer-directed opening up to the audible. In turning, listening, and hearing, it is I that hear the call of the feral parakeet. Listening to the feral parakeet, or at least its audible activity, is something that I do, even if in hearing the parakeet's call I undergo an experience caused in me, at least in part, by the calling of the parakeet.

While we have found a role for activity in hearing aspects of the distal environment, listening merely requires the potential for such activity, understood as a preparedness to act in auditorily relevant ways, in order to be sustained. Audition remains not as active as the exemplar, grasping, but it is not merely passive the way the registering of movement by the tympanic membrane is. Listening requires the perceiver's vigilance. But the perceiver's auditory vigilance over the distal environment, their being prepared to act in auditorily relevant ways to bring aspects of the distal environment into earshot, remains a stance actively sustained by the perceiver.

In the traditional, post-Aristotelian vocabulary, the distinction between listening and grasping can be described in terms of first and second actuality.

The distinction is traditionally introduced in terms of Aristotle's discussion of knowledge in *De anima* 2 3 417 a 22–417I. Thus an educable person may be ignorant of some point of grammar. But since they are educable, learning that point of grammar is not beyond their ken, and so they may be said to, in this sense, potentially know that point of grammar. Suppose the ignorant if educable person comes to learn it. In learning the relevant point of grammar, they come to actually know it. But, Aristotle observes, the knowledge of the now learned person is itself a kind of potentiality. It is the capacity to apply that knowledge in a reasonable manner given the practical circumstances. Thus the learned person might reasonably apply their knowledge of grammar in interpreting the speech of another. In reasonably applying their knowledge, in the given circumstances, the learned person actualizes their knowledge. Learning is the actualization of the educable person's capacity for knowledge. In the traditional post-Aristotelian vocabulary, it is the first actuality. But since what is learned, knowledge of the relevant point of grammar, is itself a kind of potentiality – it is the capacity to apply that knowledge in a reasonable manner given the practical circumstances – its exercise is itself a kind of actualization. It is the second actuality.

Grasping or enclosure, understood as a mode of haptic perception, requires the second actuality of the hand's activity in order to be sustained. Listening, by contrast, merely requires a first actuality, or equivalently, a second potentiality, the capacity to act in auditorily relevant ways, in order to be sustained. Nevertheless, this second potentiality, required by listening, involves the preparedness to act, a kind of perceptual vigilance, which itself requires activity on the part of the perceiver to sustain. Consider the following mechanical analogy: The operation of the clutch will only set the vehicle in motion if the drive shaft is already in motion. The first actuality, or, equivalently, second potentiality, is the vehicle's capacity for motion partly constituted by the motion of the drive shaft, and the second actuality is the motion of the vehicle when the clutch is in operation. Like the drive shaft, the perceiver must be active in sustaining the second potentiality. Moreover, listening, the psychological stance, sustained by this activity, whereby the perceiver opens themselves up to auditorily experience distal events and processes occurring in the natural environment, is itself a kind of activity directed toward its object.

I turn, and listen, and hear the call of the feral parakeet. What I hear is the audible activity of a distal body, the animate body of the feral bird. Audition affords me explicit awareness of the parakeet's call. I hear how loud it is, its distinctive timbre, and its sharpness and urgency. I hear the parakeet's call through, or in, the sound that it makes. The parakeet's call-ing generates a patterned disturbance that propagates, in every direction, through the dense and imperfectly elastic air. It is through, or in, this audible media, the sound that it makes, that the call of the feral parakeet is heard. In turning, and listening, and hearing, I alter my auditory perspec-tive on the natural environment to bring an aspect of that environment, the audible activity of the feral parakeet, into earshot. Turning, and listening, and hearing – actively changing my auditory perspective on the natural environment – is itself a sympathetic response to what is heard. Changing my auditory perspective to increase the acuity with which the feral para-keet is heard is to sympathetically respond to the call of the feral parakeet. Preparedness to act in certain ways so that the impingement of the force of the propagation of the patterned disturbance, the dynamic principle of unity of the sound event, carries information about its distal source, sensi-tivity to which constitutes, in propitious circumstances, explicit auditory awareness of that source, is what makes possible the sympathetic presen-tation, in auditory experience, of the source of the sound. The power to receive auditory stimulation from proximal perturbations may be purely passive, but it is the perceiver's perceptual vigilance, their preparedness to alter the circumstances in which such stimulation is received with the end of hearing its distal source, and the psychological stance that activity makes possible, the perceiver's listening out for, their outer-directed openness to the audible, that makes for the sympathetic presentation, in audition, of the source of the sound.

CHAPTER 5

Vision

5.1 The Biranian Principle

So far we have discussed grasping and listening and how they make sympathetic presentation possible in haptic and auditory experience, respectively. We turn now to looking. I shall argue that looking makes possible sympathetic presentation in visual experience. Our guiding idea, echoing Maine de Biran, is that in order to see well, one must look. Our task is to describe a conception of looking that could plausibly make this principle true.

Such a conception must satisfy two conditions. A conception of looking that stands a chance of making true the Biranian principle must at once be something that the perceiver does and that makes the distal environment perceptually accessible.

First, looking must be something the perceiver does. Only in this way is the analogy with grasping, enshrined in the Protagorean model, sustained. However, like the case of audition, this psychological stance may be sustained, in the Peripatetic fashion, by a capacity to act. Looking, like listening, while not a passive power, may be less than fully active. In the traditional, post-Aristotelian vocabulary, that stance may be sustained by a first actuality of a second potentiality. Looking may be a psychological stance sustained, at a minimum, by the potential to act in visually relevant ways, on some appropriate understanding of that potentiality. While looking and listening may fall short of the exemplar, grasping, since haptic perception requires the second actuality of the hand's activity to sustain it, still, they are not something done to the perceiver, but something that the perceiver does. What the perceiver does in looking may be sustained, in certain circumstances, by nothing further than a preparedness to act in perceptually relevant ways. At a minimum, then, looking merely requires vigilance (perhaps fortuitously, "vigilance" derives from the Latin *vigilare*, meaning to watch). But the perceiver's perceptual vigilance over the distal environment, their being prepared to act in visually relevant ways to bring

148

aspects of the distal environment into view or at least increase the acuity with which they are seen, remains a stance actively sustained by the perceiver. Moreover, the stance sustained is itself a kind of activity. Looking is something the perceiver does. The perceiver, in maintaining vigilance, looks outward. Looking is a kind of outer-directed opening up to the visible. Looking is something the perceiver does, even if in seeing what they do in looking they undergo an experience caused in them, at least in part, by what they perceive.

Second, looking is an activity of the perceiver whose end is to bring distal aspects of the natural environment into view. Looking makes aspects of the distal environment perceptually accessible. For the perceiver to act in visually relevant ways is for them to alter their visual perspective on the natural environment so as to present distal aspects of that environment, or, at least, increase the acuity with which those aspects are seen.

A conception of looking answering to the truth of the Biranian principle – that in order to see well, one must look – would most likely exceed the conception of looking enshrined in ordinary usage, though, perhaps, in the manner of a conservative extension. This might count against describing such a conception as an instance of "looking." However, other alternatives fare less well. "Gaze" is, by now, perhaps too ethically fraught (especially after Mulvey 1975; see also Jay 1994). Olivi's *aspectus*, while a historically important antecedent, is too technical sounding and is bound up with Olivi's Augustinian dualism. Thus, for example, Olivi distinguishes the physical *aspectus* of the sense organ, the eye pointed in a certain direction, say, from the spiritual *aspectus* of the soul. (Though Olivi's notion of *aspectus* may owe as much to Alhazen's *De aspectibus* as to Augustine, see Tachau 1988, 41 especially n. 43; on Olivi on perception, see Pasnau 1997, 121–4, 130–4, 168–81; Silva and Toivanen 2010; Spruit 1994, 215–24; Tachau 1988, 3–26, 39–54; Toivanen 2009, part 1, 2013, part 2). In the absence of an adequate alternative, we shall persist with talk of looking, mindful of the ways that the demands of making true the Biranian principle might exceed the conception of looking enshrined in ordinary usage.

Not only shall I defend the Biranian principle, but I shall offer an explanation for it in terms of the operation of sympathy. Looking makes aspects of the distal environment perceptually accessibly by making possible their sympathetic presentation in visual experience. We shall begin our search for a conception of looking that makes true the Biranian principle in an unlikely place, in what historians describe as extramission theories of perception. Extramission theories provide a false causal model of distal perception, where a part of the perceiver extends through space so that it is in contact with the perceived object such that the perceiver, or at least a part of them, is substantially located where the perceived object is. Thus Nemesius Bishop of Emesa attributes such a view to Hipparchus, a second-century BC astronomer:

> Hipparchus says that rays extend from the eyes and with their extremities lay hold on external bodies like the touch of hands. (*De natura hominis* 7; Sharples and van der Eijk 2008, 104)

This conception of perception spontaneously arises for many, outside of explicitly theoretical contexts, and is surprisingly resilient to empirical counter-evidence. As we shall see, this is because there is a phenomenological insight enshrined in extramission theories, a phenomenological insight that may be preserved even should we abandon the false causal model that it provides of distal perception. Developing that phenomenological insight will result in the advertised conception of looking that makes true the Biranian principle.

5.2   The Persistence of Extramission

Piaget (1929, 48) observed that there is a tendency for children to understand vision in terms of an active, outward influence of the eyes. This tendency was manifest in reports of looks mixing and in "a confusion between vision and light." Concerning the latter Piaget reports:

> Pat (10) stated that a box makes a shadow "*because the clouds* (Pat believes it to be the clouds which give light when there is no sun) *can't pass through it*" (i.e. because the light cannot pass through the box).

> But immediately after Pat said of a portfolio that it made a shadow "*because the clouds can't see that side.* – Are to see and to give light the same thing? – *Yes.* – Tell me the things which give light? – *The sun, the moon, the stars, the clouds and God.* – Can you give light? – *No … Yes.* – How? – *With the eyes.* – Why? – *Because if you hadn't eyes you wouldn't see properly.*"

> Duc (6 1/2) also stated that the light cannot see through a hand, alike confusing "seeing" with "giving light."

> Sci (6) said that dreams come "*with the light.*" – "How? – *You are in the street. The lights* (street-lamps) *can see there … they see on the ground.*" "Tell me some things that give light. – *Lights, candles, matches, thunder, fire, cigarettes.* – Do eyes give light or not? – *Yes, they give light.* – Do they give light at night? – *No?* – Why not? – *Because they are shut.* – When they are open do they give light? – *Yes.* – Do they give light like lamps? – *Yes, a little bit.*" (1929, 48)

And Piaget (1929, 48–9) goes on to compare these reports with Empedocles' lantern analogy. (On the lantern analogy, see Wright 1981, 240–3; on Empedocles' theory of vision, see Ierodiakonou 2005; Kalderon 2015, chapter 1; Sedley 1992.)

Winer and Cottrell (1996, 138), prompted by Piaget's observations, were "surprised – indeed shocked" by the degree and resilience of belief in extramissive perception. Not only do children hold extramission beliefs, but so do adults, though such beliefs tend to decline during adulthood. To the simple question that required a "yes" or "no" response:

> When we look at someone or something, does anything such as rays, waves, or energy go out of our eyes?

> Forty-nine percent of the first graders, 70 percent of the third graders, 51 percent of the fifth graders, and 33 percent of the college students affirmed extramission. Moreover, these beliefs proved "highly resistant to experimental intervention designed to alter them" (Winer and Cottrell 1996, 138).

Winer and Cottrell (1996) augmented their use of verbal questions with graphic displays:

> The computer graphics portrayed various interpretations of the process of vision by displaying one or more renditions of a person looking at a rectangle, with visual input and output depicted by lines that appeared to move between the person's eye and the rectangle. Thus, in one graphic, lines, presumably representing rays, appeared to move inward from the rectangle to the eye of the figure on the screen, demonstrating the process of intromission. In another graphic, lines appeared to move outward from the eye toward the rectangle, demonstrating pure extramission. (139)

They did so for two reasons. First, the graphic displays were used to filter out any misinterpretations that might have been suggested by the verbal questions. Second, they predicted that, given a hypothesized source of extramission belief, exposure to the graphic displays would increase the affirmation of extramission.

What is this hypothesized source? Winer and Cottrell (1996) hypothesize that both the tendency for extramission beliefs to persist into adulthood and their resistance to experimental intervention is partly explained by a phenomenological truth enshrined in extramission models:

> We assume that core aspects of the phenomenology of vision underlie extramission interpretations. Consider one phenomenologically salient aspect of vision, namely, its orientational or outer-directed quality. When people see, they are generally oriented toward an external visual referent, that is, they direct their eyes and attention to an object in order to see it. In fact, this

quality of vision is reflected in language. People talk about "looking at" things, and English has expressions such as "looking out of a window" and "looking out of binoculars." Even notions such as "piercing glances" and "cutting looks" suggest an outer directionality. (140)

On this basis, they predicted an increase in the affirmation of extramission because of the way that the graphics "present representations that are suggestive of the orientational aspects of vision." And subsequent studies confirmed this.

It is unclear, at least to me, what to make of this increased affirmation of extramission in response to the use of graphic displays. The displays do not unambiguously represent the intended interpretations of the process of vision. Specifically, they do not unambiguously represent lines of causal influence. As Winer and Cottrell (1996) observe, they are at least suggestive of the orientational aspects of vision. But given the iconic nature of the pictorial representation, moving lines might represent lines of causal influence, but they might just as easily represent lines of sight. Perhaps, the increased affirmation of extramission is less an expression of belief in extramission than an expression of the active, outer-directed phenomenology of vision. Perhaps, the affirmation of extramission involved belief in, not a scientific misconception, but a phenomenological truth misleading expressed (see Robbin 2003 for a similar worry). Winer and Cottrell (1996) claim to control for this, but whether they did so successfully is difficult to independently assess.

Whatever the genuine extent of extramission belief, it is the phenomenological diagnosis for it that we shall focus upon. In the next section, we shall examine the active, outer-directed phenomenology of vision that Winer and Cottrell (1996) take to underlie belief in extramission.

5.3   The Truth in Extramission

Merleau-Ponty provides a description of the active, outer-directed phenomenology of vision that would make talk of extramission apt:

> If I adhere to what immediate consciousness tells me, the desk which I see in front of me and on which I am writing, the room in which I am and whose walls enclose me beyond the sensible field, the garden, the street, the city and, finally, the whole of my spatial horizon do not appear to me to be causes of the perception which I have of them, causes which would impress their mark on me and produce an image of themselves by a transitive action. It seems to me rather that my perception is like a beam of light

which reveals the objects there where they are and manifests their presence, latent until then. Whether I myself perceive or consider another subject perceiving, it seems to me that the gaze "is posed" on objects and reaches them from a distance – as is well expressed by the use of the Latin *lumina* for designating the gaze. (1967, 185)

Merleau-Ponty is not endorsing the extramission theory as a causal model of perception. He is not denying that the object of perception is the ultimate efficient cause of that perception. Rather, in seeing the desk before him, Merleau-Ponty claims only that his experience does not present itself as the exercise of a passive power, a sensory impression caused in him by the mediate causal action of the distal object. There may be an active element to outwardly attending, in vision, to distal aspects of the natural environment, and this may be phenomenologically vivid, but that is consistent with the object of visual perception being among its causal antecedents. "My present experience of this desk is not complete ... it shows me only some of its aspects" (1967, 186). Merleau-Ponty's experience may be incomplete in that it reveals only some aspects of its object, but once we allow that perception is partial in this way, it is at least open that experience is incomplete, as well, in that it only manifests some aspects of its nature. The active, outer-directed nature of vision may be phenomenologically vivid, but vision may still require that the distal object mediately act upon the perceiver. A visual experience may be undergone, but seeing is not something done to the perceiver, but something the perceiver does.

Nor is Merleau-Ponty claiming that it appears from within that seeing involves the emission of a fiery effluence akin to light. Rather Merleau-Ponty is pressing an analogy. He is describing what visual experience, from within, is like. And not only from within, but from without as well. The analogy holds not only when Merleau-Ponty considers his own experience, but also when he considers the experience of another perceiving subject. Consider another's piercing glance or cutting look (Winer and Cottrell 1996, 140). Piaget's reports of looks mixing are cases where the analogy would hold, as well, of other perceiving subjects:

> From a boy of 5 years old: "*Papa, why don't our looks mix when they meet.*"
>
> From one of our collaborators: "*When I was a little girl I used to wonder how it was that when two looks met they did not somewhere hit one another. I used to imagine the point to be half-way between the two people. I used also to wonder why it was one did not feel someone else's look, on the cheek for instance if they were looking at one's cheek.*" (1929, 48)

Merleau-Ponty, then, is describing that aspect of our visual phenomenology, considered from within and without, that Winer and Cottrell (1996) claim to underlie extramission beliefs.

More explicitly, the awareness visual experience affords is like a beam of light that manifests the latent presence of its object. Vision, like illumination, has direction. Light is emitted outward from its source upon the scene that it illuminates. Vision too is outer-directed. In seeing, the perceiver looks out upon the scene before them. Not only do vision and light have direction, but they are both rectilinear as well. Moreover, just as illumination manifests the latent visibility of an object, seeing an illuminated object manifests its latent presence to the perceiver, revealing it to be where it is. The explicit awareness of the natural environment visual experience affords is akin to light not only in its rectilinear directionality and its power to manifest latent presence, but in the manner in which it discloses distal aspects of that environment. Just as a beam of light may "pose" on an object that it illuminates and that it reaches from a distance, the perceiver's gaze may "pose" on the object that it presents and that it reaches from a distance. The illumination alights upon the object it illuminates at a distance from its source, the perceiver's gaze alights upon the object of perception at a distance from the perceiver. The imagery here not only emphasizes that vision is a kind of perception at a distance, but invokes an active outward extension, as in Kilwardby's wax actively pushing against the seal (Chapter 1.6).

Accepting the aptness of the analogy is not tantamount to accepting the extramission theory. Consider a similar analogy of Olivi's:

> an object, to the extent that the gaze (*aspectus*) and the act of a power are terminated at it, co-operates in their specific production ... Namely, the cognitive act – and the gaze – is fixed (*figitur*) to the object and it absorbs the object intentionally to itself. This is why a cognitive act is called the apprehension of, and the apprehensive extension to, the object. In this extension and absorption the act becomes intimately conformed and assimilated into the object. The object presents itself or appears as being present to the cognitive gaze, and the object is a kind of representation of itself by an act which is assimilated to it. As an actual illumination of a spherical or quadrangular vase becomes spherical or quadrangular only because the light source generates the illumination in conformity with the figure of the object which receives and confines it; so also, because a cognitive force generates a cognitive act with a certain formative absorption of the act towards the object, and with a certain signet-like and inward (*sigillari et viscerali*) extension of the object, therefore – because it is generated thus – the act becomes a similitude and signet-like expression of the object. (*Questiones in secundum librum Sententiarum* q. 72 35–6; Toivanen 2013, 146–7)

The passage is complex and is replete with suggestive detail. But to begin with, focus on the analogy with illumination.

Despite his play with neo-Platonic imagery, no doubt an Augustinian heritage (Kent 1984, 198), Olivi is not endorsing an extramission theory of perception. Olivi explicitly denies that extension involves any real emission (*Questiones in secundum librum Sententiarum* q. 58 ad 14.8). Perceptual apprehension may be a form of apprehensive extension to its object, but this apprehensive extension is not corporeal. Though likened to illumination directed upon the object it illuminates, the perceptual act, the apprehensive extension by which that act assimilates to its object, does not consist in, or otherwise involve, the emission of a fiery substance, no matter how rarified. Nor does the apprehensive extension involve the emission of any spiritual matter. Perception is a simple, spiritual act that takes place in the soul, and the soul can only be in the body, at least when alive. So no part of the soul is substantially located where the perceived object is as would be the case if extramission were true. Likening the seeing of an object to light directed upon an object that it illuminates, by itself, carries with it no commitment to the metaphysics of extramission. Rather, Olivi, like Merleau-Ponty after him, is emphasizing the active, outer-directed nature of vision.

Moreover, like Merleau-Ponty, Olivi is presenting a conception of perception that contrasts with a mere passive reception of sensible form. Olivi, however, working in the same broadly Augustinian metaphysical framework as Kilwardby, is less concessive to Peripatetic accounts of perception.

Recall (Chapter 1.6), according to the Peripatetic account, at least as understood by the late Scholastics, the perceived object acts upon the transparent medium such that its sensible form, its species, exists, in some sense, in it, and that the medium, in turn, affects the sense organ such that the species comes to, in some sense, exist in it as well (*De spiritu fantastico* 69, 97). So understood, the eye's reception of a color species, while not a literal coloration, is the exercise of a passive power, like the power to be heated. The distal object mediately acting upon the perceiver's sense organ posited by the Peripatetic account was understood, by Kilwardby, as a necessary if insufficient condition for perception. In order for perception to occur, the perceptive soul must assimilate the species, but this requires the soul's activity.

According to Olivi, however, the affection of the sense organ by a species originating from the distal object is not even a necessary condition for its perception. Echoing Plotinus (*On Difficulties about the Soul iii*, or *On Sight, Ennead* 4 5 2 50–5; Chapter 2.7), Olivi maintains that if perception were mediated by a corporeal species, the species would be the object of perception, thus screening off the distal object in the natural environment (on Plotinus' argument, see Emilsson 1988, chapter 3; on Olivi's argument, see Tachau 1988, 43–5, especially n. 53, and Pasnau 1997, chapter 7.3). The object of perception is not an efficient cause of that perception, no matter how mediate.

Like Kilwardby, Olivi is moved, in part, by the Augustinian doctrine of the ontological superiority of the soul over the body, though perhaps Olivi interprets that doctrine more stringently than Kilwardby. The way in which the soul and its powers and acts are superior to the body is inconsistent with a body ever acting upon the soul. So an extended corporeal species could not activate the perceptual power, the power and its act being simple and spiritual (*Questiones in secundum librum Sententiarum* q. 73 83–4). Silva and Toivanen (2010, 263) observe how Olivi anticipates, here, the Cartesian distinction between *res extensa* and *res cogitans* (see also Tachau 1988, 46). The powers of the soul, even perceptual powers, are not the passive recipients of external stimuli, but are active. Like Merleau-Ponty, Olivi thinks that the active character of our perceptual powers is phenomenologically evident (Pasnau 1997, 236–47; Tachau 1988, 3–26, 39–54; Toivanen 2013, 143).

While Olivi does not deny that perception presupposes the presence of its object in the natural environment, he does deny that it is, or even among, the efficient causes of perception. In Olivi's technical vocabulary, the object of perception is a terminative cause. It is controversial how to understand Olivi's terminative causes. Are terminative causes a species of final cause, as Kent (1984, 192–5) and Pasnau (1999a) maintain? Or are they a kind of cause not classified by the traditional Peripatetic four causes (*Physica* 2 3, *Metaphysica* E 2), as Toivanen (2013, chapter 6) maintains? While it is difficult to form a clear, positive conception of terminative causes, the negative contrast with efficient causes is clear. The actualization of a perceptual power may require the presence of its object in the natural environment, but that object acting upon the power is not required for its actualization. The efficient cause of the perceptual act is the power and not the object of perception. The presence of that object merely cooperates by being the *terminus* of the perceptual act, that which it is directed upon, like light directed upon a spherical vase.

So Olivi maintains that the active, outer-directed phenomenology of vision is inconsistent with the object seen being the efficient cause of that perception. Merleau-Ponty, by contrast, merely claims that the object of perception acting upon the perceiver, however mediately, is not manifest in our experience, not that it is inconsistent with it. Perhaps this more cautious attitude is, in the end, warranted. I do not recommend this more cautious attitude merely as a beneficiary of optical knowledge unavailable to Olivi, but on philosophical grounds as well.

To bring this out, first consider an element of the Olivi passage that goes beyond what Merleau-Ponty explicitly describes. Olivi, like Merleau-Ponty, uses the neo-Platonic imagery of illumination to emphasize the active, outward extension involved in the visual apprehension of the distal environment, and where this active, outward extension is no kind of extramission. Olivi goes further than Merleau-Ponty, however, in coupling the active, outward extension of the illumination with being shaped by its *terminus*, the circular or quadrangular vase, say. In illuminating a circular vase, the area illuminated is itself circular. The shape of the area illuminated is constituted by the shape of the object illuminated. The illumination is "in conformity with the figure of the object which receives it and confines it." This is meant to be an analogy for how the perceptual act formally assimilates to its object. Extension and absorption are linked. In neo-Platonic vocabulary, extension and absorption are a kind of procession and return. Like Kilwardby before him, Olivi thinks that the perceptual act only assimilates to its object thanks to the activity of the perceptual soul. Indeed, the passage ends with Olivi echoing Kilwardby's figure of the active wax pressing against the seal. (It is unclear whether Olivi read Kilwardby. Perhaps similar paths were laid out for them by their shared Augustinian heritage. For a comparison of Kilwardby and Olivi, see Silva and Toivanen 2010.)

Extension and absorption, a kind of procession and return, is important, so it is perhaps worth a brief digression on a detail of the passage that we have so far glossed over. The perceiver's gaze, in being fixed on its object, a circular vase, say, absorbs the object intentionally to itself. It is only in intentionally absorbing the object of perception that the perceptual act assimilates to its object. Moderns should resist the temptation to understand the qualifier "intentionally" in terms of the notion of intentionality derived from Brentano (1874) (on the historical development of the concept of intentionality, see Sorabji 2003; on Olivi's role in the development of intentionality in late Scholasticism, see Pasnau 1997, chapter 2). A sensible form inhering in a body, the whiteness inhering in a circular vase, say, has natural existence in that body. Part of the point of the qualifier is to deny that the perceived sensible form has natural existence in the perceptual act. In part, then, the point of the qualifier is to rule out a position like the one Crathorn will later endorse where perception becomes colored in seeing a colored object and so avoid Theophrastus' *aporia* (Chapter 1.4). However, not only does Olivi deny natural existence to the sensible form in the perceptual act, he denies, as well, its real existence. This prompts Pasnau (1997, 67) to remark that with Olivi, there is "movement toward making intentionality mysterious."

Moreover, according to Olivi, the intentional existence of the object in the perceptual act – in virtue of which it assimilates to that object and so becomes like it, if not naturally like, in the manner of Crathorn – involves the perceptual power's virtual presence to that object (on the meaning of *virtualis* in late Latin and Olivi specifically, see Pasnau 1997, 172–3). Specifically, it is because the power is virtually present to its object that that object comes to exist intentionally in the actualization of that power:

> A power can be present to something either essentially or virtually. This is to say that it can be present to something in such a way that its essence really is beside that thing, or in such a way that the gaze (*aspectus*) of its power is so efficaciously directed to the thing that it, as it were, really touches the thing. If the power is not present to its object or recipient (*patienti*) in this second way, it cannot act, even if it were present to it by its essence or according to the first way. The visual power is present to a thing that is seen from a distance in this [second] way … This [kind of] presence suffices for an act of seeing. (Olivi, *Quaestiones in secundum librum Sententiarum*, q. 58 486–7; Toivanen 2013, 151–2)

In speaking of a power's presence to its object as opposed to the object's presence to the power, Olivi is emphasizing the active, outer-directed nature of that power. If a power is essentially present to an object, then the power and the object are contiguous, "its essence really is beside that thing," and there is a real connection between them akin to the perception by contact involved in touch. In contrast, if a power is virtually present to an object, then the object and the power are not contiguous, but are at a distance from one another. Moreover, there is no real connection between the object and the power whose act contains it. Virtual presence is a necessary condition for visual perception. It is only by the visual power being virtually present to an object that seeing that object may formally assimilate to it. Virtual presence is also a sufficient condition. The virtual presence of the visual power to an object suffices for its extensive apprehension.

The virtual presence of a power to its object precludes the need for any real connection between them. A visible object need not be palpable to vision the way in which a corporeal body must be palpable to touch if it is to be felt (though contrast the account of vision that Socrates attributes to Empedocles in the *Meno* 76 a–d; see Kalderon 2015; Chapter 1.2 for discussion). There need be no contact between sight and its object in order for the latter to be seen, not even mediate contact. And, at least by Olivi's lights, contact is required for a real connection. Olivi's notion of a terminative cause is meant to explain how a sensory power may be the total efficient cause of its act and yet its content be determined by an object in the distal environment to which that power is merely virtually present.

Like intentional existence, the virtual presence of a power to an object contrasts with, not only the natural existence of that object in that power's act, but its real existence as well. Moreover, while the presence of the object in the natural environment may be required for its perception, it is not among the efficient causes of perception. But if what is intentionally absorbed by the perceptual act lacks both natural and real existence, and the object of perception in no way acts upon the perceiver, one may well wonder how, exactly, it may shape that act such that the perceptual act formally assimilates to its object.

Contrast Olivi's position with the neo-Platonically inspired account of perception developed herein. Recall, sympathy played two roles in Plotinus' account of vision (Chapter 2.7). First, it was meant to explain the action at a distance involved in visual perception. Specifically, sympathy was the principle by which the distal object may affect the sense organ without affecting anything in between. For Plotinus, at least, this was a real connection. Plotinus denies that a real connection requires contact. There is action at a distance, and sympathy is its principle. Second, sympathy was meant to explain how the distal object, and not sensible aspects of the medium, is present in the perceiver's visual experience of it. It is this second suggestion that we have taken up and generalized. In taking the visual power to be merely virtually present to its object, Olivi overlooks the possibility of sympathetic presentation.

Linked to this is contrasting attitudes to the location of the perceptual act. Though Olivi may have inherited the neo-Platonic imagery from Augustine, one thing that he does not inherit is the neo-Platonic tendency to locate the perceptual act in its object. Thus in the *Sermones* 277 10 Augustine writes "to have opened the eye is to have arrived" at the object seen (O'Daly 1987, 82). We have seen an example of this already in a passage of Plotinus cited earlier (Chapter 2.8), though it passed by uncommented:

> It is clear in presumably every case that when we have a perception of anything through the sense of sight, we look where it is and direct our gaze where the visible object is situated in a straight line from us; *obviously it*

is there that the apprehension takes place [my emphasis] and the soul looks
outwards. (*On Sense-Perception and Memory, Ennead* 4 6 1 14–18; Armstrong
1984, 321)

Toward the end of a passage emphasizing the active nature of visual perception, Plotinus makes, at least to our post-Cartesian ears, a startling
pronouncement: the apprehension of the visible object takes place in the
object seen. Olivi, by contrast, denies that the perceptual act takes place in
its object (at least if this is understood non-metaphorically *Quaestiones in
secundum librum Sententiarum* q. 37 obj. 13, ad. 13). Rather, it is a simple,
spiritual act of the immaterial soul, and the soul is located where the body
it animates is, at least when alive (for a comparison of Olivi's conception
of perception with the neo-Platonic conception, see Toivanen 2013, 151).
Olivi, in making this denial, overlooks the possibility of sympathetic presentation. When I look where the ancient chestnut tree is and direct my
gaze at that tree situated in a straight line from me, sympathy places me in
the very heart of things, and it is there, where the tree grows too slowly to
be perceptible, that my visual apprehension of it takes place.

There is nothing virtual about the sympathetic presence of the ancient
chestnut tree in my perception of it. Even allowing that presence may be
said of in many ways, virtual presence is no presence at all. If I were merely
virtually present to the tree in seeing it, it is hard to understand how my
visual experience could be shaped by that tree. And if my visual experience
is not shaped by that tree, then it is not present in my experience. (Similar
remarks apply to Noë's 2012 more recent account of perception in terms
of virtual presence.)

To bring this out, consider the way the neo-Platonic analogy fails to
support Olivi's extreme position. Indeed, attending to its details reveals a
striking *aporia*. The object of illumination, the illuminated circular vase,
say, receives and confines that illumination. In receiving and confining
the illumination the illuminated area takes on the shape that it does. In
receiving and confining the illumination the circular vase resists that illumination. It obstructs that illumination and so casts a shadow. It is hard
to understand how the spherical vase may confine, resist, and obstruct the
activity of the illuminant without being a cause, or, at least, a countervailing force. Of course, it is the source of the illuminant that generates
the illumination, but the illuminated area takes on the shape that it does
because the illuminated object resists the activity of the illumination insofar as it can. Kilwardby's doctrine that the soul's use of a body is limited
by the passivities of matter (*De spiritu fantastico* 99–100) was meant to

address this kind of difficulty. However, the invocation of the neo-Platonic analogy just is Olivi's response. Olivi is drawing our attention to the fact that it is the source that generates the illumination and not the object illuminated. But that does not suffice to make the analogy consistent with taking the object of perception to be a terminative cause with all that that entails. Visual consciousness may extend to its object, but it must somehow come into conflict with it, as on the Protagorean model, if the subsequent absorption is to be so much as possible.

How is the Peripatetic analogy, the ancient figure of the wax and seal, meant to be understood by Olivi's lights? It occurs at the point where Olivi spells out the consequences of the neo-Platonic analogy for perception. One curious feature of Olivi's treatment is the way that extension and absorption are transposed at this point. Whereas earlier in the passage Olivi speaks of the act's extension to its object, he now speaks of the "formative absorption of the act towards the object." And whereas earlier in the passage Olivi speaks of the act's absorption of the object by which the act assimilates to it, he now speaks of "a certain signet-like and inward extension of the object." I am uncertain of the significance of this transposition, if it is not, indeed, a slip on Olivi's part. If intentional, perhaps it is meant to emphasize the unity of extension and absorption. Extension is at once a formative absorption to the object, just as absorption is at once an inward extension of the object. Notice, on this hypothesis, the unity of extension and absorption only holds for extensive apprehension, the kind of extensive activity characteristic of perception, as opposed to a non-perceptual visual experience, such as a hallucination. In cases of hallucination, there is nothing to absorb. And so while such experiences may involve extensive activity, there is no subsequent absorption, merely the illusion of such.

The *aporia* involved in Olivi's use of the neo-Platonic imagery affects his treatment of the ancient figure of the wax and seal. Even if, in line with the neo-Platonic analogy, the visual power generates the perceptual act in conformity with the figure of the object that receives it and confines it, how are we to understand this reception and confinement? "Because it is generated thus the act becomes a similitude and signet-like expression of the object." Perception formally assimilates to its object because it is generated thus. It only conforms with its object by being received and confined. But reception and confinement are naturally understood as arising in the face of a countervailing force, the upshot of a conflict between the perceptual act and its object that resists it insofar as it can. It is hard to understand how the presence in the natural environment of an object that is the *terminus* of the perceptual act could determine the content of that act, even if the act is directed upon it, like a beam of light, without somehow coming into conflict with it, as on the Protagorean model. Somehow the *terminus* must determine the content of the perceptual act without itself being a determinant. But how could that be?

Duns Scotus anticipates the present worry. Scotus at least presses a parallel point about the intellect in his *Ordinatio* and on the same general grounds. Though Scotus does not name names, Olivi is clearly a target as he reproduces a number of arguments from Olivi's *Sentences* commentary (Pasnau 1997, 148). Scotus concedes to Olivi that the object of the intellect could not be the complete cause of the intellectual act. However, Scotus insists that the object must play some causal role if the act of intellect is to be a likeness of it (*Ordinatio* 1 3 3 4 n. 486). Generalizing, Scotus' idea is that the demands of formally assimilating to the object require that the object play an explanatory role inconsistent with being a terminative cause. And it is the application of this general idea to the case of perception that constitutes the present worry (on Scotus on Olivi, see Pasnau 1997, chapter 4.4; on Scotus on cognitive powers, both sensory and intellectual, see Cross 2014; Spruit 1994, 257–66; Tachau 1988, chapter 3; for a related worry, see Pasnau 1997, 174–5).

The worry reveals the way in which Olivi's view is a step along the way toward adverbialism (see Ducasse 1942). Moreover, this is due, in part, to proto-Cartesian aspects of Olivi's view, an effect of their shared Augustinian heritage, such as Olivi's anticipation of the Cartesian distinction between *res extensa* and *res cogitans*, manifest, for example, in his denial that an extended, corporeal species may actualize the soul's perceptual power (on Descartes's Augustinianism, see Menn 1998, not to mention Malebranche's testimony in *Recherche de la Vérité*; for a non-Cartesian development of adverbialism, see Chirimuuta 2015). The perceptual power is the total efficient cause of the perceptual act. Though the act is directed upon its terminus, the object is not among the efficient causes of the perception. The perceptual power is merely virtually present to the object and so has no real connection with it. Though the presence of its object in the natural environment may occasion it, perception is a simple, spiritual act of the immaterial soul. To the extent to which the object present in the natural environment is a terminative cause, and so no determinant of the simple, spiritual act, that act is independent of its object in a way that anticipates more modern adverbialist theories. According to adverbialism, seeing blue is not a matter of being presented with an instance of blue in sight, but rather seeing bluely. On adverbialist theories, then, the perceptual act is not constitutively shaped by its object, but has its conscious character independently of that object. Olivi, of course, is no modern adverbialist. The simple, spiritual act may be determined independently of its object, but it is meant to be an intentional absorption of and assimilation to that object. The problem, of course, is to understand how Olivi could coherently maintain this.

Even if Olivi is wrong to deny that an object plays a causal role in its perception, he may be right in claiming that extension and absorption are linked. If extension and absorption are linked, if the wax only takes on the form of the seal by actively pressing against it, then the active extensive element in Merleau-Ponty's description is the basis for a subsequent absorption. The light is posed on the circular vase and is fixed there, and so the illuminated area is shaped by that vase. Merleau-Ponty's gaze is posed on his desk and is fixed there, and so his visual experience is shaped by that desk. Indeed, Olivi was criticized precisely by holding fast to the link between extension and absorption, a kind of procession and return, and drawing out what that entails, namely, that the active, outward extension's coming into conflict with the object is what explains, in part, that object's subsequent absorption. The grasping hand only conforms to a rigid, solid body by grasping it. The grasping hand extends its grip until it can no more, consistent with its ends, and so conforms to the body's contours. It is only thanks to the activity of the hand and the resistance it encounters that the perceiver's haptic experience formally assimilates to the tangible qualities of the object grasped. In this way is the hand the active wax of haptic perception. It is the force of the hand's activity coming into conflict with the self-maintaining forces of the object grasped that makes possible the sympathetic presentation of that object in haptic experience and its formal assimilation to that object, understood as a mode of constitutive shaping. The grasped object plays an explanatory role, inconsistent with being a mere terminative cause, in the conflict with the hand's grasp that discloses it. If perception's formal assimilation to its object, understood as a mode of constitutive shaping, is the basis of its objectivity, that is only so because of the explanatory priority of its object, an explanatory priority inconsistent with being a terminative cause. There is a connection, then, between perceptual objectivity and explanatory priority (Chapter 1.2).

5.4   Looking

We have been discussing the active, outward, extensive character of visual phenomenology that underlies persistent belief in extramission in some children and adults and is plausibly the font of classical extramission theories. We have done so in aid of honing in on a conception of looking that stands a chance of making true the Biranian principle – in order to see well, one must look. Such a conception must involve the active, outer-directed extension of visual awareness where this involves the emission of nothing, no matter how rarified and akin to light.

Like grasping and listening, there are three distinguishable moments in looking. The first moment corresponds to the preparatory reach in grasping, and might be performed for the end of grasping some particular object or for the end of grasping what there is to be grasped. Just as someone may reach out for something and listen out for something (Chapter 4.5), they may look out for something as well. A perceiver may look out with the end of seeing some particular object or with the end of seeing what there is to be seen. The second moment corresponds to the enclosure of the object grasped. Just as the hand, in reaching out, may come to conform to the contours of the object grasped, in listening out, the perceiver may come to audibly attend to something and so listen to it. Similarly, in looking out for something, the perceiver may come to look at something and so see it. In looking out, an object is sighted. The third moment corresponds to the sustaining of enclosure. If the activity of the hand relaxes, the object will slip from its grasp. So not only is activity required to enclose the object in the hand's grasp, but it is also required to sustain that grasp. Moreover, listening is required to sustain audible attention. Should the perceiver listen away, attending to some other audible event in a sonically complex environment, they would cease to listen to what they were initially listening to. Similarly, looking is required to sustain the explicit awareness afforded by visual experience. Should the perceiver look away, attending to some other visible aspect of the natural environment, they would cease to look at, and so visually attend to, the object of perception.

I turn, and look, and see an ancient chestnut tree. It is one of the ancient chestnut trees replanted in Greenwich Park when Charles II had the park redesigned in the 1660s. An organism of impressive size and age presents itself. The majority of its burrs remains on the tree and are brighter green than the surrounding foliage. It is early evening, and the light is long and golden. The light both articulates the fine texture of the bark and sets off the overall flow of the trunk in dramatic relief. Despite its manifest strength and solidity, the twisted trunk appears to be flowing in a wave-like form. I come to realize that I am witnessing an organic process, the growth of the trunk, occurring so slowly as to appear, from within my limited temporal perspective, frozen, static. The difference in the scale of our lives is striking. For a moment, it induces in me a kind of temporal vertigo. Just as a radical difference in spatial scale can be vertiginous – think of how small one can feel when viewing the Milky Way – a radical difference in temporal scale can be vertiginous as well. The scale of its life and the strength manifest in centuries of growth make the sweet chestnut tree a fit object of awe. I find myself musing that in a different cultural context, perhaps one more prone to animism, the tree might reasonably be reckoned a god.

In looking at the ancient chestnut tree, I do so from across the park. I look at the tree by peering through the intervening space. My gaze perceptually penetrates that space until it encounters the ancient tree. The tree's surface is the site of visual resistance. Perceptually impenetrable, it determines a visual boundary through which, and in which, nothing further may appear. The tree is opaque to a significant degree. Its opacity consists in its resistance to my gaze. The illuminated air between, by contrast, being transparent, is perceptually penetrable. One can see in it and through it. Thus a scrub brush can appear in the water of a bath, and a cherry tree can appear through a window. Appearing through a medium does not require that the object be embedded in that medium the way appearing in does, though it is consistent with the object being so embedded, at least if the perceiver is as well. Thus, it is through the illuminated air that the ancient chestnut tree is disclosed to me in sight. Looking, at least in the potentially extended sense that makes true the Biranian principle, involves the perceiver's gaze coming into conflict with what is perceptually impenetrable. (Compare the phenomenological interpretation I give of the bounded and unbounded in *De sensu*, Kalderon 2015; Chapter 3.3.)

Broad (1952) describes vision as prehensive and saltatory. It is prehensive insofar as vision involves the presentation of its object in the explicit awareness afforded by visual experience. It is saltatory insofar as this awareness seems to leap the spatial gap between the perceiver and the object. There are two separable elements to Broad's conception of saltitoriness. The first is simply the frank admission that vision is a kind of perception at a distance, that the objects of visual awareness are located at a distance from the perceiver. That much is unexceptional. The second is a phenomenological claim, that visual awareness seems to leap the spatial gap between the perceiver and the object of perception. For visual awareness to leap, the spatial gap would be for the objects of visual awareness to be confined to a remote location and so not to have traversed the space between. However, I am visually aware not only of the coloring of the ancient chestnut tree and the wave-like form of its trunk, but of the intervening space as well.

We not only see the colors of distant particulars and their shapes, but we do so by seeing through intervening illuminated media.

Two years after the appearance of "Some elementary reflections on sense-perception," Jonas (1954, 518) will deny that vision is saltatory in Broad's sense, and it is the second element of Broad's conception that he takes exception to and not the first: "in sight the object faces me across the intervening distance, which in all its potential 'steps' is included in the perception." Broad is right to emphasize the distal character of the objects of vision, but his description of vision as saltatory is inapt since it fails to heed the perceptual penetrability of the intervening medium. Vision would leap the gap between the perceiver and the distal color if the object of visual awareness were confined to the remote spatial region where that color is instantiated. Vision, so conceived, would be a kind of "remote viewing." However, vision is not so confined and so does not leap the gap between the perceiver and distal color. Rather, by means of it, the perceiver may peer through the intervening medium, in all its potential steps, and encounter objects facing them across the intervening distance, if the medium is transparent at least to some degree. In the course of an otherwise astute and insightful comparative phenomenology of the senses, Broad is misled, at this point, by overlooking the active, outer-directed phenomenology of vision. Broad, in effect, overlooks the truth in extramission.

As in the case of audition, this psychological stance may be sustained, in the Peripatetic fashion, by a capacity to act. Looking, like listening, while not a passive power, may be less than fully active. In the traditional, post-Aristotelian vocabulary, looking, a psychological stance, may be sustained by a first actuality of a second potentiality. Looking may be a psychological stance sustained, at a minimum, by the potential to act in visually relevant ways, to alter one's visual perspective on the natural environment to better bring into view distal aspects of that environment, but only on a particular understanding of that potentiality. While looking and listening may fall short of the exemplar, grasping – haptic perception requires the second actuality of the hand's activity in order to sustain it – still, they are not something done to the perceiver but something the perceiver does. What the perceiver does in looking may be sustained, in certain circumstances, by nothing further than a preparedness to act in perceptually relevant ways. Perhaps to get better sense of the trunk's flowing pattern, I must follow that pattern along with my gaze, at least to a certain degree, or in a certain way. Perhaps I need to move closer, or perhaps further away. Looking at the ancient chestnut tree may involve, at a minimum, a preparedness to act in such visually relevant ways, but such preparedness requires vigilance.

In looking at the ancient chestnut tree, I maintain vigilance over the tree and its visually manifest aspects. Being thus vigilant, being prepared to act in visually relevant ways, remains a stance that I must actively sustain. So the characteristic activity that sustains the psychological stance may be a first actuality of a second potentiality, but the relevant sense of potentiality involves a preparedness to act in a way that itself requires activity to sustain, a kind of perceptual vigilance.

Looking may be a psychological stance, sustained by a characteristic activity, where the perceiver opens themselves up, in a directed manner, to visually experience distal aspects of the natural environment, but that stance is itself an activity. In maintaining perceptual vigilance, I open myself up to the visible. My gaze, that the tree resists insofar as it can, is something I direct at the tree. Looking through a window, or into a fish tank, or across a park is something that the perceiver does. Looking at the tree, gazing upon it, remains something that I do, even if in seeing the tree I undergo an experience caused in me, at least in part, by the tree itself.

Looking, so conceived, may not be a simple, spiritual act of the immaterial soul as Olivi maintains, but its outward, extensive activity remains something that the perceiver does independently of any visible object it may encounter. In opening their eyes, the perceiver opens themselves up to visually experiencing the natural environment, and that is something they do independently of whatever they encounter in so doing. However, accommodating this insight, if it is one, does not require the object of perception to be a terminative cause. In opening themselves up, in a directed manner, to visually experiencing distal aspects of the natural environment, the content of their perception is determined by what they encounter in so looking in a manner inconsistent with the object of perception being a mere terminative cause.

Looking, understood as a psychological stance sustained by characteristic activity, is an outward gaze, a looking into the distance, an outer-directed opening up to the visible. It can sometimes happen, if circumstances are propitious, that in looking outward, aspects of the natural environment, facing us from across the intervening distance, are presented to us in our visual experience. The next section shall discuss how looking, so conceived, helps make possible the sympathetic presentation of distal objects in the natural environment. If looking, understood as an outer-directed opening up to the visible, makes possible the sympathetic presentation of distal aspects of the natural environment, then looking, so understood, suffices for the truth of the Biranian principle – in order to see well, one must look. A conception of looking that would make true the Biranian principle must at once be something that the perceiver does and that makes the distal environment perceptually accessible. Looking outward is something the perceiver does. And looking outward, insofar as it makes possible the sympathetic presentation of the distal environment in visual experience, makes that environment perceptually accessible.

5.5   Sympathy and Visual Presentation

I look where the ancient chestnut tree is and direct my gaze at that tree situated in a straight line from me. My gaze is fixed upon the tree. My gaze reaches it from a distance and is posed on it. The visual awareness afforded me by my perceptual experience is not merely confined to the remote spatial region where the tree is located. I peer through the intervening space, in all its potential steps, and encounter an ancient chestnut tree facing me from across the intervening distance. Being opaque to a significant degree, the tree is a site of visual resistance. The ancient chestnut tree determines a perceptually impenetrable boundary that resists my gaze. In resisting my gaze, the ancient chestnut tree facing me is present in my visual experience. In looking at the ancient chestnut tree in the early evening, my experience assimilates to that tree and that tree shapes my experience of it. In looking, my visual awareness extends to the tree and absorbs it. And it is the resistance that the tree offers to my visual extension that explains, in part, its subsequent absorption and formal assimilation.

In order to see well, one must look. Looking makes aspects of the distal environment perceptually accessible by making possible their sympathetic presentation in visual experience. It is the role that looking plays in making possible the sympathetic presentation of the visible that makes true the Biranian principle.

I turn, and look, and see an ancient chestnut tree. In so doing, I direct my gaze across the park. I look through the illuminated space, a space perceptually penetrated by my gaze, until I can no more. It is the resistance to my looking, my visual encounter with the perceptually impenetrable, that presents opaque objects arrayed in the distal environment. The ancient chestnut tree resists my visual activity. The ancient chestnut tree prevents me from seeing further. I can see nothing in it or through it. However, not all limits to my gaze are external. There are internal limits to how far I may look into the distance. Other perceivers possess the capacity to look further than I can. So how is it possible for an experienced limit to my visual activity to disclose the perceptually impenetrable tree? If the visual presentation of the perceptually impenetrable is due to the operation of sympathy, then we have the basis of an answer. It is only when I experience the tree's limit to my visual activity, its resistance to my gaze, its perceptual impenetrability, as a sympathetic response to a countervailing force, my gaze encountering an alien force that resists it, one force in conflict with another, like it yet distinct from it, that the perceptually impenetrable body discloses itself to visual awareness.

In *De sensu*, Aristotle distinguishes between the limit of the transparent and the limit of a body. The limit of the transparent is a perceptually impenetrable visual boundary. The limit of a body is its spatial boundaries. These are distinct limits. Whereas the former is qualitative, the latter is quantitative. However, importantly, they can coincide. A bounded body, in being perceptually impenetrable, determines a visual boundary that coincides with the limit of the body. Moreover, Aristotle's claim that color is the limit of the transparent in a determinately bounded body (*De sensu* 3 439 b 11) gives expression to just this coincidence (or so I argue, Kalderon 2015; Chapter 3.3). Color, that is, surface color, is the limit of the transparent in being the terminal qualitative state in a progression of qualitative states ordered by decreasing perceptual penetrability. A determinately bounded body is one such that, being perceptually impenetrable, determines a visual boundary through which nothing further may appear. This visual boundary is spatially coincident with the limit of the body and is where the body's surface color is seen to inhere. In experiencing the visual resistance of the colored body as a sympathetic response to a countervailing force that resists the perceiver's gaze, the perceptually impenetrable chromatic body discloses itself in visual awareness.

To get a sense of this, compare David Katz's description of the way that the appearance of surface color contrasts with the appearance of spectral color:

> The paper has a surface in which the colour lies. The plane on which the spectral color is extended in space before the observer does not in the same sense possess a surface. One feels that one can penetrate more of less deeply into the spectral color, whereas when one looks at the colour of a paper the surface presents a barrier beyond which the eye cannot pass. It is as though the colour of the paper offered resistance to the eye. We have here a phenomenon of visual resistance which in its way contributes to the structure of the perceptual world as something existing in actuality. (1935, 8)

The phenomenon of visual resistance contributes to the structure of the perceptual world as something existing in actuality. And it does so, or so I claim, by being a necessary precondition for the sympathetic presentation of what resists the perceiver's gaze. Katz's discussion also nicely brings out how, from among the many determinate forms of visual resistance, there is a distinctly chromatic form of visual resistance at work in the contrasting appearances of surface and spectral color.

Despite philosophers' penchant for limiting their visual examples to opaque bodies, such as Moore's (1903) blue bead or Price's (1932) red tomato, not all visibilia are opaque and not all are bodies, as Katz's example of spectral colors illustrates. Can the account of the sympathetic presentation in vision of opaque bodies be extended to, at least, non-opaque things? Is the principle of sympathy operative in the presentation of the visible more generally?

In *De sensu*, Aristotle observes that transparency comes in degrees. By the transparent, Aristotle means what is actually transparent, what is illuminated by the contingent presence and activity of the fiery substance. The transparent offers insufficient visual resistance to determine a perceptually impenetrable boundary. But offering insufficient visual resistance to determine a perceptually impenetrable boundary is consistent with offering visual resistance nonetheless. Something is perfectly transparent if it offers no visual resistance to sight. Something is imperfectly transparent if it offers visual resistance to sight but not sufficient to determine a perceptually impenetrable boundary. From perfect transparency, as we approach the limit of perceptual penetrability, the perceptually impenetrable that determines a visual boundary through which and in which nothing further may be seen, there is a range of states of imperfect transparency ordered by declining degrees of perceptual penetrability.

The illuminant is a perceptual medium in the way that I claimed sounds to be (Chapter 4.4). Sounds make the audible activities of distal objects perceptually accessible and are in that sense audible media. We hear the distal source through or in the sound it generates. Similarly, we may see an opaque body through or in the illumination. Whereas physical media answer to the demands of being a causal intermediary, perceptual media answer to the demands of perceptual accessibility. Light does not require physical media in which to propagate in the way that sound waves do. As the Michelson–Morley experiment of 1887 went some way toward showing, there is no Luminiferous aether. But the illuminated air may be a perceptual medium, nonetheless. Moreover, not only are perceptual media themselves perceptible, but they are perceptible in a certain way. Specifically, they are not perceptible in themselves, but owe their perceptibility to other things that are perceptible in themselves, the objects the perceptual media make perceptually accessible. So the illuminant is visible, though not visible in itself, but owes its visibility to the objects that it illuminates. One sees the brightness of a pantry, not in itself, but by seeing the brightly lit objects arranged in it. This is the way in which the perceptually penetrable presents itself to the perceiver's gaze.

The more the perceptually penetrable resists the perceiver's gaze, the more visible in its own right it becomes and so loses, to that degree, the capacity for other things to be perceived in it, or through it. Visual resistance can take many forms. For example, the determinate kind of visual resistance offered by a perceptually penetrable thing, such as a liquid mass, may consist in its possessing a volume color. A volume color pervades the perceptually penetrable mass, and that liquid mass has that color, independently of the colors of the things arrayed in it, or seen through it (though see Mizrahi 2010). If the liquid mass is sufficiently perceptually penetrable, seeing the colors of things arrayed in it may be within the bounds of normal human color constancy. That is, one may see a red bead in a yellow liquid and that bead may be seen to be red, though, of course, looking the way a red thing would when seen through a yellow liquid. The red bead will look to be red, and the same shade of red, when seen through a clear liquid, though, of course, it will look another way. In moving from the yellow liquid to the clear, the red bead's appearance changes, but the bead does not appear to change color. There are limits, however, to the normal human color constancy. If the liquid is strongly enough colored, if it offers sufficient visual resistance in that way, this will erode the perceiver's ability to visually recognize the determinate shade of the bead, or even that it is red. Volume color is not the only form of visual resistance offered by otherwise perceptually penetrable media. As Katz observed, spectral color also offers visual resistance. And refractions, reflections, specular highlights, shadows, all contribute, in determinate ways, to the visual resistance of the imperfectly transparent.

The perfectly transparent, insofar as it can be seen at all, is visually presented by the objects seen in it or through it. Its visibility is entirely parasitic on the visibility of the objects it enables. Insofar as the perceptually impenetrable is presented in sight as a sympathetic response to the experienced limit to the perceiver's gaze, and the perfectly transparent medium is thereby presented, the principle of sympathy makes possible the presentation, in vision, of the perfectly transparent. The imperfectly transparent, by contrast, offers visual resistance at least to some degree, but not to a degree sufficient to determine a perceptually impenetrable boundary. To the degree that it manifestly resists perceptual penetration, it is possible to sympathetically present it in visual experience. Think of the way in which the volume color or refraction of an imperfectly transparent medium may present that medium in our visual experience of it. However, the more visible in its own right the imperfectly transparent becomes, the more it erodes the sympathetic presentation of objects arrayed in that medium. The more we hear audible features of the sound had independently of the source that generates it, the less capable we are of hearing that source through or in that sound. The more we see visible features of the illuminated media had independently of the objects that it illuminates, the less capable we are of seeing through it or in it. Illumination may reveal the latent visibility of things, but if it is sufficiently strong, it may blind us to the scene. Perceptual media, in calling attention to themselves, erode the sympathetic presentation of distal objects they otherwise make possible.

We have explained the visual presentation of the perceptually impenetrable in terms of the operation of sympathy. The perceptually impenetrable is presented in sight when the limit to the perceiver's gaze is experienced as a sympathetic reaction to a countervailing force that resists that gaze. However, the operation of sympathy is not confined to the presentation, in vision, of the perceptually impenetrable. We see perceptually penetrable things as well. The visual presentation of the perfectly transparent, if that is so much as possible, entirely derives from the sympathetic presentation of objects seen in it. So sympathy would suffice to explain the visual presentation of the perfectly transparent, if it can genuinely be said to be visible at all (whether it can may depend upon the practical point of so saying in the given circumstances). Sympathy played an additional role in the visual perception of the imperfectly transparent. Insofar as it is perceptually penetrable to some degree, it makes possible the sympathetic presentation of perceptually impenetrable objects seen in it or through it. It is only because the gaze may penetrate to the site of visual resistance, facing it from across a distance, that the perceptually impenetrable is sympathetically presented in visual experience. However, insofar as the imperfectly transparent is visible in its own right, the resistance it offers becomes the means of sympathetically responding to it, and this erodes the sympathetic presentation of distal objects otherwise made possible.

So we have the following argument by cases. The visible exhaustively divides into the perceptually impenetrable and the perceptually penetrable. The perceptually penetrable is either perfectly perceptually penetrable, offering no visual resistance, or imperfectly penetrable, offering visual resistance to some degree. The operation of sympathy suffices to explain the visual presentation of the perceptually impenetrable. Moreover this explanation suffices, as well, for the visual presentation of the perfectly penetrable, as we have explained. Sympathy explained as well not only the presentation of the imperfectly penetrable insofar as other objects may be sympathetically presented in it, or through it, but also the respects in which it is visible in its own right and the way that this erodes the sympathetic presentation of objects seen in it, or through it. So the operation of sympathy suffices for the presentation of the visible, in sight, quite generally.

We began by explaining the visual presentation of an opaque body in terms of sympathy. Since the objects of sight are not limited to opaque bodies, this raised the question whether sympathy operates in visual presentation quite generally. The following worry might arise about the argument so far: While we have explicitly addressed the visual presentation of non-opaque things, we have failed to explicitly address the visual presentation of non-corporeal things, such as events and processes. However, perceptual impenetrability does not merely pertain to the surfaces of opaque bodies. A flame, should the fire be burning intensely enough, may be perceptually impenetrable, obstructing the view of other visibilia. Thus Herbert Mason reports that as he waited to take his iconic photograph of St Paul's on December 29, 1940, "glares of many fires and sweeping clouds of smoke" obscured the dome of St Paul's. It is not just the sweeping clouds of smoke, masses of particulate matter, that obscured the dome of St Paul's, but the glares of many fires. The general point is that the way in which we have characterized the visible, in terms of degrees of perceptual penetrability, is equally applicable to visible objects of distinct ontological categories. Perceptual penetrability applies equally to corporeal and non-corporeal things and so does not preclude the visual presentation of events and processes.

There may be further doubts about whether the taxonomy of the visible provided by degrees of perceptual penetrability is, in fact, complete. On a clear day, the sky is blue. And the sky, at night, when unobstructed by cloud cover or light pollution, is black, albeit speckled with points of irradiation that vary chromatically. Is the blue of the day sky, or the black of the night sky, a quality of something perceptually penetrable or perceptually impenetrable? And if we feel uncomfortable answering, doesn't this show that the proposed taxonomy of the visible is incomplete? The puzzlement is resolved, however, once we realize the sense in which each of these responses is at least partly right consistent with one another. And if the puzzlement is resolved in this way, the completeness of the taxonomy of the visible is not thereby challenged.

We have accepted Aristotle's claim that transparency comes in degrees, degrees to which it resists perceptual penetration. Aristotle also claims that the blue appearance of the day sky can be explained in terms of the imperfect transparency of the illuminated air (*De sensu* 3 4391–3). In this way, it is like water. From a cliff overhanging the sea, the sea may appear blue. But, if enticed by the sea, one were to descend to the beach and examine a handful of seawater, it would not be blue at all but transparent. Similarly, looking up at the sky on a clear autumn afternoon, one sees an expanse of blue. But if one were to travel to that region of the sky, by helicopter, say, nothing blue would be found. The visual resistance of an imperfectly transparent medium increases with an increase in volume. The further one sees into a transparent medium, the more resistance that medium offers to sight. In the case of a clear sky, its scattering of light is what offers progressive resistance to our gaze. And its blue appearance is the effect of this resistance. Aristotle is explicit about the effects of such resistance in *Meteorologica*: "For a weak light shining through a dense medium ... will cause all kinds of colours to appear, but especially crimson and purple" (*Meteorologica* i 5 3425–8; Webster in Barnes 1984, 8–9).

When I look into the blue of the clear autumn sky, I see as far as I can see. Other people and animals may see further than I do, but the power of sight of all finite creatures is limited in this way. So while the blue appearance of day sky is due to the degree to which it resists perceptual penetration, its scattering of light offering progressive resistance to my gaze, there is a limit to how far I may peer in it or through it. This perceptual limitation is manifest in our experience of the dome of the heavens. In a clear blue sky, in any direction I may look, there is a limit to how far I may see. The finite lines of sight extending in every direction from the perceiver's vantage point determines a sphere. This is what we experience as the dome of the heavens. I confess to recoiling somewhat from the impiety of this expression. The dome of the heavens, construed literally, is not only a reification of a perceptual limitation, but is misattributed to the heavens as well. Its impiety consists in giving expression to an anthropomorphic conceit of cosmic proportions.

Our experience of the dome of the heavens is relevant to our initial puzzlement. Recall we wondered whether the blue of the sky inhered in something perceptually penetrable or in something perceptually impenetrable. We are now in a position to see how each response is at least partly right consistent with one another. The blue of the sky inheres in the perceptually penetrable illuminated air, the resistance it offers by the scattering of light resulting in a blue appearance should one peer deeply enough into it. However, there is a limit to how far one may see, and this is reflected in our experience of the blue sky, specifically, in its apparent dome shape. The surface of the dome represents the limits of visibility, and is, to that extent, perceptually impenetrable. But the blue of the sky is not seen to inhere in the dome of the heavens. It is a volume color, not a surface color. A blue inhering in the surface of the dome would be a vulgar simulacrum of the voluminous blue of the sky, its appearance more akin to the interior design of a Vegas casino than the clear autumn sky that it apes.

In sympathetically disclosing the ancient chestnut tree, my visual experience absorbs that tree and is constitutively shaped by it. The conscious character of seeing the tree is constituted, in part, by its bright green burs and the wave-like form of its trunk sympathetically presented to my partial perspective on that tree in the given circumstances of perception. What it is like for me to see the tree depends upon and derives from, at least in part, what the tree is like, at least in visible respects. Visual experience formally assimilates to its object, relative to the perceiver's partial perspective, as a consequence of being constitutively shaped by that object as presented to that perspective, a constitutive shaping made possible by the sympathetic presentation of that object in visual experience. Constitutive shaping of visual experience by its object is a "communion" with that object – in undergoing that experience, the perceiver is united, in a way, with the object of their perception. Moreover, as with Plotinus (Chapter 2.8), this unity explains in part, the similarity between the visual experience and its object. The formal assimilation of visual perception to its object, at least relative to the perceiver's partial perspective, is the effect of constitutive shaping, and thus its conscious character depends upon and derives from, at least in part, the visible character of the object seen.

Recall, we are generalizing from Plotinus in taking the unity of visual presentation to be explanatorily prior to the operation of sympathy (Chapter 2.8). The visual presentation of distal aspects of the natural environment is not being constructed from elements and principles understood independently of their visual presentation, rather the unity of the perceiver and the distal aspects of the natural environment is presupposed, and sympathy merely analytically explicates the intelligible structure of this presupposed unity. Not only does sympathy only operate within a unity, but that unity is reducible to no other thing.

Visual presentation is an irreducible unity. If sensory presentation is a distinctive kind of unity, a "communion" with its object, then visual presentation is more distinctive still. Insofar as visual presentation, like haptic and auditory presentation, is governed by the principle of sympathy, it is a mode of being with. Turning, and looking, and seeing the ancient chestnut tree is a way of being with that tree. Sartre's overly aggressive conception of the look, in *L'Être et le néant*, blinds him to this possibility. Sartre fails to see how the look's coming into conflict with its object may be the means of the latter's sympathetic presentation to the former. (See Jay 1994, chapter 5, especially 287, where he remarks that Heidegger's conception of *mitsein* was, perhaps, too irenic for Sartre.) Like auditory presentation, and unlike haptic presentation, visual presentation is incompletely corporeal. Haptic presentation involves a conscious animate body, the perceiver, being with another corporeal body. It is a way for one body to be with another body. Auditory presentation, by contrast, is incompletely corporeal since it involves a conscious animate body, the perceiver, being with an event or process, even events or processes that do not have bodies as participants. Events and processes may be seen as well as heard, and so visual presentation is to that extent incorporeal as well. Visual presentation may, at least in certain circumstances, be a disclosure with duration, but the objects disclosed are not essentially dynamic as are the *substrata* of audible qualities. Like haptic perception, vision may disclose relatively static features of the distal environment. But even seeing relatively static features of body, such as their color, may only be disclosed over time. A color is wholly present in a body at every moment of its instantiation. Nevertheless, the unchanging color of a body may only be disclosed in the distinctive manner it interacts with changes to its relations to the perceiver, the illuminant, and the circumstances of perception (Broackes 1997; Matthen 2005; Noë 2004). And that is compatible, if circumstances are propitious, with the perceiver being able to recognize at a glance the color of a thing.

The unity presupposed by sensory presentation generally, being partial, is a lesser unity than the unity presupposed by intelligible presentation. The intelligibly differentiated image of the hyperontic One is wholly present to the Intellect. An intelligible object is wholly present in the act of intellection in the way that a sensible object never is in perception since sensory presentation is invariably relative to the perceiver's partial perspective. Though a lesser unity, being partial, it is a kind of unity nonetheless. Being the kind of unity it is, a mode of being with whose principle is sympathy, there is a sense in which, sensory presentation, despite its partial character, places the perceiver in the object perceived. As we observed earlier (Chapter 5.3), this is a neo-Platonic heritage.

In Chapter 1.4, we stopped just short of embracing that heritage. We considered, instead, a related but weaker claim about haptic experience. Beginning with the prima facie absurdity of supposing that haptic experience is in the perceiver's head (an absurdity mitigated, somewhat, in a philosophical milieu in which "Cartesianism *cum* Materialism" is the reigning metaphysical orthodoxy, Putnam 1993, 1994, 1999), we claimed, instead, that it is more natural to suppose, at least initially, that haptic experience is closer to where its object is at, in our handling of that object. The Plotinian claim, if made on behalf of haptic presentation, is stronger still. It would be the claim that haptic experience places us within the object of haptic experience. In grasping or enclosure, the haptic experience is in the perceived overall shape and volume of the object that the perceiver is handling. The earlier, weaker claim hedged at the boundary between the apparent body, the region wherein bodily sensation is potentially felt (Martin 1992), and extrapersonal space. However, if haptic perception involves a mode of sympathetic presentation, then the haptic variant of the Plotinian claim, that haptic perception places us in the object of haptic investigation, must be true, at least on a certain interpretation of that claim.

The next chapter will explore whether good sense can be made of this neo-Platonic heritage. I shall argue that the neo-Platonic heritage is best understood as articulating an aspect of the phenomenology of explicit awareness made possible by sympathetic presentation. The overall aim of the next chapter is to explicate the conception of perceptual objectivity that sympathetic presentation affords us. It will turn out that this conception of objectivity is the basis of a strong form of perceptual realism, a form of realism on which the distinction between the phenomenal and the noumenal collapses. Things in themselves are perceptible, albeit partially and imperfectly. That perception, via the operation of sympathy, places us into the very heart of things, explains how this may be so.

CHAPTER 6

Realism

6.1 Grasping and the Rhetoric of Objectivity

Haptic perception plays a privileged role in the rhetoric of objectivity. In Chapter 1.7, we discussed two historical exemplars of this rhetorical impulse, the Giants shaking trees and boulders at the Friends of the Forms as they affirm their corporealism, and Dr Johnson's kicking the stone outside of the church in Harwich as an exasperated affirmation of its material existence independent of our ideas. While by no means dead, this rhetorical trope has, perhaps, lost some of its sheen in giving birth to the late twentieth-century cliché of the table-pounding realist.

Being a cliché is no proof against existence. I once attended a lecture where the speaker pounded on the podium at each mention of an objective worldly correlate of our conceptual scheme. Through this performance, the philosopher was expressing the objectivity of the worldly correlate, and, in a rather bullying fashion, demanding our assent to it. Like Dr Johnson's performance, it was a multimodal affair (Chapter 1.7; Campbell and Cassam 2014, 71). The audience, in sympathetically responding to the philosopher's tactile experience, is meant to vividly experience the tangible resistance of the podium, revealed, in part, in the loud, sharp sound it produced when pounded. It is this resistance to touch that is meant to disclose the podium to be objectively there, independently of the speaker's pounding, just as the worldly correlate is meant to be there, independently of our conceptual scheme.

Haptic perception plays a privileged role in the rhetoric of objectivity. It does so, in part, because the experience of felt resistance to touch is phenomenologically vivid and primitively compelling. Though in no doubt about the presence or solidity of a thing, we may, nevertheless, be drawn to touch it. Thus we must endeavor to teach children to keep their hands to themselves, and even in maturity, polite notices are required to remind adults to not touch the display cabinet. Aristotle discerns an existential concern in touch. While the distal senses, such as sight and audition, are for the well-being of an animal equipped with locomotion, touch is for that animal's very existence. The tangible may be of vital concern, be it predator or prey. Perhaps this existential dimension is part of what makes touch so primitively compelling. Haptic perception plays a privileged role in the rhetoric of objectivity, in part, because the experience of felt resistance to touch is phenomenologically vivid and primitively compelling. Moreover, and for our purposes more importantly, it plays a privileged role, as well, because grasping provides a model for perceptual objectivity quite generally, in the assimilation of the hand, and the haptic experience it gives rise to, to the object of haptic investigation.

6.2   Perceptual Objectivity

That perception assimilates to its object is the manifestation of its objectivity. Perceptual assimilation is formal rather than material. The conscious qualitative character of the perceptual experience becomes like, if not exactly like, the presented object without materially absorbing it. Moreover, the formal assimilation of perception to its object is not exact in the way that would entail the sharing of qualities. The experience of our hominid ancestor, in seeing the alien obelisk, does not itself become black. The qualitative character of their visual experience in seeing the obelisk may be like, in some sense, the blackness presented in it. But that blackness enjoys no natural existence in our hominid ancestor's perception of it the way it enjoys natural existence in the alien obelisk. Perception may be a capacity to become like, as Aristotle contends, but it is not chameleon-like, as Crathorn imagined, and Holcot complained of (Chapter 1.4), thus avoiding Theophrastus' *aporia*.

An ineliminable source of the inexactness of perception's formal assimilation to its object consists in its perspectival relativity. Perception only formally assimilates to its object relative to the perceiver's partial perspective (Chapter 1.4, Chapter 3.6). I have not done enough to defend the general claim that all sensory experience is perspectival. I have not, for example, argued that olfaction is perspectival. I have, however, argued that, in addition to visual perspectives, there are, as well, haptic and auditory perspectives. Each allows for better or worse perspectives, and each involves the potential disclosure of previously hidden aspects of a sensible object. Moreover, each does so in an egocentrically structured space. Finally, each is such that the perceptual appearance of an object can vary between its presentation to distinct perspectives. While there are similarities among them in virtue of which they each count as perspectives, haptic, auditory, and visual perspectives are also, importantly, distinct. While each structures a space, not only may the space differ, be it peripersonal or extrapersonal space, but the manner of its structuring may differ as well. Vision is rectilinear in a way that audition, in providing the perceiver with 360 degree awareness of the natural environment, is not.

Perception provides only a partial perspective on the natural environment. The object of perception may not be wholly present to the perceiver's partial perspective on it. To that extent, their perception is imperfect in the sense of being incomplete – there are perceptible aspects of the object not disclosed to the perceiver's perspective. As Merleau-Ponty stresses, however, perception is not imperfect in a further, normative sense:

> But in immediate consciousness this perspectival character of my knowledge is not conceived as an accident in its regard, as an imperfection relative to the existence of my body and its proper point of view; and knowledge by "profiles" is not treated as the degradation of a true knowledge which would grasp the totality of the possible aspects of the object all at once. Perspective does not appear to me to be a subjective deformation of things but, on the contrary, to be one of their properties, perhaps their essential property. It is precisely because of it that the perceived possesses in itself a hidden and inexhaustible richness, that it is a "thing." ... Far from introducing a coefficient of subjectivity into perception, it provides it on the contrary with the assurance of communicating with a world which is richer than what we know of it, that is, of communicating with a real world. The profiles of my desk are not given to direct knowledge as appearances without value, but as "manifestations" of the desk. (1964, 186)

In most cases, the object of perception, in all its particularity, exceeds what is disclosed of it in perceptual experience. Touch provides a vivid example of this in what I earlier described as the allure of the tangible (Chapter 1.2). The allure of the tangible is the sense, or premonition, that, at any given moment, the body exceeds what is disclosed to us by touch. We have the sense, when touching an object, that it is tangibly determined in ways that we have yet to feel. Our tactile sense of a body's "thingness" – its concrete particularity – consists, in part, in this allure. While, perhaps, particularly vivid in tactile phenomenology, Merleau-Ponty maintains that something like this is true of perceptual phenomenology more generally, that perception's partial disclosure is an objective manifestation of an object that exceeds what is disclosed of it in experience. Far from being an obstacle to perception's objectivity by introducing a coefficient of subjectivity into perception, the perspectival character of perception is what makes possible its objective disclosure of the natural environment. Objectivity and the parochial are linked (for an insightful exploration of this theme, though not within the philosophy of perception, see Travis 2011).

To bring out one way in which objectivity and the parochial may be linked in perception, consider the limits to normal human color constancy. Human color constancy is imperfect. Not only does human color vision display constancy for only some scenes and some conditions of illumination, but human color vision displays different degrees of constancy in different kinds of scenes in different ranges of illumination. Human color constancy is imperfect in that it displays these various kinds of incompleteness. Hilbert explains how human color constancy is imperfect in a further important sense:

> Many theories of color constancy take the form of explaining how it is that the visual system manages to extract information about the reflectance of the objects in a scene from the color signal from those objects. Since this involves separating the contributions of the reflectance and the illuminant to the color signal these theories are often characterized as "discounting the illuminant." Perfect color constancy in these terms would involve accurate recovery of reflectance for any scene under any lighting conditions. The perceived color of objects would be perfectly correlated with their reflecting characteristics and not vary at all with changes in the illuminant of the composition and arrangement of objects in view. This type of perfect color constancy is not possible. (2005, 143)

Human color constancy is imperfect. As Merleau-Ponty emphasizes, this should not be thought of as a deficit. Suppose there could be a perceiver whose perception displayed perfect color constancy in Hilbert's sense. What would perfect color constancy, so conceived, be like? If we bracket Hilbert's reflectance physicalism, apparent color would be perfectly correlated with real color and would not vary with a change in the illuminant or with a change in the composition and arrangement of the other elements of the scene. What would it be like for a perceiver with perfect color constancy, so conceived, to see a field of grass set against a blue summer sky? The field would appear uniformly green and the sky uniformly blue. Moreover, no difference in color appearance would differentiate any portion of the uniformly green field. The experience of the scene would be not unlike a young child's drawing of the scene. The grass would be uniformly green and lack the golden cast that we might observe in viewing the same scene, nor would it be dappled, as we observe the scene to be, by sunlight and shadow, for these variations in appearance are due to variations in illumination. Furthermore, no difference in color appearance would differentiate any portion of the uniformly blue sky. The sky would be uniformly blue and would manifest no deepening azure to the east, for, again, these variations in appearance are due to variations in illumination. Children's drawings also intimate what perfect size constancy might be like – they will draw a car as larger than an adult even if the car is at a great distance from that person. Just as with perfect size constancy we would lose information about distance, so with perfect color constancy we would lose information about the illuminant. So the partial and variable character of human color constancy is no deficit. And not merely because it lacks the garish character of children's crayon drawings, but because we would be insensitive to important aspects of our environment. Our environment is only objectively disclosed in sensory experience to the partial perspective we have on it.

Not only does perception formally assimilate to its object, relative to the perceiver's partial perspective, but this formal assimilation is a kind of constitutive shaping. The object present in perceptual experience constitutively shapes that experience, the way that St Paul's constitutively shapes the London skyline. What that skyline is like is determined, in part, by what St Paul's is like. St Paul's determines what the London skyline is like, at least in part, by virtue of being a part or contour of that skyline. Similarly, what the perceiver's experience of an object is like is determined, in part, by what that object is like. The object of perception determines what the perceiver's experience of it is like, at least in part, by virtue of being a constituent of that experience. Constitutive shaping entails formal assimilation, though formal assimilation need not involve constitutive shaping. Consider Locke on primary quality perception. In perceiving a primary quality, the perceiver's experience resembles its object, but not by having that object as a constituent. The object constitutively shaping the perceiver's perceptual experience of it is, as Ardley (1958) stressed, the result of the perceiver's "communion" with that object. It is the unity of the perception with its object that ultimately explains the similarity between the conscious qualitative character of perceptual experience and the qualitative character of the object presented to the perceiver's partial perspective. (Recall, according to Plotinus, it is because of the unity provided by the World-Soul that potentially distant parts of the sensible cosmos that are suitably disposed to become like or unlike may sympathetically interact. See Chapter 2.7. For the generalization and application of this point to the case of haptic perception, see Chapter 2.8.) Perception, so conceived, is a kind of incorporation in a metaphorical and anti-Cartesian sense (Chapter 1.5). Perception is a kind of incorporation insofar as its formal assimilation to its object, relative to the perceiver's partial perspective, is understood on the model of constitutive shaping.

It is because this feature of grasping or enclosure, understood as a mode of haptic perception, generalizes to other forms of perception, such as vision and audition, that grasping is an apt metaphor for perception, more generally. If this feature carries over to perception generally, if the object of perception constitutively shapes the perceiver's perceptual experience, then it is easy to see its epistemic significance. If perception involves becoming like the perceived object actually is, then it is a genuine mode of awareness. One can only perceptually assimilate what is there to be assimilated. If perceptual experience is a formal mode of assimilation understood as a mode of constitutive shaping, then one could not undergo such an experience consistent with a Cartesian demon eliminating the object of that experience. If there is no external object, then there is nothing to which the perceiver, or perhaps their experience, could assimilate to. If the phenomenological character of perception is constitutively shaped by the object presented to the perceiver's partial perspective, then we can begin to see the epistemic significance of perceptual phenomenology. If the phenomenological character of perception is constitutively shaped by the object presented to the perceiver's partial perspective, then it is the grounds for an epistemic warrant for the range of propositions whose truth turns on what is presented in that perceptual experience (Johnston 2006b, 2011; Kalderon 2011c).

The warrant, here, should be understood as an entitlement to judge (in the ordinary sense of "entitlement" and not in Burge's 2003 technical sense of the term; compare McDowell 2009b, 132n). Entitlements may be possessed without being exercised. In being aware of some aspect of the natural environment, the perceiver may possess an epistemic warrant that entitles them to know various things without the perceiver, in fact, coming to know these things. The perceiver is knowledgeable of the object of perception in the sense that knowledge is available to the subject in perceiving the object, whether or not such knowledge is in fact "activated" (in Williamson's 1990 terminology). The epistemic warrant grounded in perceptual awareness is not a factor in terms of which knowledge could be analyzed or otherwise explained. Moreover, it is an epistemic entitlement: the object of awareness is an epistemic warrant for the range of propositions whose truth turns on what the perceiver is aware of. Perception confers this epistemic entitlement given the alethic connection between the particular that is the object of perceptual awareness and the proposition potentially known. Awareness of the sensible particulars affords the subject with a reason that is in this way akin to proof – it is logically impossible for the particular to exist and the proposition to be false (see Cook Wilson 1926; Kalderon and Travis 2013; Travis 2005). Because in seeing the bright green burrs of the ancient chestnut tree, I possess a reason that would, in the given circumstance, warrant my coming to know that the burrs are bright green, I am authoritative about the color of the chestnut tree's burrs. My seeing the bright green of the burrs can stand proxy for any inquiry on your part about the color of the burrs. If in coming to know that the burrs are bright green, I express my knowledge by stating it, I extend to you an offer to take it on my authority that the burrs are the color that I see them to be.

The present metaphysics of perception, while inconsistent with a Cartesian demon eliminating the object of experience, is not, by itself, sufficient to refute skepticism. Even conceding the conception of perceptual experience as a kind of formal assimilation understood as a mode of constitutive shaping, that conception is nevertheless consistent with the possibility of ringers. This possibility can arise in two ways. The objects of perception, what we perceive, may have ringers. I may see Castor and shake his hand, but his twin, Pollux, is a dead ringer. Moreover, not only do the objects of perception, those sensible aspects of the natural environment that we encounter in experience, admit of ringers, but our perceptual episodes, our experiences, may themselves admit of ringers. A perception of Pollux is a ringer for a perception of Castor, as is a perfectly matching hallucination of Castor. And a skeptic might try to exploit this latter possibility to undermine the epistemic warrant afforded by perception, a warrant not shared with its experiential ringers. The mere existence of experiential ringers is, by itself, insufficient for the skeptic's conclusion. The skeptic would need, in addition, the claim that if a perceptual episode affords the perceiver with epistemic warrant, it must not admit of ringers that do not. So conceived, epistemic warrant requires ringer-less proof. Though this is not the place to go into it, I doubt very much that these further skeptical maneuvers could succeed. They rely on an over-demanding conception of epistemic warrant that is difficult to coherently maintain. (For a sense of this, see how these ideas work themselves out in the tradition of Oxford realism as discussed in Kalderon and Travis 2013, especially their discussion of "the accretion." See also Williamson's 2000 discussion of luminosity. For more on Oxford realism, see Marion 2000a, 2000b.)

Perception is a fundamental form of objectivity in our cognitive economy since it affords us explicit awareness of sensible aspects of the natural environment. It is not a fundamental form of objectivity, however, by being a primitive form of objective representation as Burge (2010) contends. Sensory awareness is a mode of assimilation, and something can only assimilate to what is there to be assimilated. Consider the following analogy. Knowledge is factive, let us suppose. If the perceiver knows something, then there is some fact that they know. If there is no fact that they know, then there is nothing that they know. Similarly we might say that perception is objective. If the perceiver perceives something, then there is some object that they perceive ("object," here, is not the ontological category, but perception's *terminus*, namely, what is perceived). If there is no object that they perceive, then there is nothing that they perceive. Perception involves the objective presentation of its object in the explicit awareness afforded by that experience. That object, of which the perceiver is explicitly aware, is only subsequently re-presented, if at all, in imagination and memory. *Pace* Burge, I favor, instead, the Peripatetic doctrine that imagination and memory, and not perception, are the basic forms of intentional or representational capacities in our cognitive economy. That is, we are presented aspects of the natural environment in our perceptual experience of it, and these aspects are only subsequently re-presented, if at all, in imagination and memory. Such re-presentations are the primitive forms of objective empirical representation, in Burge's sense, not perception. Though the explicit awareness afforded by perceptual experience makes objective empirical representation possible, such awareness has no veridicality or accuracy conditions, its object being presented, not re-presented. Perception is the basis of an epistemic warrant not by making the perceiver aware of a truth, though recognition of what one is perceiving may afford such awareness. Rather perception affords awareness of those aspects of the natural environment upon which the truth of a variety of propositions depend.

Moreover, sensory awareness, the explicit awareness afforded by perception of the natural environment, as opposed to awareness of truths about that environment, is epistemically distinctive. Information can go stale. What once passed for knowledge may accrete into dogma if the world changes without a corresponding change in cognitive state. The explicit awareness afforded by perceptual experience, in contrast, keeps the perceiver *au courant* with their environment (Travis 2013, 173–174). In disclosing, partially and imperfectly, that environment, their perceptual experience will change with every change of what is presented in it. If timeliness is important in your practical circumstances, perception offers a distinct advantage over, not only belief, but what passes for knowledge. If you value timeliness, given your practical circumstances, if being *au courant* with some aspect of the natural environment is of particular practical significance, then you should keep an eye on it or, at the very least, be perceptually vigilant, more generally.

That perception assimilates to its object, in the sense that it does, is due, in part, to the activity of the perceiver. Perhaps that is why Olivi describes the outward extensive activity of perception as being, at the same time, a formative absorption toward its object. The haptic experience of our hominid ancestor only assimilates to the stone thanks to the activity of their hand's grasp and the resistance it encounters. It is when the limit to the hand's activity is experienced as a sympathetic response to an alien force, like it yet distinct from it, that the stone is presented in their grasp. Haptic touch discloses the overall shape and volume of the stone by grasping it. Its roughness is disclosed by feeling it. Its heft, by weighing it. Grasping, feeling, weighing, listening, and looking are all outward extensive activities by which the perceiver opens themselves up, in a directed manner, to the sensible, in all its varieties. The activity of the perceiver is a necessary precondition for the objective disclosure of the perceived object. For it is the resistance that such activity encounters in the natural environment that makes possible the sympathetic presentation of the sensible world without.

I have been discussing perceptual objectivity and its epistemic significance. Specifically, I have been spelling out the conception of perceptual objectivity that one arrives at once one conceives of perception, in the hylomorphic fashion, in terms of the assimilation of form without matter, as sustained by the perceiver's activity, and the epistemic significance of the resulting conception of objectivity. However, much of what was claimed would remain true on any conception of perception that merely postulates an indispensable presentational element. Thus, for example, McDowell (2008) believes that perception affords the perceiver with a non-propositional mode of awareness that grounds an epistemic warrant, understood as an epistemic entitlement. McDowell neither endorses a hylomorphic conception of sensory presentation (though he does help himself to the Peripatetic metaphor of shaping, McDowell 1998) nor even entertains its neo-Platonic elaboration in terms of sympathy with the natural environment that resists the force of the perceiver's activity. However, the metaphysics of sensory presentation that I have defended offers not only an explanation of the epistemic significance of perceptual phenomenology in the form of an analytic explication of its intelligible structure (Chapter 2.4), but also a further, distinct possibility.

If perceptual presentation is sympathetic presentation, then perception places us into the very heart of things, thus allowing us to experience them from within. Perhaps the sympathy at work in fellow-feeling would provide the most vivid and suggestive example. Fellow-feeling involves feeling along with the object of sympathy. One experiences their plight from within. The sympathetic presentation of an object in perceptual experience involves the perceiver placing themselves in the object, coinciding with it, and so experiencing it from within. The present account of sensory presentation in terms of sympathy naturally belongs to the broader neo-Platonic heritage of thinking of perception as placing the perceiver in its object. There is a way in which the present account, where sensory presentation is governed by the principle of sympathy, can make sense of this neo-Platonic heritage, though perhaps it is not the only way. On the understanding of this neo-Platonic heritage afforded by sympathy, perception presents how things are from within. Sympathy makes possible the presentation of a thing's inner nature, and thus one may perceive how a thing is in itself. Echoing Johann Friedrich Herbart, we may say that the world is a world of things in themselves and things in themselves are perceptible. Things in themselves are what appear in our perceptual experience. They are the objects of sensory awareness. If perceptual presentation is governed by the principle of sympathy, then the distinction between the phenomenal and the noumenal collapses.

6.3   Kantian Humility

Sympathy allows the perceiver to experience the presented object from within. In sympathetically presenting that object in their experience of it, the perceiver coincides with that object and experiences how that thing is in itself, its inner nature, albeit imperfectly, from a partial perspective. We can begin to make sense of these claims through a critical examination of Langton's (1998) defense of Kantian Humility.

Consider the following puzzle for Kant's position, first raised by Jacobi. According to Kant, things in themselves exist and are the cause of phenomenal appearances. But if Kant's critical philosophy is correct, then it would seem that we can have no knowledge of things in themselves. But if we have no knowledge of things in themselves, then how could we know that they exist and are the cause of phenomenal appearances? This puzzle prompts Jacobi (1815, 304) to remark of the first edition of the *Kritik der reinen Vernunft* that without the presupposition of the thing in itself I "cannot enter into the system, yet with this presupposition I cannot remain in it" (Guyer 1987, 335; for discussion of Jacobi's puzzle, see Allison 1983, 247–54, Guyer 1987, chapter 15, Langton 1998, chapter 1).

Langton's interpretation of Kant provides a straightforward solution by qualifying our ignorance of things in themselves. The qualification proceeds on the back of a metaphysical interpretation of the distinction between phenomena and things in themselves. Things in themselves are substances that have intrinsic properties whereas phenomena are relational properties of substances (Langton 1998, 20). Our ignorance pertains not to the existence of things in themselves, nor to their relational effects, such as their causing in us phenomenal appearances, but to their inner natures. We cannot know how things are in themselves. We cannot know, specifically, their intrinsic properties (Langton 1998, 13).

Kantian Humility is the name that Langton bestows upon the doctrine that we cannot know how things are in themselves, that we are irredeemably ignorant of the intrinsic natures of things in themselves. Part of the interest of Langton's book is not just the interpretation of Kant she provides, but her conviction that Kant, so interpreted, might just be right. The case Langton makes for Kantian Humility inspired Lewis (2009) to construct a Ramseyan variant. (For discussion of Ramseyan and Kantian Humility, from a standpoint that similarly takes perception to have an indispensable and irreducible presentational element, see Brewer 2011.) What case for Kantian Humility does Langton claim that we can find in Kant's writing?

In the *Bounds of Sense*, Strawson doubts that there is any such case to be found:

> Knowledge through perception of things existing independently of perception, as they are in themselves, is impossible. For the only perception which could yield us any knowledge at all of such things must be the outcome of our being affected by those things; and for this reason such knowledge can be knowledge only of those things as they appear – of the appearances of those things – and not of those things as they really are or are in themselves. The above is a fundamental and unargued complex premise of the Critique. (1966, 250)

Strawson, however, hints at potential grounds for Kantian Humility in the receptivity of human sensibility, its propensity to be affected from without. Indeed it is partly on these grounds that Langton herself sees a case for Kantian Humility.

According to Langton, Kant's case for Kantian Humility rests upon another doctrine of Kant's:

> the *receptivity* of our mind, its power of receiving representations in so far as it is in any way affected, is called sensibility ... Our nature is so constituted

that our intuition can never be other than sensible, that it contains only the way in which we are affected by objects. (Kant, *Kritik der reinen Vernunft*, A51/B75; Smith 1965, 93)

From this and other passages, Langton attributes to Kant the thesis she describes as Receptivity: "Human knowledge depends on sensibility, and sensibility is receptive: we can have knowledge of an object only in so far as it affects us" (1998, 125).

Langton's Kant is driven to embrace Kantian Humility, in part, by working out the consequences of Receptivity for human knowledge. Specifically, Langton sees the case for Kantian Humility as resting upon the distinction between the phenomenal and the noumenal (on its metaphysical interpretation), the irreducibility of relational properties to intrinsic properties (an issue she sees as at stake between Leibniz and Kant, Langton 1998, chapters 4 and 5), and Receptivity as formulated earlier.

That things in themselves cause in human subjects phenomenal appearances is a phenomenal, that is to say, relational feature of these substances. These phenomenal appearances might yet acquaint human subjects with how things are in themselves if relations somehow reduced to intrinsic properties. But no such reduction is in the offing (Langton 1998, chapter 5). So it would seem that perception, being essentially receptive, only affords human subjects with knowledge of the phenomenal features of the world, of the relational properties of substances whose intrinsic nature remains forever hidden from us.

I must confess to a lingering Strawsonian worry. Langton's argument only works on the assumption that the object of perception is relational in character. Without that assumption, the argument simply has no grip. To see how there may be a further issue here, look closely at the difference between Langton's official formulation of Receptivity and the passage from A51/B75. According to Receptivity, we can perceive an object only insofar as it affects us. That is a relatively weak claim. Perhaps only Olivi, Malebranche, and Leibniz deny it. However, among our predecessors who accept that claim, many would deny that the content of perception is restricted to the relational properties of substances. Notice, however, how the claim in A51/B75 is stronger. Kant claims that our nature is such that sensible intuition "contains only the way in which we are affected." If sensible intuition contains only the way in which we are affected, then the content of a sensible intuition is restricted to the subject being affected from without. The way in which we are affected is a causal, relational feature. So the content of sensible intuition would be relational in the way required. The lingering Strawsonian worry concerns what grounds there could be for this stronger Kantian claim, for without it, Langton's case for Kantian Humility collapses.

Why assume that the content of perception is restricted to relational properties of substances? It does not follow from the mere fact that perception requires being affected from without. So what grounds this restriction? The lingering Strawsonian worry is that this is a fundamental and unargued assumption of Langton's case for Kantian Humility. Notice Langton could not legitimately reformulate Receptivity in terms of the stronger Kantian language of A51/B75. That would have "the advantages of theft over honest toil" (Russell 1919, 71). For suppose she did. Then since the content of perception is restricted to the relational properties of substances, the content of perception would exclude the intrinsic properties of substances. A perception, so conceived, would not be a way of becoming knowledgeable of the intrinsic properties of substances since these do not figure in its content. And given a minimal empiricism, that is tantamount to Kantian Humility.

Suppose that Kant and Langton in fact provide no further grounds for this assumption. Perhaps the claim that the content of perception is restricted to relational properties of substances is grounded, not in an argument, but in an inability to conceive of the alternative. Perhaps in thinking about the passive reception of sensory impressions they could frame for themselves no positive conception of how, being affected thus, perception could present how things are in themselves. I shall not here speculate on the source of this inability. (Though a more complete anti-Kantian polemic, of a similar scale and ambition as Prichard's 1909, would provide a diagnosis of this.) Rather, I shall try to provide the wanted positive conception. Interestingly, doing so in the terms argued for in the present essay parallels, in certain respects, an anti-Kantian argument of Bergson's.

6.4   Bergson contra Kant

In *Introduction à la métaphysique* Bergson (1903) marks a distinction between relative and absolute knowledge. Surprisingly, at least to readers of *Matière et Mémoire*, Bergson counts perceptual knowledge as relative knowledge. It is hard to understand how perceptual knowledge being relative could be consistent with the conception of pure perception developed in chapter 1 of *Matière et Mémoire*, for there Bergson rejects indirect realism, arguing, instead, that pure perception, at least, directly acquaints us with its object (though see Moore 1996, for a reconciliationist reading,

39–41). That perceptual knowledge is relative is, perhaps, merely a dialectical concession to a Kantian opponent and not a claim that Bergson is himself endorsing. We shall not resolve this exegetical matter here, for our focus is not on relative knowledge, but on absolute knowledge and what, according to Bergson, makes that possible.

What is the distinction between relative and absolute knowledge? Bergson introduces the distinction this way:

> philosophers, in spite of their apparent divergencies, agree in distinguishing two profoundly different ways of knowing a thing. The first implies that we move round the object; the second that we enter into it. The first depends on the point of view at which we are placed and on the symbols by which we express ourselves. The second neither depends on a point of view nor relies on any symbol. The first kind of knowledge may be said to stop at the *relative*; the second, in those cases where it is possible, to attain the *absolute*. (1912b, 1)

Absolute knowledge, whatever else it might be (for discussion, see Lacey 1989, chapter 6), involves knowledge of things in themselves precluded by Kantian Humility. How is such knowledge obtained? How may we enter into the object of knowledge and so know it absolutely?

It is impossible to obtain absolute knowledge of an object merely by integrating partial perspectives on that object into a harmonious, unified whole. "Were all the photographs of a town, taken from all possible points of view, to go on indefinitely completing one another, they would never be equivalent to the solid town in which we walk about" (Bergson 1912b, 5). According to Bergson, one may come, instead, to have absolute knowledge by means of the faculty of intuition whose principle is sympathy:

> By intuition is meant the kind of *intellectual sympathy* by which one places oneself within an object in order to coincide with what is unique in it and consequently inexpressible. (1912b, 7)

Intuition, here, is intellectual as opposed to sensible. Intuition involves a kind of intimate unity between the act of intuition and its object (and presumably, it displays a greater degree of unity than that at work in perception, which yields only relative knowledge). Sympathy, as the principle of intuition, allows the thinker to enter into or coincide with the object of absolute knowledge. In this passage, Bergson makes the rather strong claim that one places oneself within the object in order to coincide with what is unique in it. And this, Bergson claims, has the consequence that the content of that intuition is inexpressible. Bergson obviously thinks that what is expressible is a kind of generality. But intuition, in presenting

what is unique in its object, lacks the kind of generality that would otherwise make it expressible (compare Aristotle *De Interpretatione*, 7 1737–8,
Categoriae 2 120–19; Frege 1882, 4; Lewis 1929, 52; Prichard 1909, 44). That
the content of the intuition is inexpressible might seem incompatible with
its being intellectual (hence Russell's 1912 charge of anti-intellectualism).
But notice that there is precedent for this. According to Plotinus, the
image of the hyperontic One intuited by the Intellect is a higher form
of intelligibility than what can be expressed in discursive rationality. The
intuition that apprehends the image is intellectual, but its content is inexpressible by finite discursive means. Similarly, Bergson's thought is that
the intuition that yields the absolute knowledge of metaphysics is at once
intellectual and its content inexpressible. Notice how Bergson, in this passage, is cleaving to what I earlier described as a neo-Platonic heritage – in
intuiting an object one places oneself within that object. This is, perhaps,
no accident. Bergson regularly lectured on Plotinus. The important point
for us is that Bergson took intellectual sympathy to explain the way intuition places one within its object. Thanks to the operation of sympathy, in
intuition one experiences the object from within and so may gain absolute
knowledge of it.

So, Bergson maintains, as against Kant, that absolute knowledge,
knowledge of how things are in themselves, is possible on the basis of
intuition and that sympathy makes this so. Some, admittedly, have been
unimpressed. And not only Russell (1912), who was writing as a polemicist,
as was Stebbing (1914). Jay (1994, 202), by no means a polemicist working
on behalf of an emerging analytic philosophy, for one, pronounces it lame.
However, I suspect such judgments are not informed by an appreciation of
the role of sympathy in Stoic and neo-Platonic physics. Bergson's thought
was so informed, and his work is best appreciated when read in light of
these ancient sources. We have endeavored to understand haptic, auditory,
and visual perception in terms of the operation of sympathy. If sensible
intuition, though a lesser unity than intellectual intuition, if such there be,
operates too by means of sympathy, could it not also disclose how things
are in themselves, if partially and imperfectly, despite its perspectival character? Could not perception, so understood, make the perceiver knowledgeable about how things are in themselves?

6.5   Perceiving Things in Themselves

Throughout this essay I have argued that sensory presentation – at least
as it occurs in haptic, auditory, and visual perception – is governed by

the principle of sympathy. So sympathy has a broader domain of application than in an intellectual intuition that makes the absolute knowledge of metaphysics available as Bergson contends. Moreover, the operation of sympathy in sensory presentation is perspective-relative. An object is only sympathetically presented to the perceiver from their partial perspective on the natural environment. However, the perspectival relativity of sensory presentation is no obstacle to its objectivity. As Merleau-Ponty (1967) stresses, it is, rather, a precondition of perceptual objectivity (Chapter 6.2). Objectivity and the parochial are linked.

There may be a higher degree of unity involved in an act of intellectual intuition, if such there be, than in a perceptual act. And this may be reflected in the fact that the content of intellectual intuition is more than just what would be disclosed in the totality of potential perspectives on its object. But that is not yet grounds for maintaining that perception discloses only the relations the perceiver bares to its object. All that really follows from the perspectival relativity of sensory presentation is that it is partial and imperfect, in the sense of being incomplete, if not in a normative sense that implies a kind of deficit. A world independent of our awareness of it may exceed our perception of it. Sensory presentation may disclose how things are in themselves, but being partial and imperfect, it may disclose only some of these and with different degrees of acuity in different circumstances of perception.

Just as sympathy, as it operates in fellow-feeling, allows us to experience from within what another undergoes, sympathy, as it operates in perception, allows us to experience from within what something external to us is like. It is this aspect of sympathetic sensory presentation that vindicates what I earlier described as a neo-Platonic heritage, that perception places us in the object perceived. If sensory presentation operates by means of sympathy, then the sensory presentation of an object in perceptual experience is a way of entering into or coinciding with that object, albeit partially and imperfectly. Perception places us into the very heart of things and reveals their inner natures. This remains a metaphor, but we may unpack two aspects of it. The first aspect is a claim about the phenomenology of explicit awareness, and the second is a claim about the object of that explicit awareness.

Begin with the first aspect, the claim about the phenomenology of explicit awareness. Consider again Olivi and Merleau-Ponty's claim that in looking at a distal object, the perceiver's gaze is posed on that object. The active, outer-directed, opening up to the visible comes to rest on a distal body that resists this activity insofar as it can. It is only in experiencing the body's limit to the perceiver's visual activity, its resistance to the perceiver's gaze, its perceptual impenetrability, as a sympathetic response to a countervailing force, the perceiver's gaze encountering an alien force that resists it, that the perceptually impenetrably body discloses itself to visual awareness. If the visual resistance of the body is the means by which conflicting forces are sympathetically presented in visual experience, then in being sympathetically presented with a distal body, the perceiver is naturally attending to the distal body, the object of visual perception. The perceiver's gaze is posed on the body. This is the effect of the body's sympathetic presentation in visual experience that arises when the perceiver looks to that body. Perception places us in the body. That is where the perceiver's explicit awareness is. In selectively attending to an object of your experience, where is your attention? On the object selectively attended to, of course. The query "Where's your head at?" gives expression to this. Your "head" is where the object of your attention is. In general, an act or episode of attention is where its object is. Attention is not the kind of thing that has location in itself. Insofar as it can be said to have location, it must inherit this location from the location of its object. This, then, is the first aspect, the claim about the phenomenology of explicit awareness, that attention is located where its object is.

Consider now the second aspect. Whereas the first aspect, unpacked from the metaphor, concerned the phenomenology of explicit awareness, the second aspect concerns its object. The perceiver's gaze is posed on the body located at a distance from it. And the perceiver's explicit awareness, in alighting upon the distal body, may disclose how that body is in itself. A body's shape, for example, is an aspect of its corporeal nature. A body's shape is part of what it is to be a body and the particular body that it is. A body's shape is not only, in this way, an aspect of its corporeal nature, but it is perceptible as well. It may be felt and seen. So at least some aspects of how the body is in itself are within the range of the explicit awareness afforded by the perceiver's sensory experience. This, then, is the second aspect, the claim about the objects of explicit awareness, that how a thing is in itself may be an object of the explicit awareness afforded by perception.

Putting these two aspects together we arrive at what the neo-Platonic heritage amounts to in the present account: perception places us in the very heart of things in the sense that the explicit awareness afforded by perceptual experience is directed upon the body, and so located where its object is, in such a way as to disclose how that body is in itself, apart from other things, in that awareness. And it is the principle of sympathy that makes this possible. Sympathy, in this way, allows us to experience, from within, what an external body is like, in and of itself.

That we must be affected in some way by the object of perception is no obstacle to the sympathetic presentation of a thing's inner nature. Rather, as the Protagorean model reveals, at least as herein elaborated, the force of the perceiver's activity coming into conflict with the self-maintaining forces of the object perceived is what makes its sympathetic presentation possible. It is only when the perceiver experiences the limit to their perceptual activity as a sympathetic response to a countervailing force from without that sympathy may disclose what is external to us. What appears to us in perceptual experience are things in themselves, both in their relational and intrinsic aspects. The fallen burr resting upon the grass may be to the left of a foraging squirrel and bright green. Vision discloses such things to us. But if things in themselves are what appear to us in perceptual experience, then the phenomenal–noumenal distinction collapses. A thing may at once be a thing in itself, a substance if you like, and appear in perceptual experience. More than that, how that thing is in itself may itself be disclosed, partially and imperfectly, in perceptual experience. What is disclosed is an aspect of the substance's inner nature, how that thing is in itself apart from other things, how it is intrinsically. We confront the burr's greenness in seeing it. Sympathy is what presents the world without the mind in sensory experience and discloses how things are in themselves, at least partially and imperfectly.

Bibliography

Allison, H. E. 1983. *Kant's Transcendental Idealism: An Interpretation and Defense*. New Haven, CT and London: Yale University Press.

Ardley, G. 1958. The nature of perception. *Australasian Journal of Philosophy*, 36(3): 189–200.

Armstrong, A. 1984. *Plotinus Ennead iv*. Loeb Classical Library. Cambridge, MA: Harvard University Press.

Arnim, I. A. 1964a. *Stoicorum Veterum Fragmenta*, volume 1. Stuttgart: B.G. Teubner.

1964b. *Stoicorum Veterum Fragmenta*, volume 2. Stuttgart: B.G. Teubner.

1964c. *Stoicorum Veterum Fragmenta*, volume 3. Stuttgart: B.G. Teubner.

Austin, J. 1962. *Sense and Sensabilia*. New York: Oxford University Press.

Bach-y Rita, P. and S. Kercel. 2002. Sensory substitution and augmentation. *Intellectica*, 2(35): 287–97.

Barnes, H. E. 1958. *Being and Nothingness*. London: Methuen & Co.

Barnes, J. 1984. *The Complete Works of Aristotle: The Revised Oxford Translations*, volume 1 of Bollingen Series. Oxford: Oxford University Press.

Bayne, T. and M. Spener. 2010. Introspective humility. *Philosophical Issues*, 20(1): 1–22.

Benedetti, F. 1985. Processing of tactile spatial information with crossed fingers. *Journal of Experimental Psychology: Human Perception and Performance*, 11(4): 517–25.

Bergson, H. 1903. Introduction à la métaphysique. *Revue de Métaphysique et de Morale*. Reprinted in Bergson 1938 and translated as Bergson 1912a.

1912a. *Introduction to Metaphysics*. Translated by T. E. Hulme. London: G.P. Putnam & Sons.

1912b. *Matter and Memory*. London: George Allen & Co.

1938. *La Pensée et le Mouvant: Essais et conférences*. Paris: Presses Universitaires de France.

Berkeley, G. 1734. *Three Dialogues between Hylas and Philonous*. Oxford: Oxford University Press.

Blackmore, S. J., G. Brelsta, K. Nelson, and T. Troscianko. 1995. Is the richness of our visual world an illusion? Transsaccadic memory for complex scenes. *Perception*, 24: 1075–81.

Boehm, M. D. 1929. *The Influence of Habit on the Faculty of Thinking*. Baltimore, MD: Williams & Wilkins.

Boswell, J. 1935. *Boswell's Life of Johnson*. Oxford: Oxford University Press.

Bower, M. and S. Gallagher. 2013. Bodily affects as prenoetic elements in enactive perception. *Phenomenology and Mind*, 4(1): 78–93.

Bregman, A. S. 1990. *Auditory Scene Analysis: The Perceptual Organization of Sound*. Cambridge, MA: MIT Press.

Brentano, F. 1874. *Psychologie vom Empirischen Standpunkte*. Translated by A. C. Rancurello as Brentano 1973. Leipzig: Duncker & Humblot.

   1973. *Psychology from an Empirical Standpoint*. New York: Routledge.

Brewer, B. 2011. *Perception and Its Objects*. Oxford: Oxford University Press.

Brisson, L. 2005. *Porphyre Sentences Tome 2*. Paris: Librairie Philosophique J. Vrin.

Broackes, J. 1997. The autonomy of colour. In *Readings on Color: The Philosophy of Color*, A. Byrne and D. Hilbert, eds., volume I, pp. 191–225. Cambridge, MA: MIT Press.

Broad, C. 1952. Some elementary reflections on sense-perception. *Philosophy*, 27(100): 3–17. Reprinted in Broad 1965.

   1965. Some elementary reflections on sense-perception. In *Perceiving, Sensing, and Knowing*, R. J. Swartz, ed., pp. 29–48. Garden City, NY: Anchor Books, Doubleday & Company, Inc.

Broadie, A. 1993. *Robert Kilwardby O.P. On Time and Imagination*, volume ix 2 of Auctores Britannici Medii Aevi. Oxford: Oxford University Press for the British Academy.

Brogaard, B. 2014. *Does Perception Have Content?* Oxford: Oxford University Press.

Brouwer, R. 2015. Stoic sympathy. In *Sympathy: A History*, chapter 1. Oxford: Oxford University Press.

Burge, T. 2003. Perceptual entitlement. *Philosophy and Phenomenological Research*, 67(3): 503–48.

   2010. *Origins of Objectivity*. Oxford: Oxford University Press.

Burnyeat, M. 1979. Conflicting appearances. In *Proceedings of the British Academy*, volume lxv, pp. 69–111.

   1982. Idealism and Greek philosophy: What Descartes saw and Berkeley missed. *The Philosophical Review*, 91(1): 3–40.

   1995. How much happens when Aristotle sees red and hears middle C? Remarks on *De Anima* 2.7–8. In *Essays on Aristotle's De Anima*, M. C. Nussbaum and A. O. Rorty, eds., pp. 421–34. Oxford: Clarendon Press.

Campbell, J. and Q. Cassam. 2014. *Berkeley's Puzzle: What Does Experience Teach Us?* Oxford: Oxford University Press.

Casati, R., E. D. Bona, and J. Dokic. 2013. The Ockhamization of the event sources of sound. *Analysis*, 73(3): 462–66.

Casati, R. and J. Dokic. 1994. *La philosophie du son*. Nîmes: Éditions Jacqueline Chambon.

   2014. Sounds. *Stanford Encyclopedia of Philosophy* (Fall 2014 Edition), Edward N. Zalta (ed.). https://plato.stanford.edu/archives/fall2014/entries/sounds/.

Cassam, Q. 2007. *The Possibility of Knowledge*. Oxford: Oxford University Press.

Caston, V. 2005. The spirit and the letter: Aristotle on perception. In *Metaphysics, Soul, and Ethics in Ancient Thought: Themes from the Work of Richard Sorabji*, R. Salles, ed., chapter 11, pp. 245–320. Oxford: Clarendon Press.

Chalmers, D. 2006. Perception and the fall from Eden. In *Perceptual Experience*, T. S. Gendler and J. Hawthorne, eds., chapter 2, pp. 49–125. Oxford: Clarendon Press.

Charles, D. 1988. Aristotle on hypothetical necessity and irreducibility. *Pacific Philosophical Quarterly*, 69(1): 1–53. Reprinted in Charles 1995.

1995. Aristotle on hypothetical necessity and irreducibility. In *Aristotle, Metaphysics, Epistemology, Natural Philosophy*, T. Irwin, ed., volume 7 of Classical Philosophy, Collected Papers, pp. 11–26. New York and London: Garland Publishing, Inc.

Chirimuuta, M. 2015. *Outside Color: Perceptual Science and the Puzzle of Color in Philosophy*. Cambridge, MA: The MIT Press.

Cohen, J. 2008. Colour constancy as counterfactual. *The Australasian Journal of Philosophy*, 86(1): 61–92.

Collingwood, R. 1938. *The Principles of Art*. Oxford: Clarendon Press.

Cook Wilson, J. 1926. *Statement and Inference*. Oxford: Oxford University Press.

Cooper, J. M. 1997. *Plato Complete Works*. Indianapolis, IN: Hackett Publishing Company.

Cross, R. 2014. *Duns Scotus's Theory of Cognition*. Oxford: Oxford University Press.

Davidson, D. 1969. The individuation of events. In *Essays in Honor of Carl G. Hempel*, N. Rescher, ed., pp. 216–34. Dordrecht: D. Reidel.

Davidson, D. and G. Harman, eds. 1972. *Semantics of Natural Language*. Dordrecht: D. Reidel.

Deleuze, G. and F. Guattari. 1987. *A Thousand Plateaus, Capitalism and Schizophrenia*. Minneapolis: University of Minnesota Press.

Derrida, J. 2005. *On Touching – Jean-Luc Nancy*. Stanford, CA: Stanford University Press.

Ducasse, C. 1942. Moore's "Refutation of idealism." In *The Philosophy of GE Moore*, P. A. Schilpp, ed., pp. 232–3. La Salle, IL: Open Court Press.

Emilsson, E. K. 1988. *Plotinus on Sense-Perception: A Philosophical Study*. Cambridge: Cambridge University Press.

2015. Plotinus on *sympatheia*. In *Sympathy, A History*, chapter 2. Oxford: Oxford University Press.

Everson, S. 1997. *Aristotle on Perception*. Oxford: Oxford University Press.

Farkas, K. 2008. *The Subject's Point of View*. Oxford: Oxford University Press.

Fine, K. 1995. Ontological dependence. *Proceedings of the Aristotelian Society*, 95: 269–90.

2006. In defense of three-dimensionalism. *The Journal of Philosophy*, 103: 699–714.

Fish, W. 2009. *Perception, Hallucination, and Illusion*. Oxford: Oxford University Press.

200

Bibliography

Frege, G. 1882. 17 kernsätze zur logik. In *Schriften zur Logik und Sprachphilosophie aus dem Nachlass*, G. Gabriel, ed. F. Meiner Verlag. Translated by Peter Long and Roger White Frege 1979.

1979. *Posthumous Writings*. Chicago, IL: University of Chicago Press.

Fulkerson, M. 2014. *The First Sense, A Philosophical Study of Human Touch*. Cambridge, MA: MIT Press.

Gallagher, S. 2005. *How the Body Shapes the Mind*. Oxford: Oxford: Clarendon Press.

Gaskin, R. 2008. *The Unity of the Proposition*, volume 64. Oxford: Oxford University Press.

Gerson, L. P. 1994. *Plotinus, The Arguments of the Philosophers*. London and New York: Routledge.

Guyer, P. 1987. *Kant and the Claims of Knowledge*. Cambridge: Cambridge University Press.

Halligan, P. W. and J. C. Marshall. 1991. Left neglect for near but not far space in man. *Nature*, 350: 498–500.

Hamilton, E. and H. Cairns. 1989. *The Collected Dialogues of Plato Including the Letters*, Bollingen Series lxxi, 14th edition. Princeton, NJ: Princeton University Press.

Hamlyn, D. 2002. *Aristotle De Anima Books ii and iii (with passages om Book i)*. Oxford: Clarendon Press.

Handel, S. 1995. Timbre perception and auditory object identification. In *Hearing*, B. Moore, ed., pp. 425–61. San Diego, CA: Academic Press.

Harman, G. 2005. *Guerrilla Metaphysics: Phenomenology and the Carpentry of Things*. La Salle, IL: Open Court Press.

Hatwell, Y., A. Streri, and E. Gentaz. 2003. *Touching and Knowing, Cognitive Psychology of Haptic Manual Perception*. John Benjamins Publishing Company.

Hawthorne, J. 2008. Three-dimensionalism vs four-dimensionalism. In *Contemporary Debates in Metaphysics*, T. Sider, J. Hawthorne, and D. Zimmerman, eds. Oxford: Blackwell.

Heidegger, M. 1935/2000. The origin of the work of art. In *Basic Writings: Martin Heidegger, Revised and Expanded Edition*, D. F. Krell, ed., pp. 139–212. Routledge.

Hilbert, D. R. 1987. *Color and Color Perception: A Study in Anthropocentric Realism*. Center for the Study of Language and Information.

2005. Color constancy and the complexity of color. *Philosophical Topics*, 33(1): 141–58.

Hilbert, D. R. and M. E. Kalderon. 2000. Color and the inverted spectrum. In *Color Perception: Philosophical, Psychological, Artistic, and Computational Perspectives*, S. Davis, ed., volume ix of Vancouver Studies in Cognitive Science, pp. 187–214. Oxford: Oxford University Press.

Holmes, B. 2015. *Reflection*: Galen's sympathy. In *Sympathy, A History*, E. Schleisser, ed., Oxford Philosophical Concepts, pp. 61–9. Oxford: Oxford University Press.

Huang, L. and H. Pashler. 2007. A Boolean map theory of visual attention. *Psychological Review*, 114: 599–631.

Ierodiakonou, K. 2005. Empedocles on colour and colour vision. In *Oxford Studies in Ancient Philosophy*, D. Sedley, ed., volume 29, chapter 1, pp. 1–38. Oxford: Oxford University Press.

   2006. The Greek concept of sympatheia and its Byzantine appropriation in Michael Psellos. In *The Occult Sciences in Byzantium*, P. Magdalino and M. Mavroudi, eds., chapter 2, pp. 97–117. Geneva: La Pommed'or.

Jackson, F. 1982. Epiphenomenal qualia. *Philosophical Quarterly*, 32: 127–36.

Jacobi, F. 1815. *Werke*, volume 2. Leipzig: Gerhard Fleischer.

Jansen, B. 1922–6. *Quaestiones in secundum librum Sententiarum*. Florence: Collegium S. Bonaventurae: Bibliotecha Franciscana Scholastica Medii Aevi.

Jay, M. 1994. *Downcast Eyes, the Denigration of Vision in Twentieth-Century French Thought*. Berkeley and Los Angeles: University of California Press.

Johnston, M. 2006a. Better than mere knowledge? The function of sensory awareness. In *Perceptual Experience*, T. S. Gendler and J. Hawthorne, eds., chapter 7, pp. 260–90. Oxford: Clarendon Press.

   2006b. Hylomorphism. *Journal of Philosophy*, 103(12): 652–98.

   2007. Objective minds and the objectivity of our minds. *Philosophy and Phenomenological Research*, 75(2): 233–69.

   2011. On a neglected epistemic virtue. *Philosophical Issues*, 21(1): 165–218.

   2013. Aristotle on sounds. *British Journal for the History of Philosophy*, 21(4): 631–48.

Jonas, H. 1954. The nobility of sight. *Philosophy and Phenomenological Research*, 14(4): 507–19.

Jones, L. A. and S. J. Lederman. 2006. *Human Hand Function*. Oxford: Oxford University Press.

Jones, W. 1957. *Hippocrates*, volume 1 of Loeb Classical Library. Cambridge, MA: Harvard University Press.

Kalderon, M. E. 2007. Color pluralism. *The Philosophical Review*, 116(4): 563–601.

   2008. Metamerism, constancy, and knowing which. *Mind*, 117(468): 549–85.

   2011a. Before the law. *Philosophical Issues*, 21:219–44.

   2011b. Color illusion. *Noûs*.

   2011c. The multiply qualitative. *Mind*, pp. 1–22.

   2015. *Form without Matter, Empedocles and Aristotle on Color Perception*. Oxford: Oxford University Press.

   forthcoming. Experiential pluralism and the power of perception. In *Themes from Travis*. Oxford: Oxford University Press.

Kalderon, M. E. and C. Travis. 2013. Oxford realism. In *Oxford Handbook of the History of Analytic Philosophy*, M. Beaney, ed. Oxford: Oxford University Press.

Katz, D. 1935. *The World of Colour*. London: Routledge, Trench, Trubner & Co., Ltd.

Kent, B. D. 1984. Aristotle and the Franciscans: Gerald Odonis' Commentary on the Nichomachean Ethics. PhD thesis, Columbia University, New York.

King, J. C. 2007. *The Nature and Structure of Content*. Oxford: Oxford University Press.

King, J. C., S. Soames, and J. Speaks. 2014. *New Thinking about Propositions*. Oxford: Oxford University Press.

Knuuttila, S. and J. Sihvola. 2014. *Sourcebook for the History of the Philosophy of Mind*, volume 12 of Studies in the History of Philosophy of Mind. Dordrecht: Springer.

Kripke, S. A. 1972/1980. *Naming and Necessity*. Cambridge, MA: Harvard University Press. Reprinted from Davidson and Harman 1972, with a new preface.

Kulvicki, J. 2008. The nature of noise. *Philosophers' Imprint*, 8(11): 1–16.

2014. *Images, New Problems of Philosophy*. London and New York: Routledge.

Lacey, A. 1989. *Bergson: The Arguments of the Philosophers*. London and New York: Routledge.

Langton, R. 1998. *Kantian Humility: Our Ignorance of Things in Themselves*. Oxford: Oxford University Press.

Leddington, J. 2014. What we hear. In *Consciousness Inside and Out: Phenomenology, Neuroscience, and the Nature of Experience*, R. Brown, ed., volume 6 of Studies in Brain and Mind, chapter 21, pp. 321–34. Dordrecht Heidelberg New York London: Springer.

Lederman, S. J. and R. L. Klatzky. 1987. Hand movements: A window into haptic object recognition. *Cognitive Psychology*, 19: 342–68.

Lemmon, E. 1967. Comments. In *The Logic of Decision and Action*, N. Rescher, ed., pp. 96–103. Pittsburgh: University of Pittsburgh Press.

Lewis, C. 1929. *Mind and the World Order: Outlines of a Theory of Knowledge*. Charles Scribner and Sons.

Lewis, D. 2009. Ramseyan humility. In *Conceptual Analysis and Philosophical Naturalism*, D. B. Mitchell and R. Nola, eds., pp. 203–22. Cambridge, MA: MIT Press.

Liberman, A. M. and I. M. Mattingly. 1985. The motor theory of speech perception revised. *Cognition*, 21(1): 1–36.

Lindberg, D. 1977. *Theories of Vision from al-Kindī to Kepler*. Chicago: Chicago University Press.

1996. *Roger Bacon and the Origins of Perspectiva in the Middle Ages, a Critical Edition and English Translation of Bacon's Perspectiva with Introduction and Notes*. Oxford: Clarendon Press.

1998. *Roger Bacon's Philosophy of Nature, a Critical Edition, with English Translation, Introduction, and Notes, of De multiplicatione specierum and De speculis comburnetibus*. South Bend, IN: St. Augustine's Press.

Long, A. and D. Sedley. 1987. *The Hellenistic Philosophers*, volume 1. Cambridge: Cambridge University Press.

Marion, M. 2000a. Oxford realism: Knowledge and perception i. *British Journal for the History of Philosophy*, 8(2): 299–338.

2000b. Oxford realism: Knowledge and perception ii. *British Journal for the History of Philosophy*, 8(3): 485–519.

Martin, M. 1992. Sight and touch. In *The Contents of Experience*, T. Crane, ed. Cambridge: Cambridge University Press.

1998. Setting things before the mind. In *Contemporary Issues in the Philosophy of Mind*, A. O'Hear, ed., Royal Institute of Philosophy Supplements. Cambridge: Cambridge University Press.

2004. The limits of self-awareness. *Philosophical Studies*, 120: 37–89.

2012. Sounds and images. *The British Journal of Aesthetics*, 52(4): 331–51.

Matthen, M. 2005. *Seeing, Doing, and Knowing: A Philosophical Theory of Sense Perception*. Oxford: Oxford University Press.

2015. Active perception and the representation of space. In *Perception and Its Modalities*, chapter 2, pp. 44–72. Oxford: Oxford University Press.

McDowell, J. 1998. Having the world in view: Sellars, Kant, and intentionality. *Journal of Philosophy*, xcv(9): 431–91. Reprinted in McDowell 2009b.

2008. Avoiding the myth of the given. In *John McDowell: Experience, Norm, and Nature*, pp. 1–14. J. Lindgaard, ed. Oxford: Blackwell. Reprinted in McDowell 2009b.

2009a. Conceptual capacities in perception. In *Having the World in View: Essays on Kant, Hegel, and Sellars*, pp. 127–44. Oxford: Oxford University Press.

2009b. *Having the World in View: Essays on Kant, Hegel, and Sellars*. Cambridge, MA: Harvard University Press.

Meillassoux, Q. 2008. *After Finitude*. London and New York: Continuum.

Menn, S. 1998. *Descartes and Augustine*. Cambridge: Cambridge University Press.

Merleau-Ponty, M. 1964. *The Primacy of Perception and Other Essays on Phenomenological Psychology, the Philosophy of Art, History and Politics*, Northwestern University Studies in Phenomenology and Existential Philosophy. Evanston: Northwestern University Press. James M. Edie, ed.

1967. *The Structure of Behavior*. Beacon Press.

Meyer, S. S. 2009. Chain of causes: What is Stoic fate? In *God and Cosmos in Stoicism*, R. Salles, ed., chapter 3, pp. 71–92. Oxford: Oxford University Press.

Mizrahi, V. 2010. Color and transparency. *Rivista di Estetica*, 43(1): 181–92.

Mole, C. 2009. The motor theory of speech perception. In *Sounds and Perception: New Philosophical Essays*, M. Nudds and C. O'Callaghan, eds., chapter 10, pp. 211–33. Oxford: Oxford University Press.

Moore, A. 2012. *The Evolution of Modern Metaphysics: Making Sense of Things, The Evolution of Modern Philosophy*. Cambridge: Cambridge University Press.

Moore, F. 1996. *Bergson, Thinking Backwards*. Cambridge: Cambridge University Press.

Moore, G. 1903. The refutation of idealism. *Mind*, 12: 433–53.

Mulvey, L. 1975. Visual pleasure and narrative cinema. *Screen*, 16(3): 6–18.

Nagel, T. 1979. What is it like to be a bat? In *Mortal Questions*. Cambridge: Cambridge University Press.

2012. *Mind and Cosmos*. Oxford: Oxford University Press.

Noë, A. 2004. *Action in Perception*. Cambridge, MA: MIT Press.

2012. *Varieties of Presence*. Cambridge, MA: Harvard University Press.

Nudds, M. 2009. Sounds and space. In *Sounds and Perception: New Philosophical Essays*, C. O'Callaghan and M. Nudds, eds., chapter 4, pp. 69–96. Oxford: Oxford University Press.

2010. What sounds are. In *Oxford Studies in Metaphysics*, D. Zimmerman, ed., volume 5, chapter 13, pp. 279–302. Oxford: Oxford University Press.

2014. Commentary on Leddington. In *Consciousness Inside and Out: Phenomenology, Neuroscience, and the Nature of Experience*, R. Brown, ed., volume 6 of Studies in Brain and Mind, chapter 23, pp. 343–50. Dordrecht, Heidelberg, New York, and London: Springer.

O'Callaghan, C. 2007. *Sounds*. Oxford: Oxford University Press.

2009. Sounds and events. In *Sounds and Perception: New Philosophical Essays*, M. Nudds and C. O'Callaghan, eds., chapter 2, pp. 26–49. Oxford: Oxford University Press.

2014. Audible independence and binding. In *Consciousness Inside and Out: Phenomenology, Neuroscience, and the Nature of Experience*, R. Brown, ed., volume 6 of Studies in Brain and Mind, chapter 22, pp. 335–42. Dordrecht, Heidelberg, New York, and London: Springer.

O'Daly, G. 1987. *Augustine's Philosophy of Mind*. Berkeley and Los Angeles: University of California Press.

O'Shaughnessy, B. 1989. The sense of touch. *Australasian Journal of Philosophy*, 67(1): 37–58.

1995. Proprioception and the body image. In *The Body and the Self*, J. Bermúdez, A. Marcel, and N. Eilan, eds., A Bradford Book. Cambridge, MA: MIT Press.

2003. Sense data. In *John Searle*, B. Smith, ed., Contemporary Philosophy in Focus, chapter 8, pp. 169–88. Cambridge: Cambridge University Press.

2009. The location of perceived sound. In *Sounds and Perception: New Philosophical Essays*, M. Nudds and C. O'Callaghan, eds., chapter 6, pp. 111–25. Oxford: Oxford University Press.

Pasnau, R. 1997. *Theories of Cognition in the Later Middle Ages*. Cambridge: Cambridge University Press.

1999a. Olivi on human freedom. In *Pierre de Jean Olivi (1248–1298). Pensée sholastique, dissidence spiritue e et sociéteé*, A. Boureau and S. Piron, eds., volume 79 of Études de philosophie médiévale, pp. 15–25. Paris: Librairie Philosophique J. Vrin.

1999b. What is sound? *Philosophical Quarterly*, 50(196): 309–24.

2000. Sensible qualities: The case of sound. *Journal of the History of Philosophy*, 38(1): 27–40.

2002. *The Cambridge Translations of Medieval Philosophical Texts*, volume 3, Mind and Language. Cambridge: Cambridge University Press.

2009. The event of color. *Philosophical Studies*, 142(3): 353–69.

Paterson, M. 2007. *The Senses of Touch: Haptics, Affects and Technologies*. Oxford and New York: Berg.

Patey, D. L. 1986. Johnson's refutation of Berkeley: Kicking the stone again. *Journal of the History of Ideas*, 47(1): 139–45.

Peramatzis, M. M. 2011. *Priority in Aristotle's Metaphysics*. Oxford: Oxford University Press.

Phillips, I. 2012. Afterimages and sensation. *Philosophy and Phenomenological Research*, pp. 1–37.

Piaget, J. 1929. *The Child's Conception of the World*. London: Routledge & Kegan Paul.

Price, H. 1932. *Perception*. London: Methuen & Co.

Prichard, H. 1909. *Kant's Theory of Knowledge*. Oxford: Oxford University Press.

  1950a. The apprehension of time. In *Knowledge and Perception*, chapter 3, pp. 47–51. Oxford: Clarendon Press.

  1950b. *Knowledge and Perception*. Oxford: Clarendon Press.

Putnam, H. 1993. Realism without absolutes. *International Journal of Philosophical Studies*, 1(2): 179–92.

  1994. Sense, nonsense, and the senses: An inquiry into the powers of the human mind. *The Journal of Philosophy*, 91(9): 445–517.

  1999. *The Threefold Cord: Mind, Body, and World*. New York: Columbia University Press.

Richardson, L. 2013. Bodily sensation and tactile perception. *Philosophy and Phenomenological Research*, 86(1): 134–54.

Ricoeur, P. 2004. *Memory, History, Forgetting*. Chicago, IL: University of Chicago Press.

Riedl, C. C. 1942. *Robert Grosseteste, On Light (De Luce), Translation from the Latin with an Introduction*. Milwaukee, WI: Marquette University Press.

Robbin, B. D. 2003. The phenomenological truth of visual emissions. *American Psychologist*, 58(6/7): 494–5.

Ross, G. 1906. *Aristotle De Sensu and De Memoria, Text and Translation with Introduction and Commentary*. Cambridge: Cambridge University Press.

Ross, W. 1924. *Aristotle's Metaphysics, A Revised Text with Introduction and Commentary*, volume 1. Oxford: Clarendon Press.

  1961. *Aristotle De Anima, Edited with Translation and Commentary*. Oxford: Clarendon Press.

Russell, B. 1912. The philosophy of Bergson. *The Monist*, 22: 321–47.

  1919. *Introduction to Mathematical Philosophy*. London: George Allen & Unwin, Ltd.

Ryle, G. 1949. *The Concept of Mind*. New York: Barnes & Noble, Inc.

  1971. Autobiographical. In *Ryle, A Collection of Critical Essays*, Modern Studies in Philosophy, pp. 1–16. London and Basingstoke: Macmillan.

Samburksy, S. 1959. *Physics of the Stoics*, volume 11. Princeton, NJ: Princeton University Press.

Schwitzgebel, E. 2008. The unreliability of naive introspection. *Philosophical Review*, 117(2): 245–73.

Searle, J. R. 2015. *Seeing Things as They Are: A Theory of Perception*. Oxford: Oxford University Press.

Sedley, D. N. 1992. Empedocles' theory of vision and Theophrastus' *De Sensibus*. In *Theophrastus: His Psychological, Doxographical and Scientific Writings*, W. W. Fortenbraugh and D. Gutas, eds., chapter 2, pp. 20–31. New Brunswick, NJ: Rutgers University Studies in Classical Humanities.

Sellars, W. 1956. Empiricism and the philosophy of mind. In *Minnesota Studies in the Philosophy of Science*, H. Feigl and M. Scriven, eds., volume I. Minneapolis, MN: University of Minnesota. Reprinted in Sellars 1997.

    1997. *Empiricism and the Philosophy of Mind*. Cambridge, MA: Harvard University Press.

Sharples, R. and P. van der Eijk. 2008. *Nemesius: On the Nature of Man*. Liverpool: Liverpool University Press.

Sider, T. 1997. Four-dimensionalism. *The Philosophical Review*, 106: 197–231.

Silva, J. F. 2008. Robert Kilwardby on sense perception. In *Theories of Perception in Medieval and Early Modern Philosophy*, volume 6 of Studies in the History of Philosophy of Mind, chapter 6, pp. 87–100. Springer.

    2012. *Robert Kilwardby on the Human Soul, Plurality of Forms and Censorship in the Thirteenth Century, Investigating Medieval Philosophy*. Leiden: Brill.

Silva, J. F. and J. Toivanen. 2010. The active nature of the soul in sense perception: Robert Kilwardby and Peter Olivi. *Vivarium*, 48: 245–78.

Silva, J. F. and M. Yrjönsuuri. 2014. *Active Perception in the History of Philosophy*, volume 14 of Studies in the History of Philosophy of Mind. Springer.

Simons, D. J. and C. F. Chabris. 1999. Gorillas in our midst: Sustained inattentional blindness for dynamic events. *Perception*, 28:1059–74.

Slakey, T. J. 1961. Aristotle on sense perception. *Philosophical Review*, 70(4): 470–84.

Smith, A. D. 2002. *The Problem of Perception*. Cambridge, MA: Harvard University Press.

Smith, A. M. 2001a. *Alhacen's Theory of Visual Perception, a Critical Edition, with English Translation and Commentary, of the First Three Books of Alhacen's De Aspectibus, the Medieval Latin Version of Ibn al-Haytham's Kitāb al-Manā ir*, volume I. Introduction and Latin Text of *Transactions of the American Philosophical Society Held at Philadelphia for Promoting Useful Knowledge*. Independence Square, PA: American Philosophical Society.

    2001b. *Alhacen's Theory of Visual Perception, a Critical Edition, with English Translation and Commentary, of the First Three Books of Alhacen's De Aspectibus, the Medieval Latin Version of Ibn al-Haytham's Kitāb al-Manā ir*, volume ii, English Translation, of *Transactions of the American Philosophical Society Held at Philadelphia for Promoting Useful Knowledge*. Independence Square, PA: American Philosophical Society.

Smith, N. K. 1965. *Immanuel Kant's Critique of Pure Reason*. New York: St. Martin's Press.

Snowdon, P. 2014. *Persons, Animals, Ourselves*. Oxford: Oxford University Press.

Soames, S. 2010. *What Is Meaning?* Princeton, NJ, and Oxford: Princeton University Press.

Sorabji, R. 1971. Aristotle on demarcating the five senses. *The Philosophical Review*, 80(1): 55–79.

    1974. Body and soul in Aristotle. *Philosophy*, 49(187): 63–89.

    2003. Intentionality and physiological process: Aristotle's theory of sense-perception. In *Essays on Aristotle's De Anima*, M. C. Nussbaum and A. O. Rorty, eds., chapter 12, pp. 195–226. Oxford: Clarendon Press.

2004. *Aristotle on Memory*, second edition. London: Bristol Classical Press.

Sorensen, R. 2004. We see in the dark. *Noûs*, 38(3): 456–80.

2008. *Seeing Dark Things: The Philosophy of Shadows*. Oxford: Oxford University Press.

2009. Hearing silence: The perception and introspection of absences. In *Sounds and Perception: New Philosophical Essays*, M. Nudds and C. O'Callaghan, eds., pp. 126–45. Oxford: Oxford University Press.

Spruit, L. 1994. *Species Intelligibis From Perception to Knowledge*, volume 1 of *Brill's Studies in Intellectual History*. Leiden, New York, and Kóln: E.J. Brill.

Squire, M. 2016. Introductory reflections, Making sense of ancient sight. In *Sight and the Ancient Senses*, M. Squire, ed., *The Senses in Antiquity*, pp. 1–35. London and New York: Routledge, Taylor & Francis Group.

Stebbing, S. 1914. *Pragmatism and French Voluntarism*, number 6 in Girton College Studies. Cambridge: Cambridge University Press.

Strawson, P. F. 1966. *The Bounds of Sense: An Essay on Kant's Critique of Pure Reason*, 1973 edition. London: Methuen & Co.

Struck, P. T. 2007. A world full of signs: Understanding divination in ancient Stoicism. In *Seeing with Different Eyes: Essays in Astrology and Divination*, P. Curry and A. Voss, eds., chapter 1, pp. 3–20. Newcastle: Cambridge Scholars Press.

Tachau, K. H. 1988. *Vision and Certitude in the Age of Ockham: Optics, Epistemology, and the Foundations of Semantics, 1250–1345*, Studien und Texte zur Geistesgeschichte des Mittlealters. Leiden: E.J. Brill.

Toivanen, J. 2009. *Animal Consciousness, Peter Olivi on Cognitive Functions of the Sensitive Soul*, volume 370 of *Jyväskylä Studies in Education, Psychology and Social Research*. Jyväskylä: Jyväskylä.

2013. *Perception and the Internal Senses, Peter of John Olivi on the Cognitive Functions of the Soul*, volume 5 of Investigating Medieval Philosophy. Leiden and Boston: Brill.

Travis, C. 2005. A sense of occasion. *The Philosophical Quarterly*, 55(219): 286–314.

2008. *Occasion-Sensitivity: Selected Essays*. Oxford: Oxford University Press.

2011. *Objectivity and the Parochial*. Oxford: Oxford University Press.

2013. The inward turn. In *Perception*, chapter 5, pp. 144–77. Oxford: Oxford University Press.

van Fraassen, B. 1989. *Laws and Symmetry*. Oxford: Clarendon Press.

Whitehead, A. N. 1978. *Process and Reality, An Essay in Cosmology, Gifford Lectures Delivered in the University of Edinburgh During the Session 1927–28, A Corrected Edition*. New York: The Free Press, A Division of Macmillan Publishing Co., Inc.

Williams, B. 1981. The truth in relativism. In *Moral Luck*, pp. 132–44. Cambridge: Cambridge University Press.

Williamson, T. 1990. *Identity and Discrimination*. Oxford and Cambridge: Basil Blackwell.

2000. *Knowledge and Its Limits*. Oxford: Oxford University Press.

Winer, G. A. and J. E. Cottrell. 1996. Does anything leave the eye when we see? Extramission beliefs of children and adults. *Current Directions in Psychological Science*, 5(5): 137–42.

Witt, C. 1995. Dialectic, motion, and perception: *De Anima*, Book I. In *Essays on Aristotle's De Anima*, M. C. Nussbaum and A. O. Rorty, eds., chapter 10, pp. 169–84. Oxford: Clarendon Press.

Wright, M. R. 1981. *Empedocles: The Extant Fragments, Edited with an Introduction, Commentary, Concordance*. New Haven, CT: Yale University Press.

Wu, W. 2014. *Attention*. London and New York: Routledge.

Wyschogrod, E. 1981. Empathy and sympathy as tactile encounter. *The Journal of Medicine and Philosophy*, 6: 25–43.

Yoshioka, T., J. C. Craig, G. C. Beck, and S. S. Hsiao. 2011. Perceptual constancy of texture roughness in the tactile system. *Journal of Neuroscience*, 31(48): 17603–11.

Yrjönsuuri, M. 2008. Perceiving one's own body. In *Theories of Perception in Medieval and Early Modern Philosophy*, S. Knuuttila and P. Kärkäinen, eds., volume 6 of Studies in the History of Philosophy of Mind, chapter 7, pp. 101–16. Dordrecht: Springer.

Index

St. Paul's, 23, 27, 173, 182
Stebbing, Susan, 192
Steenhagen, Maarten, xvii
Stockhausen, Karlheinz, 92
Stoics, 64, 66, 68, 76, 78
Stout, G. F., 49, 88
Strawson, Peter, 188
Strong Experiential Dependence, 43, 44, 48
Struck, Peter, 66
surface color, 175
sympathy, 50–57, 191
    analytic approach, 53, 54, 56, 76, 141
    auditory, 135–41, 147
    general characterization, 74
    mode of being with, 82, 83, 141
    Plotinus, 66–75
    similarity condition, 69, 76
    Stoics, 63–66
    synthetic approach, 53, 56
    unity, 66, 68, 76, 77, 140, 141, 175
    visual, 168–77

Tachau, Katherine, 149, 156, 162
tactile metaphors, xii–xiv, 1–3, 4, 6, 16, 30, 86
tapir, 1, 2, 18, 31
Tati, Jacques, 11
terminative cause, 156
Thames, 89
Theaetetus, 12, 24, 87, 90
    Secret Doctrine, 12, 87
    twin births, 12, 13
Themistius, 16
Theophrastus, 16, 21, 77, 158
Timaeus, 65, 66, 68, 103, 104
timbre, 97, 99, 116, 140

Toivanen, Juhanna, 30, 31, 32, 149, 156, 157, 160
transparency, 135, 165, 170, 171
    degrees of, 170
Travis, Charles, xviii, 54, 112, 184, 185
2001: A Space Odyssey, 1

unity of all souls, 67
the unity of the proposition, 54

van Fraassen, Bas, 67
virtual presence, 158, 159
visuocentrism, 18
voice, 98
volume color, 171, 175

The Wave Theory, 89, 94, 103, 110
    final formulation, 124–25
    objections, 113–25
wax analogy, 24, 25, 26, 161
    active wax, xvii, 30, 31, 32, 33, 34, 41, 85, 154, 157
Whitehead, Alfred North, 52, 68, 81
Williams, Bernard, xi
Williamson, Timothy, 183, 184
Winer, Gerald, 151, 152, 153, 154
Witt, Charlotte, 122
World-Soul, 65, 77, 182
Wright, M. R., 151
Wu, Wayne, 46
Wyschograd, Edith, 52, 81

Yoshioka, Takashi, 8
Yrjönsuuri
    Mikko, 55

Zabarella, Jacopo, 2

For EU product safety concerns, contact us at Calle de José Abascal, 56–1°, 28003 Madrid, Spain or eugpsr@cambridge.org.